"Peter Gabel is one of the grand prophetic voices in our day. He also is a long-distance runner in the struggle for justice."

—*Cornel West, Professor of the Practice of Public Philosophy, Harvard University*

"This book is a major contribution to critical social theory and to the ongoing project of respiritualizing our lives in the family, the market, and the state. It is broad and deep at the same time, with grace and pleasure to be had on every page."

—*Duncan Kennedy, Carter Professor of General Jurisprudence Emeritus, Harvard Law School*

"Karl Marx considered the class struggle the engine of human history. In *The Desire for Mutual Recognition*, however, Peter Gabel boldly asserts the existence of a deeper underlying motive factor: the dynamic of our human yearning, whether towards frustration or fulfillment, to co-create and inhabit a universe of authentic, loving connection, and mutual recognition. Human liberation requires us to intentionally embed social-spiritual strategies within socio-political movements to radically challenge social fear while generating powerful experiences of mutual recognition that support the evolution of humanity toward its full realization. To read this entrancing work is itself to gain entrance into a re-sacralized dimension, evocative of a new future."

—*Fania E. Davis, long-time activist, civil rights lawyer, and restorative justice scholar and practitioner*

"Peter Gabel's *The Desire for Mutual Recognition* may soon reshape the landscape of contemporary social theory. With great sophistication and yet accessibility for those with no previous background, Gabel reveals the key to healing and transforming our world. Demonstrating why those who seek liberation must move past liberalism, Marxism, and deconstruction, Gabel shows how a respiritualization of every aspect of our world can move us beyond the alienation that characterizes so much of human interactions and the institutions in which we are continually imagining ourselves to be stuck. Far from utopian, liberation is in our own hands and could be achieved very quickly once we break through the false vision of reality that can be overcome if we follow Gabel's sage advice."

—*Rabbi Michael Lerner, editor of* Tikkun; *author of* The Left Hand of God *and* Jewish Renewal

"Peter Gabel is a God-wrestler and has been one for years and decades. In this important and needed book he brings his passion for justice and healing of our world along with his well honed analytical skills to bear on the pressing issue of our time: How to let go of the "false self" and the "false we" that poisons our political discourse and stifles our social imaginations. A deep contribution to a needed movement of sacred activism and the return of conscience to our civic life. Dr Martin Luther King Jr. reminded us that "true peace is the presence of justice." In this regard, this is a book about true peace-making."

—*Matthew Fox*

"In *The Desire for Mutual Recognition*, Peter Gabel unfurls a nuanced phenomenology of the social world, a theory of human interbeing as experienced from within its often confounding relational depths. Gabel's ability to think and reflect with his whole organism (with his heart as well as his head) illumines both the uncanny inertia of a destructive civilization seemingly unable to change course, and the erotic energy-flows that provide the ever-present wellspring for such transformation."

—*David Abram, author of* The Spell of the Sensuous *and* Becoming Animal

"Now more than ever, progressives need a transformed way to understand ourselves, our world, and the future we imagine. Peter Gabel's extraordinary book demonstrates the revolutionary truth that meaningful social change depends on ordinary people overcoming the alienation from the social world and from each other that frames each of our lives in liberal societies. Contemporary radical theory has been adept at identifying the myriad forms in which social power is manifest, but it has paid little attention to how power works at the level of consciousness and everyday experience to provide a (false) substitute for the mutual recognition and connection that we all desire. *The Desire for Mutual Recognition* reveals the spiritual and psychological dynamics that form the existential ground for social alienation and that must be addressed for redemptive social change to take hold. It is a beautifully written and evocative work of social theory, and a prophetic and practical call for social change."

—*Gary Peller, author of* Critical Race Consciousness: Reconsidering American Ideologies of Racial Justice

"Peter Gabel's synthesis of political and spiritual activism is exactly what we need for the future. Gabel offers insights into how we can overcome our "fear of the other" and expand authentic social connections into peaceful and loving communities. This book's fresh perspective on movement building should be widely read and discussed."

—*George Katsciaficas, author*

THE DESIRE FOR MUTUAL RECOGNITION

The Desire for Mutual Recognition is a work of accessible social theory that seeks to make visible the desire for authentic social connection, emanating from our social nature, that animates all human relationships.

Using a social-phenomenological method that illuminates rather than explains social life, Peter Gabel shows how the legacy of social alienation that we have inherited from prior generations envelops us in a milieu of a "fear of the other," a fear of each other. Yet because social reality is always co-constituted by the desire for authentic connection and genuine co-presence, social transformation always remains possible, and liberatory social movements are always emerging and providing us with a permanent source of hope. The great progressive social movements for workers' rights, civil rights, and women's and gay liberation, generated their transformative power from their capacity to transcend the reciprocal isolation that otherwise separates us. These movements at their best actually realize our fundamental longing for mutual recognition, and for that very reason they can generate immense social change and bend the moral arc of the universe toward justice.

Gabel examines the struggle between desire and alienation as it unfolds across our social world, calling for a new social-spiritual activism that can go beyond the limitations of existing progressive theory and action, intentionally foster and sustain our capacity to heal what separates us, and inspire a new kind of social movement that can transform the world.

Peter Gabel is the former president of New College of California and was for over thirty years a professor at its public-interest law school. He is a founder of the critical legal studies movement and the Project for Integrating Spirituality, Law, and Politics. Editor-at-Large of the progressive Jewish magazine *Tikkun*, he is the author of numerous books and articles on law, politics, and social change. He lives in San Francisco with his partner Lisa Jaicks, a union organizer for the hospitality workers union, and they have one son, Sam, 22, a hip-hop artist and emcee.

The Desire for Mutual Recognition

Social Movements and the Dissolution of the False Self

Peter Gabel

NEW YORK AND LONDON

First published 2018
by Routledge
711 Third Avenue, New York, NY 10017

and by Routledge
2 Park Square, Milton Park, Abingdon, Oxon, OX14 4RN

Routledge is an imprint of the Taylor & Francis Group, an informa business

Library of Congress Cataloging-in-Publication Data
A catalog record for this book has been requested

ISBN: 978-1-138-09527-4 (hbk)
ISBN: 978-1-138-09528-1 (pbk)
ISBN: 978-1-315-10575-8 (ebk)

Typeset in ITC Legacy Serif
by Apex CoVantage, LLC

To Lisa

True sanity entails in one way or another the dissolution of the normal ego, that false self competently adjusted to our alienated social reality: the emergence of the "inner" archetypal mediators of divine power, and through this death a rebirth, and the eventual re-establishment of a new kind of ego-functioning, the ego now being the servant of the divine, no longer its betrayer.

—R.D. Laing, *The Politics of Experience*

Contents

Preface

If you were to sit opposite me here in my living room, and if we sat together quietly for perhaps a few minutes, we might quite suddenly become present to each other, or more accurately discover a mutuality of presence that was already here but was masked by our selves, these outer garments of personality that we have been wearing, without realizing it, to separate us. In that moment, we would experience ourselves not as "individuals" with two separate centers of Being, but as social beings already connected by a spiritual bond that unites us. From the relatively withdrawn detachment of everyday life, we would quite suddenly find ourselves pulled into the immediacy of co-presence, meeting like a Holy Spirit "in front of" the seemingly separate beings we had been but a moment earlier. And such a meeting, if it were able to occur, would lead us to see, however briefly, that we are all actually co-present to each other in just this way, that we are not lost in our heads and our personalities and selves, but are truly united in a living latticework of interbeing, "caught in an inescapable network of mutuality, tied together in a single garment of destiny" whose ground is love itself. I am he as you are she as you are me and we are all together.

This book seeks to illuminate both the immediate and present truth of this mutuality of presence and its potential to become visible through "mutual recognition," and also the legacy of fear of the other that routinely disables us from seeing one another as the scattered, shattered shards of light seeking reunification that we actually are. I hope that the book will contribute to the emerging movement that is insisting that attending to the spiritual dimension of our social existence is an essential part of transforming the world, that we cannot accomplish this transformation by remaining tied to the inherited paradigms of social theory and action that focus only on the material, external aspects of life. Marxism, psychoanalysis, feminism, deconstruction, queer theory, identity politics, and environmentalism have all made important contributions to understanding what is wrong with the world, but a new pathway of thought and action is needed to illuminate the social-spiritual distortions that keep reproducing the conditions of separation that create so much human suffering. If 20,000 children die of starvation each day, and if we have sufficient food to feed them, then it is morally required that we discover the reason that we are not doing so. "We" are not experiencing the spiritual bond that unites us to each other and through each other, to each of these children. I hope this book succeeds in showing why this is so, and how a new kind of social-spiritual activism can begin to heal the fear at the heart of Being that continues to hold us back (in part by tricking us into remaining loyal to mistaken theories).

I first developed the central ideas put forward in the first few chapters of this book in my doctoral dissertation in psychology written at the Wright Institute in Berkeley almost forty years ago. In the subsequent decades I have written many articles in law reviews and in *Tikkun* magazine of which I have long been an editor, and I have published some of my writings in my two prior books, *The Bank Teller and Other Essays on the Politics of Meaning* and *Another Way of Seeing: Essays on Transforming Law, Politics, and Culture*. Much of this work has been based on the ideas originally formulated, at least in outline, in that early dissertation, but I have never sought again to write down the entire theory in one place, in a single text. While much of the core of the first two chapters of this book expresses ideas first appearing in my dissertation, I could not have written Chapters 3 through 10 without having lived the intervening decades and learned slowly how the fear of the other that we first internalize in childhood is linked to the fear circulating from one to the other in the wider world, including within our own movements for social change. So in some respects it is better to have waited this long to publish these ideas; I'll hope with Hegel that the owl of Minerva takes flight at dusk.

True mutual recognition of each other's full and vulnerable humanity, if we could begin to more fully realize it in the world, would begin to dissolve the false self that keeps us sealed off from one another and would allow us to move more decisively toward the moral redemption of the loving impulse that is already at the heart of our social existence. That loving impulse is expressed most palpably in the mutuality of presence that emerges in idealistic social movements, but its expression remains possible in every human encounter and points in every such encounter toward the possibility of the completion of our social being through one another that we have aspired to from birth and that we carry with us as a longing in our hearts for as long as we are here. I hope that this book contributes to making that possibility more visible, and by doing so, increases our confidence that it can become so in reality.

– Peter Gabel, June 21, 2017

Introduction

We are born as living beings and emerge into direct experiential contact with the world, but almost immediately an envelope is cast over us. This envelope is often referred to as our "conditioning," and in truth we begin to sense it sometime before birth, in the mood that surrounds us even prenatally. This mood almost always transmits love—our mothers carrying and later holding us, the joy and affection that spontaneously flows from others toward, around, and through us, a true circuit of radiant social humanity—but it also transmits the limitations on love that have been inherited from prior generations as these limitations are manifested in the world of our parents.

Thus each of us exists as a plenitude of being miraculously bursting into the world at a particular time and place—wow! incredible!—and yet because we are inherently social creatures, we are right away folded into a social embrace that envelopes us in a blend of love and doubt that establishes from the very start the psychospiritual field within which we must exist ourselves forward and thus make our journey.

In this book I present as best I can in written words my sense of how this process of existing ourselves forward as social beings inmixed in an ambivalent psychospiritual field actually occurs, with the hope of supporting the love side of the equation, of moving us forward toward the realization of a fully loving world that will be the full realization of ourselves as loving beings. The point is to build a world in which we can reciprocate what we ourselves long for, to respond with a loving embrace, as a society, to the core loving impulse that pulses through each of us. Surely this is doable.

A main problem that inhibits our ability to move forward toward this more loving and caring world is that the cultural envelope into which we have been cast from our earliest days assimilates us to a way of seeing and a way of thinking that prevents us from apprehending the world as it actually is—as an existential, intersubjective terrain in which we are perpetually struggling to make authentic contact with the Other, with others, and are discouraged by a rotating fear that our longing will not be realized. We cannot easily see this terrain, this psychospiritual field in perpetual motion inflected by desire and fear, because the fearful aspect of this field has led us, through our conditioning from our earliest years, to perceive ourselves as separated entities—abstract individuals—scattered within an abstract entity called "society." When we do so perceive the world, we actually unconsciously withdraw ourselves back from the immediacy of our existential enmeshment *in* the world to an imaginary "mental space" in which we look "at" the world from a protective distance. From this outside position, we then think "about" the world as an entity outside us (but in which we also "are" as one of the people in it, within the mental entity). Once our immediate presence has been erased in this way through withdrawal back and up into the head, so to speak, we then participate in the conditioned way of "conceiving" of the world, which since the Enlightenment of the sixteenth and seventeenth centuries has roughly involved the use of mental concepts, or word-forms transmitted initially through speech sounds, that signify a mental picture made up of scattered individuals and the State and other entities, all presupposing our essential ontological separation.

Thus when the existential world is in its normal, inert state—held in place by our fear of each other through dynamics I will discuss in this book—our way of seeing the world and thinking about the world reflects this fear and unconsciously seeks to cement the inert state through withdrawn perception and conceptual representations carrying images that convey, defend, and legitimize it. In reality I am here in a room with you in the present moment in what I am calling an intersubjective psychospiritual field of desire and fear or doubt, perhaps of tentative mutual presence, as are all others who are not outdoors across the geological landscape stretching from coast to coast. But instead of seeing this "horizontal" existential reality, we may think, "I am a citizen of the United States, an individual among 350 million other individuals, living in a democracy started by our Founding Fathers and encoded in our constitution and legal system." While this latter statement is true enough if understood as a provisional and culturally specific way of seeing and describing the existentially grounded world of our actual world—the world of people in rooms (if we are not outdoors) aspiring to authentic connection and fearing it at the same time—it is not true if it is reified or treated as a "fact" so as to obscure the visibility of our being-together-in-rooms.

The vast majority of philosophy, political theory, social theory, economics, social change thinking, and most important, "common sense" participates in seeing and thinking "about" the world starting unconsciously from the withdrawn stance and then constructing mental concepts which are superimposed on the world and taken as accurate descriptions of the way things are. Because of the reified, grid-like nature of these conceptually signified congeries of images, and because they emerge from the fear-generated presupposition of our separation, they prevent us from becoming conscious of the inherently-already-connected existential life-world that grounds social reality in lived experience and that when seen clearly, illuminates the possibility of a loving transformation of the psychospiritual field that is our real life.

This insight first came to me as I was being drawn in to the social movements of the 1960s (most of which for me happened in the early to mid-70s) because the experience of "movement" (and the experience of being drawn in) itself involved a more or less spontaneous reversal of this fear-based stance, a reversal that revealed my otherwise unconscious, largely invisible, prior withdrawn state. The very reason we call these social upsurges "movements," as I have written about previously, is that through them we arise from our separation, liberate each other from the psychospiritual prison in which we had previously confined each other, and discover through an emergent connection that we are *here*, present to each other, and are co-creating an existential life-world that we had previously been detached from, had been observing and then "thinking about" from a kind of self-erasing infinite distance. The social movement is actually a movement forward toward the other of each of us liberating the other through the experience of mutual recognition in a great ricochet. And from an epistemological point of view, this emergence of our collective being engenders a new, horizontal perceptual experience in which our prior concepts "about" the world dissolve, replaced by the actual life-world itself. We suddenly experience ourselves as *actually existing*, the world fills out like a great balloon of horizontal presence and mutuality, and the spiritual radiance that had previously been contained through collective social withdrawal suddenly becomes visible, illuminated. Not to idealize the experience—we have a long way to go still before we can endure this enlivening and enlightening experience of social transformation without internal and social conflict because our very safety as social beings appears (from our fear-saturated conditioning) to be as much at stake as our physical bodies are in the presence of a wild animal—but the experience is nevertheless fundamental in its grant of sight. Through the grace provided by each of us to the other, we can suddenly see the world as it actually is and as it actually was in our prior state of unconscious separation. As Van Morrison put it in "I Forgot That Love Existed":

> If my heart could do my thinkin'
> And my head begin to feel,
> I would look upon the world anew
> And know what's truly real.

Thus the proper way to see the world in its social being is as a vast intersubjective life-world of social energy that is either primarily blocked and collectively withdrawn, or unblocked and collectively fully-present-to-each-other. This either/or characterization does not do justice to the truth of lived experience because when we are primarily collectively withdrawn, the fearful impulse is countered at every moment by the pulse of desire moving through it, longing to and actually trying to overcome the withdrawn condition that is spiritually painful and imprisoning. And at the present time of our still limited stage of human evolution (or revolution), when we are more fully present and extended outward in spirit in a greater plenitude of loving connection, we are haunted by the anxiety that our tentative vulnerability will be undermined, that we will each pull the rug out from the other because of the legacy of fear of the other that has been the weight of our inheritance. This is why when we dare to hope, we feel special collective pain when the hope is unrealized, as was the case, for example, after the 2008 election of Barack Obama.

But the essential point is that wherever we are in the continuum of mutual presence and the mutual distance of the withdrawn state, we are at all times social through and through: While we exist as distinct presences, we are never actually "individuals" to the extent this word implies ontologically distinct and separated "entities." In truth, when we criticize the existing world as being "too individualistic," what we really mean is that we are existing our social life together in a state of painful mutual withdrawal, in the withdrawn state of peering out from a distance at each other and mediating our connection through conditioned, ungrounded personae or masks (please see Chapter 2). Even more, when we say that the problem with our society is that it is too individualistic, we inadvertently participate in the illusion we are longing to change, because we erase our own social presence in our "way of seeing" itself—we treat the world as "out there" and implicitly contrast that too individualistic world with a more socially connected world that would also be "out there." To the extent that this "out there" way of seeing and describing reality silently conveys the erasure of our own presence *in* the world, we cannot convince people of what we are saying because the description participates in the very withdrawnness that is what needs to be overcome. There is no "world in here" and "world out there"—there is only the withdrawal of mutual presence that we must see and describe while being present in the world speaking out from our withdrawn state ourselves, so as to take the risk that others may think that we're incomprehensible or crazy. Our listeners are withdrawn themselves, without fully knowing it, and we are trying to reach them . . . and embolden ourselves . . . by seeing and describing and speaking from within the existential social field rather than going along with outside description.

Those of you with a background in philosophy may recognize that this perhaps unfamiliar way of speaking and writing that I'm engaging in here has a tradition in philosophy—the phenomenological tradition manifested in the work of Kierkegaard, Nietzsche, Husserl, and many others, especially Heidegger (in *Being and Time*) and Sartre (in *Being and Nothingness*), and R.D. Laing in the field of psychology, all of whom tried to express that we need to recover the truth of our subjective experience in describing being-in-the-world, and stop talking about the world as some kind of entity out there, a thing cut off from Being that could be described by a hypothetical observer standing outside of it. Even more, they too made the point that this very mistaken way of seeing is what needs to be described and illuminated in its mistakenness. But all of these writers, also without realizing it, unwittingly wrote from inside the envelope, contrasting the authentic perception they aspired to with the mistaken perception they sought to clarify as voices from the withdrawn space rather than as voices from the movement looking back at the withdrawn state. Something in their upbringing and later lives (i.e. religious community in Kierkegaard's case) induced them to see into the subjective ground of being as lived experience, but they may not have yet had enough experience of social movement to fully pull themselves out of their detachment. So Sartre in *Being and Nothingness* and in his early plays interposed a Cartesian distance between self and other, and self and world, that still conveyed "the man/woman alone" heroically shouldering his or her freedom and responsibility, and Heidegger, who so keenly saw into the fallen state of the "they-self" of social conformism in *Being and Time*, catastrophically projected that a kind of superhero authentic being was needed to rescue us from our alienation, which played a role in leading him to Hitler and the Fuhrer principle that he defended in the 1930s as Rector of the University of Freiberg. In fairness to Sartre, his later writing in especially *The Critique of Dialectical Reason* transcended this unconscious attachment to separation precisely because of the influence of having plunged into social activism and the movement experience, but that work also retained the tendency toward externalization of the totality that is the continuing limitation of Marxism and that despiritualizes the social field and erases its erotic energy, silently by so doing reaffirming an a priori collective withdrawnness that it was Sartre's main objective to overcome. Thus for all the contributions these writers have made in illuminating the existential qualities of our lived experience, they still tend to confirm our condition rather than capturing the life-world in a way that promotes healing, transformative, social action.

We must go further out toward each other in our way of seeing and really surrender our separation. We are withdrawn together looking out "at" the world, and we must release our erotic longing out toward each other toward true mutual recognition and affirmation . . . starting with how we talk about the life-world itself. We must let out the leash that we have ourselves on, so that our erotic aspirations to connect with each other in a spirit of love and recognition of each other's present humanity at every moment informs and "respiritualizes" our descriptions of the life-world and in so doing injects a moral dimension into our descriptions themselves, so that listeners or readers who can recognize themselves in our descriptions of the world will at the same time want to change the world, or rather know (possibly for the first time) that they have always wanted to change it and know in what moral direction to go.

Let me give a simple example of such an enriched method of description. A conventional statement about our current world might be, "We live in a market system." Please note that this sentence signifies—creates a mental picture—of an entity outside of you yourself and me myself that we are "in." And who are "we" in this sentence? We are also serially separated entities who are clumped together within this other entity, the market system, that exists outside us. If it is a "system," it is presumably in motion, but outside us, affecting how we live "in" it. And what is the nature of this motion? We know the main thing about the market as a system is that it involves competition among economic actors. People who like markets could say that this is a good thing; those who don't could say it's a bad thing—the description itself is morally neutral. So if we now summarize this barest surface of this short descriptive sentence, we could say that what it communicates is a morally neutral mental picture of an entity outside of us in which we are and live, which we are "in" and are in some way appended to as it moves us around like a system, in some kind of systemic motion.

Note how different the description is if we "respiritualize" it, enlivening the description with our own erotic energy. Instead of "we live in a market system," we could better say that while we long to authentically connect with each other and to co-create our world in a mutually affirming and co-present way toward bringing into being a meaningful emergent social reality (including the economy if we focus on the material aspect of the market), we have inherited a fearful surrounding environment that leads us to suppress our natural brotherliness and sisterliness toward instead using each other to maximize our "money" to mediate and sustain our separation, even as we still seek in small ways at every moment to transcend that spiritual distance in informal ways. Our need for food and shelter to sustain our physical bodies and keep up the vitality of our life-force does exert a profound pressure in support of the legacy of fear that separates us, and this blend of material need and fear of each other leads us to participate, against our will and with varying levels of intensity, in co-creating this spiritually painful state of affairs as we grow, make, and distribute material goods to each other, even as we continue to try to connect in many, many small ways in spite of that.

This latter description is just another way of saying we live in a market system, but it "spiritualizes" the description by restoring to it its existential human quality and by linking the spirit of the describer and the description to the spirit of the "thing" being described. Instead of presenting the world as a kind of mechanism in motion outside of the describer (and therefore outside of all of us, since the validity of the statement by the describer depends upon our identification with it as valid), my latter description recasts this same world in a way that restores its lived, spiritual, erotic quality.

Here is the critical point: When I as the perceiver and describer of the social reality *release myself into it*, when I "let out the leash" on myself and release myself from my "di-stance" and self-erasure and by so doing join the world of my own description, I also at the same time release the listener or reader from the withdrawnness that he or she is longing to be released from. When we perceive and then describe the world, we take a stand on how it actually is and implicitly bring the force of this descriptive truth-claim to bear on the listener, silently confirming his or her withdrawn condition, or on the other hand affirming his or her erotic aspiration to transcend that condition.

If the "market system" example is an example of an economic narrative, we can now return to the mini political narrative I presented earlier about citizens and the State to more easily see how the same descriptive force works on us in the political sphere, in the mental space we call political thought. In its opening sentence on the topic, Wikipedia presents the following description of democracy:

> Democracy is a form of government in which all eligible citizens are meant to participate equally—either directly or, through elected representatives, indirectly—in the proposal, development and establishment of the laws by which their society is run.

We can now see that this way of seeing so to speak "instantly" despiritualizes the intersubjective life-world by offering a description of disconnected citizens somehow getting together "equally," meaning in an additive fashion that includes each citizen-entity, to make an entity separate from them, called society, "run." If we contrast that with my sentient longing to connect with the person next to me, to overcome my alienation in a mysteriously inherited world of reciprocally-enforced isolation and to come into a communion of empathy while engaging in common, cooperative, meaningful activity, we can see that the Wikipedia description presents a mental picture of the intersubjective life-world that consigns me and you to solitude in perpetuity by designating us, through the signifying power of mental concepts, as ontologically separated figures inside some larger entity ("their society") that we together make run. On the other hand, if we "respiritualize" democracy, if we seek to redescribe it beginning with the illumination of ourselves as socially-connected spiritual beings seeking each other's recognition and affirmation, we can understand that the realization of the idea of government by the people requires the transcendence of our mutual alienation/solitude/withdrawnness/separation so that a "people" can actually come into existence and in so doing *become* a *together* that can shape a world. To have democracy, we must emerge into the connection of mutual presence through gatherings that foster empathy, mutual understanding, and dialogue with the intention of collectively becoming present to shape our life-world. This is quite a difference from the citizen-units in the Wikipedia's version of democracy slogging out to touch a computer screen on one day a year, the first Tuesday in November.

To say that our new way of seeing and knowing involves a respiritualization of the social world will likely raise at least two red flags among readers committed to the liberation of humanity from injustice, suffering, and oppression.

First, you may be put off by the very idea of "spirituality," or of "respiritualizing" first social interpretation and then social activism, because the word spirituality is associated with either religion, which you do not believe in or think of as an opiate that distracts people from the injustices of the real world, or new-age beliefs and practices that you believe involve pursuing private, quasi-mystical fantasies of transcendence that also involve a denial of reality as it actually is. At the core of these concerns is a conviction that spirituality is both false in the sense of made-up and not really referring to anything real, and also a denial of the reality of economic inequality and power relations in the really existing, empirically visible world.

To the extent that spirituality can be guilty of these charges, I would ask you in reading this book to suspend these concerns, at least temporarily, because I am not using the term in either the religious sense or the new-age privatized sense (though I should say I am drawn to what I consider the best and most binding-together-again [or re-ligious] elements of religious and other spiritual practice). When I speak of respiritualizing the world, what I mean is simply that we human beings are bound together by spirit, that there is a vibrant life-force that unites us and that is social in nature, although invisible to the "naked" objectifying eye—and more, that the longings of this social spirit are at the core of our search for meaning in life and are at the core of all human motivation in the realm of economics, politics, psychology, personal life, everything. There are to be sure objective material motivations in life having to do with the survival and well-being of the physical body—the need for food, clothing, and shelter—but I am saying that there is a social-spiritual aspect of life that is at the heart of the meaning of our social existence. Reincorporating that into the way we describe what is occurring in our social existence is what I mean by the need to respiritualize our way of seeing and knowing and speaking about that existence. If you like and if it helps, the emphasis is on "spirit" rather than "spirituality"—I am trying to illuminate the radiant texture of psychospiritual meanings, the previously for the most part invisible longings of the heart channeled into our intersubjective intentions and actions, that are at the heart of what Sartre calls "le vecu," the lived. My use of the term has nothing to do with religion or spiritual practices as such.

The second red flag that some may see in my emphasis on respiritualizing the way we see things is the concern that I am emphasizing the "inner" at the expense of the "outer"—that there is a real struggle going on in the world between, for example, the owners of capital and workers who can only survive by selling their labor-power to these capital owners, and that my approach minimizes the importance of this kind of real struggle that many on the Left see as underlying the psychospiritual factors that I emphasize. In response to this let me say at the outset that my interest is in showing not that this material struggle does not exist or is not important, but rather that it is itself an expression of a psychospiritual alienation that underlies it rather than the converse. Thus I will attempt to describe the hierarchies of the capitalist workplace as socially cemented manifestations of social fear and to show how this fear is actually spread through and reinforced within the hierarchy—the hierarchy of classes and within hierarchies as a whole in which some imagine themselves "above" and others "underneath" others (although as we shall see, everyone not present here with others imagines him/herself "underneath" in order to remain withdrawn from others). In this way of seeing the same reality that the Marxist sees, I wish to show that the owner of capital is caught up in and has internalized a social network characterized by Fear of the Other, meaning not particularly fear of the worker, but fear of everyone—his wife, his children, the person next to him—that makes it difficult for him to see that sharing his resources in seeking to create a more loving community is his actual salvation. I will be trying to show in my descriptions that it is this network of social fear that motivates him to be an economic oppressor, that shapes the pretensions of his character, and that isolates him in a silent social paranoia that leads him to see the worker (mainly) as a mere factor of production, that makes him mostly indifferent to, or really blocked against recognizing, the humanity of others.

Therefore although my descriptions advocate a respiritualization of how we perceive and understand the world, they are just as social and political in nature as Marxist descriptions in the sense that only social action and effort, including struggle against strong resistance, will transform the social reality. It is true that the implications of my psychospiritual emphasis point to more diverse opportunities for transformative action than ways of seeing requiring contradictions of economic interest to generate collective agency, because in my way of seeing, the longing for human connection at all times co-exists with and transcends the fear that contains it. Thus rather than being restricted to a materially-based concept of class struggle, the opportunities for transformation exist at all points in the social context where love and hope can emerge through the blend of spiritual anxiety and material fear that maintains the inertia of existing life-patterns—and in fact, coming to see the existence of these opportunities and coming to understand how to organize through and against the network of social fear is a purpose of this book. But although the terrain that I emphasize is the spiritual dimension of our common existence, the approach to social change I am offering remains a social-political approach, and is equally opposed, with Marxism and other related traditions on the Left, to the idea that social change can result from a private transformation of consciousness in socially separated persons (though such so-called personal efforts, which turn out on investigation to also be social insofar as they always require a liberating internalization of an other human being, also have their place).

This spiritualization of a socio-political analysis of class and other hierarchical dynamics in the present moment also indicates that we must shift our way of understanding historical dynamics. One of the most compelling features of the Marxist analysis of society has been and continues to be its understanding of history: In fact, most people on the Left were at one time drawn to Marx by a common experience of revelation: We are born inside capitalist culture and therefore initially internalize the common sense and ideology of the system, including its individualism, its message that we are all free and equal, that each of us succeeds according to our own merit, that we live in a democracy where we the people decide, and that therefore the world is as it should be, or will be eventually as we move forward in collective liberty. But then this internalized common sense and ideology comes into contradiction with some aspect or aspects of our real experience, as pain and suffering and injustice (witnessed in others but also experienced in ourselves) become evident to us in a way that does not appear justified by the justifying common sense and ideology. And then, one encounters Marx and the Marxist tradition and suddenly the contradiction seems resolved at least in thought—the common sense and ideology was a mask, underlying socio-economic forces are exposed as what was and is real, with great detail and intricacy of historical analysis. I myself remember the moment in my early 20s when I as a second-year law student in the library first read *The German Ideology* by Marx and Engels, and felt the blinds were being lifted from my eyes as I read their compelling historical description of the rise and fall of class societies.

And yet this experience of revelation may have been misleading precisely to the degree that it was and remains persuasive. I recently watched a television drama on the Wars of the Roses called *The White Queen*, which presented the struggle for royal power in the fifteenth century between the Yorks and the Lancasters as simply the result of vicious in-fighting between the two families in which "to be king" was the self-evident sole objective of the warring sides. There are many ways to understand the description of social reality in a television presentation like this, including the appeal in the present day of a symbolic, fear-saturated and rage-filled melodrama as ideology that legitimizes our current world by suggesting that this is how human beings simply are in their being but also suggesting that we have surpassed, in our enlightened liberal democracy, this kind of primitive monarchical governance by inter-familial bloodbath. But one thing that was clear to me and my partner Lisa was that the rest of England and the wider world were a part of the superstructural battle over the State that we were witnessing.

So in pursuit of a quick education in what might have been really going on, we went to counterfire.org's "Marxist History of the World, Part 34," which briefly and convincingly analyzed the underlying factors behind the Wars of the Roses—the stage they represented in the struggle of the landed gentry and rising bourgeois class against the feudal lords that characterized this historical period ("market feudalism"), the shift of consciousness toward absolutist monarchy and national identity that mediated the conflict in productive forces, the role of new inventions and new legal forms facilitating the rise of urban crafts, industrial enterprise, long-distance trade, and money-lending, new forms of military bombardment under royal control. According to this narrative, these were the complex underlying economic and social forces shaping the civil wars among royal families, with contesting socio-economic groups backing one or the other of the contestants for the crown, based upon their respective economic interests, across a period of a few hundred years prior to the ultimate defeat of feudalism and victory of the capitalist class.

When I say that this Marxist interpretation of the television show's events is convincing, I mean that it is so far superior in practical detail and narrative plausibility to the show's version of reality as a war among a dozen or so royal family members that one would naturally be inclined to say "of course, this is what was really going on," or something like it. But the Marxist description presents in a completely unproblematic way what it means to say someone "is" or "was" a feudal lord, or a member of the landed gentry or any of the other roles in the description, and even more it covertly envelops these social roles in a story that places the engine moving the role(s) forward in historical time in the economy, the struggle therefore of socio (roles)-economic (underlying material motivation) forces. The explanatory power of the Marxist interpretation results from the reification of the socio-economic narrative as a totality, which the writer presents as objective observation from outside the events themselves.

But as I will show, a "feudal lord" is not a flat entity-like designation of an identity, but is rather an evocation of an alienated manifestation of social being longing to transcend its alienation and afraid of doing so. A respiritualized way of seeing the same phenomena described by the Marxist historian requires that we get inside the existential life-world of the feudal lord, that we "grasp" him in his style, pretense, and effortful authority, that we show why he might anxiously be shifting an imaginary allegiance as an isolated fearful being from the family and its coat of arms to being "English" during this period of the rise of a unifying nationalistic imaginary, that we feel his erotic ties to a sado-masochistic relationship to his "vassals" whom he protects and how this may protect him from becoming vulnerable to their true humanity.[1] And I will show how the same alteration of social being inflects the other actors in the historical dynamic—the landed gentry, the rising class of merchants, the King himself—insofar as these historical actors give themselves over to being "roles" in an inter-group, fear-saturated struggle. My intent is not to reject the Marxist's socio-economic elements in the situation, but to show we can engage in this enlivened description of the existential life-world of social being as it was lived at a particular time while acknowledging the proper weight and influence of the fear of starvation and scarcity, the need to maintain control over land and crops, and other survival needs of one's own body and other bodies with whom one is identified. In other words, if we can respiritualize the psychospiritual field of the present moment that we ourselves live in, we must also accomplish this in trying to recover the existential life-world of those who preceded us in precisely the same way, to conserve the Marxist attention to the empirical detail of historical reality, while going inside these details to restore to them their social-spiritual "heart" or core or foundation.

How do I know that the approach I am proposing to the feudal lord is truer to the reality of the feudal lord than the Marxist approach? My answer to that question must be addressed to you, dear reader, as simply an appeal: The method that this book flows from is to begin from inside myself and to call upon you to respond from inside yourself, to let go of your holding back and looking at things from a distance, and instead throw yourself forward into the world so as to illuminate it with the light of your own existence. The Marxist, like the liberal describer who posits that we are all "free and equal individuals," withdraws him-/herself from the vortex of life and writes and speaks "about" the world as seen from the outside. The next great shift of consciousness in theory and practice, in perceiving, thinking through, and acting on our situation, requires that we respiritualize all of these ways of seeing and thinking so that we a) surrender our detachment, b) connect the heart and the head, c) describe the world from the inside by throwing ourselves forward via an intuitively-based description into the inside of the life-world itself, and d) because the life-world is inherently social, make visible its interior social distortions in such a way as to point the listener or reader toward a healing redemption of our longing to live in a loving and authentically connected community. To accomplish this evolution of our way of seeing and thinking and speaking of our life-world, we must begin by clarifying what it is that has gotten so distorted, a distortion that keeps reproducing itself generation after generation.

Note

1 The erotic nature of these ties is illuminated by the enfeoffment kiss which might accompany a serf's enfeoffment to his or her lord. See the following remarkable account of one such ceremony given in Fordham University's Internet Medieval Handbook, drawn from Galbert de Bruges's Chronicle of the Death of Charles the Good:

> Homage and Fealty to the Count of Flanders AD 1127 . . . : First they did their homage thus; the count asked if he was willing to become completely his man, and the other replied, "I am willing"; and with clasped hands, surrounded by the hands of the count, they were bound together by a kiss. Secondly, he who had done homage gave his fealty . . . in these words: "I promise on my faith that I will in future to count William, and will observe my homage to him completely against all persons in good faith and without deceit." Thirdly, he took this oath to this upon the relics of the saints. Afterward, with a little rod which the count held in his hand, he gave investitures to all who by this agreement had given their security and homage and accompanying oath.

The Marxist might understand this kiss as an eroticization of a hierarchical relationship in the service of class domination, with the material relationship being the "underlying" driving force. In this book, my emphasis is rather on the eroticization of domination as a kind of cementing of the false self within what I will later call a rotating patterning of social alienation in which hierarchy is a central constituting element. In my framework, the spiritual distortion of the interhuman within the enfeoffment kiss itself is what is essential, not the material dimension that for me is an expression of social separation rather than the cause of it.

Works Cited

"Democracy." *Wikipedia*. www.wikipedia.org, Accessed 23 May 2017.

Griffen, John, Faber, George, and Pattinson, Charles, Creators. *The White Queen*. Company Pictures, London, 2013.

Heidegger, Martin. *Being and Time*. Translated by John Macquarrie and Edward Robinson, Harper & Row, 7th ed., New York, NY, 1962.

"A Marxist History of the World Part 34." *Counterfire*. www.counterfire.org, Accessed 23 May 2017.

Sartre, Jean-Paul. *Being and Nothingness*. Translated by Hazel E. Barnes, Philosophical Library, Inc., New York, NY, 1956.

Sartre, Jean-Paul. *Critique of Dialectical Reason*. Translated by New Left Books, Verso, New York, NY, 1984.

Van Morrison. "I Forgot That Love Existed." *Poetic Champions Compose*, Mercury Records, London, 1987.

Chapter 1

The Desire for Mutual Recognition

The fundamental social desire of all human beings is the desire for mutual recognition.[1] This desire is an unmediated movement of being outward toward the other, emanating directly from my very center, that seeks to make contact with the being of the other. Thus coming-into-contact is a singular movement that has two experiential poles: my desire to recognize, and my desire for a reciprocating recognition. But you can't have one without the other. What is aspired to and what occurs when it occurs is an indissoluble co-presence. And this co-presence made manifest through mutual recognition is the realization of our social being, a social being that pre-exists our realization of it—if we are out of contact, we are actually in flight from that contact rather than truly "disconnected." The inherent mutuality of our social being is always pulling us back toward each other—in every moment, the desire for the immediacy and co-presence of mutual recognition pulses through us, moves us out toward each other, and seeks to realize, reciprocally and through the draw of a mutual magnetic pull, our inherent social nature.

Consider the color portrait of a woman by photographer Robert Bergman, located at www.therobertbergmanarchive.org/photo-color-portraits-14.html, and presented here in black-and-white (Figure 1.1).

In looking at this portrait in its full color presence, at first you might only see the face of a woman. Most likely, you will start out looking at her "from a distance," as one often looks at a portrait or really at any object

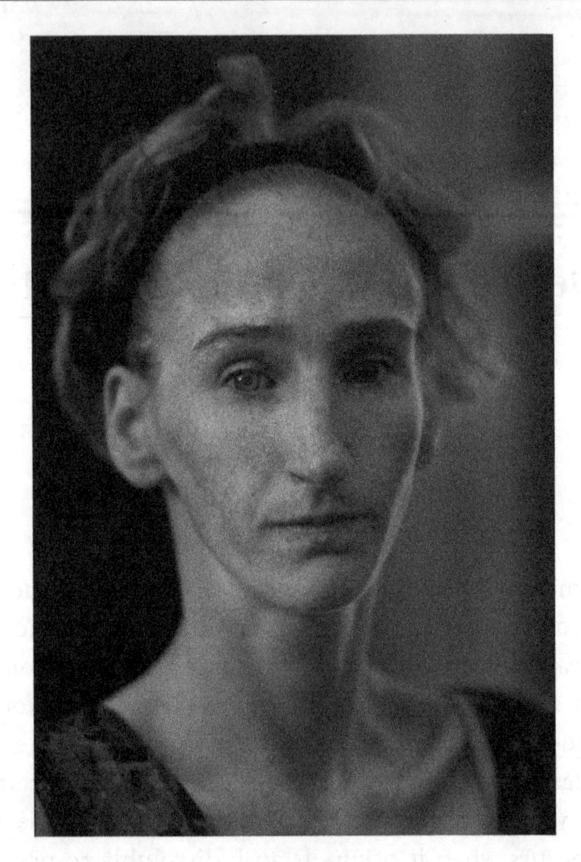

Figure 1.1

in the world, and she might at first appear to you as sad, or troubled, or thoughtful, and perhaps also resilient in carrying life's burdens. Her freckles might stand out, or you might notice particularly the redness of her dress and hair against the red light behind her. But if you allow yourself to stay with her for a full thirty seconds and don't pull away or allow her image to simply glance off your gaze, you may suddenly encounter her directly as a fully present human being. At first you may have this disturbing, disorienting encounter through her right eye as her gaze penetrates the shield of your normal distance as a withdrawn observer. But if you stay with her and don't avert your own gaze, you will see that you are experiencing her presence as a totality and not only through the eye, as a radiant energy manifesting her living being as a whole social person. And at the same moment, as you are pulled into relation with her, you will feel your own presence that you did not feel an instant before. You were "lost in thought," floating inside the withdrawn mental space of your head. And now you are for a moment, or for longer if you can tolerate it, fully present in relation to another human being.

I have described this as disorienting and disturbing, and this is so because the photograph has the uncanny power to dissolve the withdrawnness and accompanying distance that we ourselves have learned to construct to protect us from a vulnerability to the other that, due to our conditioning, frightens us. We have all learned to fear this vulnerability to the other, just as in Freudian terms the ego fears and defends itself against the impulses of the id. And what we fear is the loss of the mediating "moat" that we have learned to lay down in the interspace between ourselves and others, a moat that co-exists with and is monitored by our moment-to-moment mental activity, the anxious monkey-mind of thought. But while it is therefore disorienting and disturbing to have that moat suddenly erased as we encounter the woman in red, we also experience relief. She graciously and beautifully brings us back into contact with the other, with others, with the entire social world, with ourselves as social beings. She reminds us of the potential that exists in the next moment; she gives us hope; she makes us want to change the world so that what we experience in encountering her can become real for our social lives and for social life as a whole. Right this moment, if you have been or are regarding the portrait and if you have allowed yourself to encounter her, you will feel your heart beating faster.

What makes Robert Bergman a great artist is not something unique or special that he has "added" to the portrait of this woman, but rather that he has revealed her as the true presence-in-the-world that she actually is as she lives her existence from within her own experience. His portrait brings forth the person behind the outer appearance, the being who actually inhabits the eyes that we otherwise experience as ocular globes. Through his way of capturing her in a single moment, he is reminding us all of the presence that we actually are, and he is calling upon us to emerge from our isolation, to gain the confidence that we are really all here together, to release ourselves from the imprisonment of our separation, and discover the beauty of our co-present collective humanity, not as a collection of individuals, but as an interconnected unity of differentiated social being.

We have the same experience of discovery when we encounter newborn children, at least once they are old enough to make eye contact with us. Like the woman in red, the newborn child suddenly pulls us out of our distanced mental selves, surrounded by the moat, into the fullness of his or her presence. Not having learned to be wary of the other, or to develop "stranger anxiety" to use the term through which psychology currently naturalizes as an inevitable stage the laying down of our alienation, the child makes us burst into a smile when we encounter him or her. Like the woman in red, the newborn child instantly relieves the suffering of our normal spiritual imprisonment and helps us to return, momentarily, to who we really are. This is why every newborn child brings us the possibility of salvation from the suffering of separation, from the paralytic self-reproducing distance that blocks our capacity to fully recognize each other.

But like Martin Buber, who sought to capture the aspiration to unmediated relational encounter in his famous book *I and Thou*, I have thus far presented the desire for mutual recognition in a way that might suggest I am mainly speaking about a psychospiritual relation between two people. This then could give the impression that the world can be understood through the lens normally used by psychology, as an infinite series of private encounters. But while I do mean to say that authentic mutual recognition can occur between two people–a couple falling in love, for example, or in an encounter between any two people who are able, by intention or accident, to break on through to the other side of the learned experiential boundary that has divided them–while I do mean to affirm that possibility, the fact is that the desire for mutual recognition and the fear of the other that opposes it undergirds the entire nexus of intersubjectivity that we call the social world. Thus when transformative social movements "emerge" and "break out," what actually takes place is a ricochet of recognition in which millions of people can sometimes become suddenly present to each other in a new way and in which the sedimented layers of separation that had divided people into discrete, alienated social pockets are emulsified very quickly by the movement's rising force.

In the late 1960s, for example, the fusion of the civil rights, women's, and anti-war movements, along with the generative creativity of the worldwide 60s counterculture, led to a ricochet of recognition that leaped like a flame from one city in the world to another very quickly, from Berkeley, to Mexico City, to Prague, and to countless other locations. The "rising force" that generated this experience of movement was actually the desire for authentic mutual recognition gaining the social confidence to erupt across vast social spaces, creating a new social ground for millions of people to stand on, an unmediated, radiant ground of joyful co-presence. No matter what the roles and customs and identities that these masses of people had felt allegiance to and had been conditioned to be bound by prior to the movement's emergence, "something in the air" allowed people to leap forward toward each other and become present to each other on a new ground of being that transcended the particularities of their previous conditioning (at least temporarily—much more than the hot moment of a movement's emergence is required to solidify a new ontological ground like this). And we will return to this later in this book.

But the point to be emphasized here in this first chapter is that the desire for mutual recognition is a social force that radiates throughout and across the social fabric of the world, as a vector emerging (as a force and a longing) out from the center of each person as a pole of social being toward each other person. Insofar as the world precedes our birth and acculturates us to a conditioning—by gender, race, nationality, economic status, and many, many other forms of conditioned particularity—that conditioning provides a vast differentiated envelope of identity that we must conform ourselves to because it is the vehicle of the recognition by which we become social at all. To take myself as an example, when I became "conditioned" in my childhood, I became all at once male, white, upper middle-class, half-Jewish (actually three-quarters), a child of actors, American, somewhat tall, and was conditioned in countless other ways. *All* of these elements of my conditioning were transmitted to me through the way I was recognized by others. All of these elements were impossible to resist had I even wanted to because they provided in significant part the channel to my actually being able to exist at all as a social person, and had something kept me from properly identifying with the way I was recognized, I would have become schizophrenic or died from failure to thrive. And at the same time, all of these elements of my conditioning linked me to the wider social world by virtue of who shared my identifications and who did not share them, by the cascade of interlocking, intersubjective recognition that actually constitutes the social world and brings it into being.

The desire for mutual recognition both supports our social conditioning (since we must seek the recognition of our parents and other adults who are here to receive us if we are to realize our social nature) and transcends our social conditioning insofar as our conditioning is alienated, insofar as it does not actually make possible the realization of the fully present interhuman encounter. In our being, we seek the direct, unmediated co-presence to which Bergman's portrait aspires—this is the life-force that moves the social world forward and also makes true Martin Luther King's statement that "the moral arc of the universe . . . bends toward justice". But in our conditioning, we are bound by the conditions of how we are actually recognized from birth, with all its limitations, with the fear of the other that it transmits and contains. Yet because the longing for authentic mutual recognition always exerts a transcendental pressure on the limitations of our conditioning, we are only bound by our conditioning so long as the web of recognition that produced it remains stable, remains more or less the same from an ontological point of view. The possibility of going beyond those limitations, and the constant unconscious search to go beyond them, exists at all times, and is our source of hope.

Now in order to more fully link this description with socio-historical interpretation and place these still seemingly psychological insights in relation to how we normally think about large-scale social processes, let me return to our description of the feudal lord of the middle ages. When Marxists or other socio-economic interpreters think of the feudal lord, they think of him in relation to his interests, as if he were a kind of cog in an external system of socio-economic relations. In this way of seeing, he might have had a psychological life, but it would have been understood as "on the side" in the way that everyone has a psychological or spiritual life—shaped, for example, by his family and by life circumstances. But his "real" existence in a social and historical setting would be understood in terms of his interests within the functioning of the whole system, as a member of the ruling class, overseeing his landed estate, appropriating the labor of the serfs and increasingly of wage workers (assuming we are again viewing him in the late feudal period of the fifteenth century), protecting those workers as an incident of fealty, and supporting and benefiting from the legitimacy of the monarchy and the church and the ideology that these prevailing political and religious institutions generated.

What I am proposing is that we revise this entire way of seeing the feudal lord and recover his lived existence through apprehending him as a living being desiring to fully recognize and be recognized by others—to be recognized by, for example, the person next to him—but with that desire also contradicted by the envelope of alienation and fear of the other that he by birth and social reproduction was thrown into. Thus, his "lordship" as a totality of mannerisms, style, pretense, beliefs, condescension and deference, dehumanization of his vassals (both as factors of production of agricultural goods and as imaginary "others" occupying a lesser place in the feudal hierarchy)—all of these and countless other ways of being-a-lord are shaped by and transcended by the conflict between desire and fear that actually incarnates him in relation to all others as a real, existential, living social being. Within this way of seeing the feudal lord, what drives the historical process forward is not his formal relationship to an external system (for Marxism, a division of classes pursuing their respective interests that are in contradiction under conditions of material scarcity), but the transcendent longing for mutual recognition organizing itself through not entirely predictable socio-historical "emergences," which sometimes have a class character (as in the overall struggle of the rising merchant and capitalist class to break asunder the restraining feudal relations), sometimes have an ideological character (the eventual coalescing of Protestant revolts against the Catholic Church), and sometimes through cultural upsurges like the forms of dress, popular song and poetry, and liberatory sexuality that give voice to each rising "movement," which we can now understand as a movement of social being seeking its own realization through transcendent and authentic community.

This is not to say the material factors shaping the feudal lord's life are unimportant but rather that they refer to those aspects of the lord's social existence that pertain to the survival of his body, and, under conditions of scarcity, provide an important channel for the longing of the desire for mutual recognition to express itself. When the peasants revolt, they are in fact starving, and they want to overthrow those who are depriving them of food, but if they lived in a beloved community, human beings would not turn on each other driven by material need. Thus there is a co-existing mutual influence of material and social-spiritual factors that must always be understood by linking the survival and health of the body, with the full social realization of our relational collective being. I will address this further in Chapter 6, but first we must fill out our description of the encounter of the desire for mutual recognition with the social envelope into which it is born and contained. How exactly does social desire that exists in everyone come to alienate itself in actual human relations?

Note

1 Several other writers–notably G.W.F. Hegel in philosophy, Jessica Benjamin in psychoanalysis, and Alix Honneth in political theory–make use of the concept of "mutual recognition" in their work. From what I have thus far read of their writings, my use of this term is different from theirs because by the desire for mutual recognition I mean a desire for an unmediated co-presence with the other, with each other, that dissolves the false self that separates us and brings us into a pre-reflective and immediate social connection. The other writers to whom I refer seem to have a somewhat more developmental notion of "mutual recognition" as something to be achieved through historical, psychological, or political growth. As I indicate in the Preface, for me the desire for mutual recognition means the desire for the completion of our very social being that we aspire to from birth and that is realized through that mutuality of presence that is most palpable in social movements but that remains possible in every human encounter. The pull of that always-present desire is the silent anchor fostering all growth and development, whether personal or social.

Works Cited

Bergman, Robert. "Portrait of Cindy Tyler." *A Kind of Rapture*. Pantheon, New York, NY, 1998.
Buber, Martin. *I and Thou*. Touchstone, New York, NY, 1971.
Freud, Sigmund. *The Ego and the Id*. W.W. Norton & Company, New York, NY, 1990.
King, Martin Luther Jr. Wesleyan University Commencement, quoting Theodore Parker, 8 June 1964, Hartford, CT, Wesleyan Baccalaureate.

Chapter 2

The Denial of Desire, Fear of the Other, and Formation of the False Self

When the newborn child encounters an adult, one aspect of the encounter is certainly, in most circumstances, a radiant experience of love. The child spontaneously seeks to recognize and be recognized by the adult—in fact, the child spontaneously pulls the adult out of his or her "world" and into a direct, unmediated encounter with the child. By "unmediated" I mean that the child's presence, though of course manifested through physical features like the eyes and mouth, emerges through and transcends those features with the animation of what is sometimes called an aura, just as the woman in red in the last chapter manifests herself as an aura of presence beyond her appearance in the photograph; each is "there" as an invisible, radiant someone that surpasses the physical incarnation through which their presence is made manifest.

The adult, if the adult is not seriously emotionally disabled or, more precisely, *dissociated*, will reciprocate the child's love, but as I have said, the already conditioned adult must do so by being pulled out of his or her "world." The adult, with relief and joy, overcomes his or her distance, or more precise the di-stance, the doubleness, of his or her own adult conditioning. The adult crosses the moat, almost against his or her will, so powerful is the child's presence-in-the-world. But the child will inevitably very quickly also begin to experience this di-stance, this conditioned withdrawnness that the adult has internalized within his or her own life history insofar as that history has been, in significant part, a transmission of alienation characterized by a fear of the other internalized first during the adult's own early childhood. Unlike the child's loving presence that extends itself fully vulnerable in anticipation of the unconditional love of mutual recognition, the adult's presence is haunted by a shadow, the legacy of a fear of the other that opposes the vulnerability of unmediated presence.

Thus the child experiences both the adult's spontaneous desire for mutual recognition that carries forward his or her loving energy as a genuine and immediate presence, and at the same time, a distance that tends to empty this presence by "denying" this desire and limiting, decisively, the adult's vulnerability. To use myself as an example, as I said in the last chapter I "am" all at once male, white, upper middle-class, half-Jewish (actually three-quarters), a child of actors, American, somewhat tall, English-speaking–I carry into my encounter with the newborn child all of the qualities of my social self that were passed on to me as the available channels for being social, for being connected to others, and so I cannot but bring this limited transmission of social being to the presence I extend to the child. From the point of view of the child's experience, he or she therefore experiences me as a presence insofar as I am pulled toward him or her with the immediacy and spontaneity of love, but also a presence haunted by an absence, insofar as my conditioned social qualities limit how I can "be."

To get a sense of what I mean by "absence," think of the newscaster who addresses you on CNN or MSNBC, or in a more familiar, almost folksy way on the local news. He or she of course manifests a vestige of the suppleness and groundedness of authentic human presence, but his or her being is semi-masked by a performance–if we assume we're speaking of a man, he casts up a "role" over his presence that he has taken from the outside, from watching other newscasters, and he speaks as if he *is* the role. When he says, to use a true example I have often used that I first encountered while watching the news in law school, "the Red Sox Win and a Fire in Dorchester!"–when he speaks thusly, we cannot but notice silently that his gestures are slightly "behind," that this voice is a bit too loud, that his eyes are blank as if he's not seeing through them but rather is focused on making "the sounds of the other," that he is not aware of the meaning of a possible fire to those affected by it and is in that moment equating it to a sports victory, all as "the news."

This hollow character is what I mean by an "absence," an absence of presence that of course co-exists with and–in the case of the newscaster–swamps his actual presence as the existential, unique, really living being that he actually is. In truth, most of his true presence is preoccupied precisely with making himself absent, not-present, through his performance, since this kind of hollowing-out of presence requires much focus and tension, since it requires both the "enacting" of an outer role-performance, and a withdrawing from sight of one's true, authentic being that would leave one vulnerable to the other's gaze. If proof of this is needed, think of the consequences you yourself may have seen when the newscaster loses his place or stumbles over a word—the anxiety that breaks out as he scrambles to cover the mistake in a way that relegitimizes the role and conceals his own vulnerability revealed by the slight and insignificant error by recementing his outward appearance.

I will return momentarily to the reason for this fear of "the viewer," the other, but the key point that I am making about the newscaster here is not to single him out for his alienation, but to describe in a recognizable way the outer "casting" of the self, the transformation of our being into alienated performances, which occurs not just in the extreme case of the newscaster, but is suffered by all of us. The newscaster is simply filling his already existing alienation—the form or existential "mould" of his conditioned and fearful ego—with newscasting, but it is a kind of structure of the self which has existed since early childhood, since he first internalized the conditions of being a person in a world that, for a reason unknown to him, requires it of him and makes it a condition of social recognition, of group membership, of existing as a social person at all. Except to the extent that we have experienced the power of loving authentic mutual recognition with another, or better, with others, through participation in liberatory social movements of some kind (for social change, in a theater group, through religious gatherings, at Burning Man), except to that extent, we are all the newscaster because the hollowing-out of authentic being and the casting up of an absenting "role" of the self, is the only alternative to authentic mutual recognition, leaving aside the withdrawal and splitting of so-called mental illness, or suicide.

Thus it is most accurate to see the newscaster as one of myriad manifestations of historically and culturally shaped role-performances that "fill up" the alienated outer structure of the self, that fill up what I have called the moat with historically and culturally specific content. But there is an additional feature of the newscaster's role-performance that is essential to the effectiveness of its coercive power, and that is that it is accompanied by a meta-message—a latent message behind the manifest message—that says, silently, "this is who I really am." The newscaster casts up a "false" role-performance that is actually an absence-of-presence and *not* who he really is, and accompanies it silently with the background claim that this *is* who he really is. And that is why we initially cannot become conscious that the newscaster is throwing up an absence of being, a false self—that he is (mainly and in significant part) a non-person pretending to be a person: the newscaster transmits to us not only his delayed and artificial persona, but also the assertion that his persona is real.

If we now discipline ourselves to realize that we all are the newscaster and have him in us insofar as we have inherited from prior generations the legacy of an alienated culture, then we can see more clearly what the child experiences in the early phase of life, during the first phase of his or her experience of social recognition. For while the child experiences the presence of the adult as a relational human being, as a co-presence actually *with* him or her, the child also experiences the limits of the adult's capacity for presence through what we may call the adult's "personality," through the adult's having internalized the totality of the culture's inherited content and the alienated form through which it was transmitted. And because the child as an inherently social being is "recognized into social existence" by the adult, the child must immediately internalize and re-externalize him-/herself the way that he or she has been recognized.

One extreme way to picture what I am saying here is to imagine the newscaster himself as this parental adult, this First Recognizer: We can well imagine that the newscaster, if he were to step out of the television screen to greet the child, might well say, "Why hello Johnny! Aren't you cute!" and in so doing throw the child from the hereness of true presence to a kind of strange thereness in which the child—now named an alienated sound "Johnny" that has some kind of designating meaning to the adult—feels himself in his being the counterpoint to the newscaster's persona. The child has no choice but to become a self as he is recognized insofar as becoming a self is an inherently social process of recognition, or in this case of both recognition (via the actual residual presence of the newscaster) and misrecognition (via the artificiality of the imposition of "Johnnyness" onto him as the recipient and carrier of the newscaster's alienated projection). And since the adult has also transmitted the meta-message that "this is who I really am," the child must internalize the corresponding injunction that this "Johnny" is who he the child really is, even as he knows and will know forever, at a deeper level, that Johnny is not who he really is and does not correspond to his authentic presence, a living being longing for authentic human contact.

Thus the child—all of us—begins to develop a split being. We retain a residue of authentic presence; indeed you can sense this in yourself right now as you read these words by attending to your presence as a grounded being. But we also superimpose on top of that presence an "otherness" that lacks the weight of presence, that is accompanied by a mental image, or really made up of a congeries of fractured mental images, of the self for the other. This image, and the otherness that is its existential quality as an absence of being, is inherently lacking because it is precisely an absence of true presence, a "role"-mould that we are cast into by the prior generation that conditions us. As we will see, this experience of lack, or hollowness, of the misrecognized self has immense consequences for the construction and reproduction of social reality. And the only way to heal this existential gap between our withdrawn presence and our relatively absent, or empty, or hollow, social self is through a steady healing encountering of authentic social presence in others, and from others into us through authentic mutual recognition. We will see that when a progressive social movement arises, this awakening and healing becomes possible—indeed the awakening actually *is* the movement, is what we mean by the moving of the movement itself, no matter what social content the movement may be carrying forward (for example, the various ways that the labor, civil rights, women's, LGBTQ, anti-war, and environmental movements manifested their "upsurge of being"). But before we turn to this social dimension of both the circulation of alienation and the potential overcoming of it through mutual recognition, let me fill out certain key elements of what occurs during our conditioning-to-alienation, certain key elements that I have not yet described of the collective internalization of the moat.

First of all, it is important to see that when the adult (inadvertently) alienates the child, the adult actually denies a desire for authentic mutual recognition—for true connection—that impels him or her in all his interactions, that always remains his ground as an at all times social being. This desire the child also experiences, but in denied form insofar as it is mediated through the role. That is, the role, or the persona, is all that the child "sees" because it is the social form of the adult as social being, but the child unconsciously experiences the adult's longing for authentic recognition at the same time, a longing that is denied in the "enactment" of the adult's self, and is therefore *revealed* in denied form. Thus if we imagine our exaggerated parody of the newscaster as adult encountering the child, when he says, "Why hello Johnny, you're so cute" in the equivalent of his newscaster voice, the child simultaneously experiences the artificiality of the projection being cast over him and at the same time the denied strain and anxiety manifested in the newscaster-adult's pulling back of his true presence from his persona, a presence that the newscaster longs to release from its withdrawn state and have recognized by the other, in this case by the child who is at first pulling for precisely this kind of authentic recognition, in a way that the adult simply does not know how to do. Thus the child experiences both the coercive projection of the artificial persona, backed by the meta-claim of the adult that "this is who I really am," and the underlying denied desire in the adult to transcend that very compulsive artificiality. If the unconscious could speak, the adult would burst into tears and join the child in a relation of innocent co-presence. But that will only become possible for the adult if circumstances permit him to experience a sustained encounter with others who can actually elevate his unconscious longing into awareness and social incarnation through recognizing that desire and reciprocating it. But the child cannot do this because the child has not yet been recognized into existence in such a way that he would have a social anchor for his own presence . . . he begins simply as an as yet unrecognized social being desiring mutual recognition, and he encounters, as his First Recognizer, an adult (or, of course, adults) who demand through the transmission of the necessity of artificiality that this desire for mutual recognition must be denied.

Thus the core double-message of the adult to the child in the very way the child is at first recognized into social existence is: "Desire me, but deny that you desire me on pain of the extinction of our connection. Instead, to be 'with' me you must become the artificial role that I claim that I really am and that I claim that you really are." The process of alienated recognition thus establishes for the child the very conditions of social membership, the very conditions of being "with" other human beings at all, and these conditions are compulsory for the simple reason that the child is a social being who seeks being-with-others as a necessary manifestation of his social essence. As contradictory as this initial double-message is for the child under conditions of alienation, we should see that it also offers hope, to the child and to all of us, for transcendence and social healing . . . because the authentic desire for mutual recognition, to see and be seen in a transparent and loving relation to the other, pulses through us at all times, even in denied form. Thus the newscaster-adult who says "Why hello Johnny, you're so cute" is self-evidently longing with all his being to be released from his own psychospiritual prison and is transmitting that as he denies it by claiming that this artificial persona is who he really is.

If drawings are helpful, Figure 2.1 is an illustration of what I am saying mapped onto the child-adult dyad in an alienated milieu—that is, onto the world as it actually is that we are all seeking to transcend.

Please recall that I have used the child-adult paradigm here to describe this process of alienation so as to emphasize the child's being thrown, as he initially seeks to be recognized into social existence, from his initial full presence into the alienation of his conditioned self. But Figure 2.1 captures equally well the paradoxical pull and push of all social relations among humans insofar as they are predominantly characterized by alienation and consequent separation.

A second point about the experience of the child when he or she is "thrown" through misrecognition into his or her alienated or false self is that because the self thus recognized lacks the weight of true presence—because this alienated self is relatively "ungrounded" and lacking—the child cannot anchor it in his or her being. It, so to speak, "floats" on the outside of the child's experience and is actually the origin of the split in

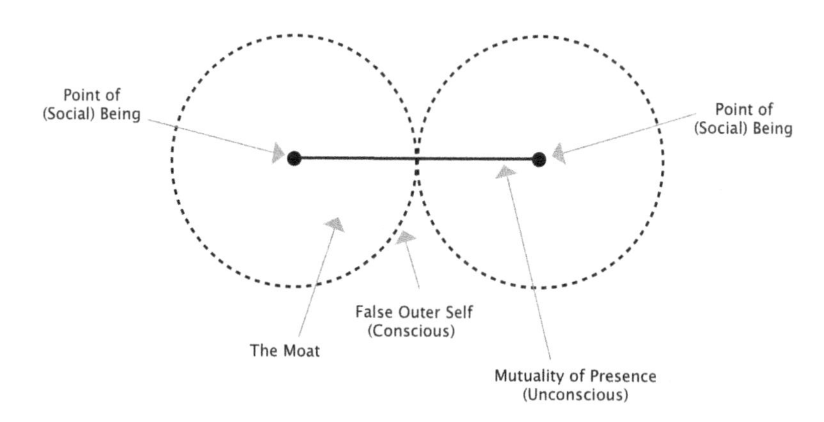

Figure 2.1 Experiential "Map" of Alienated Child-Adult Dyad

the child's subjective experience between a sense of an outer and an inner self. The suffering of many women about their appearance provides a clear insight into the adult manifestation of this split: Many women report feeling "from the inside" where their sense of realness is located that their "outer self" is constantly lacking in its appearance-for-the-other, but there is no way to take hold of this "outer" appearance and ground it "from the inside" because within the wider culture, girls are misrecognized in early childhood as "having" an outer appearance that is disengaged from the ground of their being, that is simply "how they look."[1] This experience of a "lacking outer appearance" is therefore a constant source of pain, because for girls and women, outer appearance still forms a part of the nucleus of social identity. "Outer appearance" is a key element in how they were recognized into social existence. But the point to be made here is that this particular split experience of many women is actually but one easily recognizable form of a universal aspect of alienated recognition by the other—the aspect of it that creates the "floating" character of the false or outer self.

Once the child has been seen as "Johnny" by the newscaster-adult, once he has been thrown from the anticipation of true mutuality into the insubstantiality of the outer-self-for-the-other, we can see that the only way he will be able to gain any mastery of this outer self is by also, gradually, identifying with the adult who has projected it onto him. This point is well-recognized in most psychoanalytic theory from Freud to the present, through such ideas as internalization of the superego, mastery through reversal of voice, identification with the aggressor, and the like, but as we can see from the phenomenological description I am giving here the origin of this identification is that it simply completes the child's process of becoming socially alienated. When the adult misrecognizes the child into an alienated social existence, the child first becomes how he is seen, and then adds to that within his alienated sense of self the persona of the adult who sees him, a persona that he takes in as an "authority" enforcing his alienation from himself. Precisely to the degree that the adult transmits the message of "this is who I really am" when he enacts himself, and correspondingly transmits "this is who you really are" in his misrecognition of the child, the child then takes that adult voice or imago into himself, into his own sense of who he really is. By internalizing that authoritative adult persona, the child simultaneously completes his relation to the other, or his sense of himself as social, at an intrapsychic level, and he gives a kind of imaginary anchor to what would otherwise be a floating and unanchored outer self.

Thus instead of experiencing and remembering the continuing sense of true mutual presence, of authentic social connection emanating from true mutual recognition, the child internalizes as his *sense of being social and of self and other* the alienated dyad: the "outer" seen self and then, gradually, the corresponding "outer" seeing self. And completing the divided alienated self is the residue of true mutual presence that has been transmitted in what I have called denied form, a residue that the child experiences as an "inner" longing that peers out across the moat of social separation. Paradoxically, the child imagines that his "floating" outer self, his seen self, is grounded by an authority that is "above" him and that he is "underneath," but that authority is also now a part of him.[2] Figure 2.2 seeks to capture this divided self with deference to a common projected authority as it exists reciprocally in the child-adult dyad.

While the example of women struggling with their sense of a lacking outer appearance may be the best example of the alienation of the floating outer self, men may provide the most easily recognizable example of

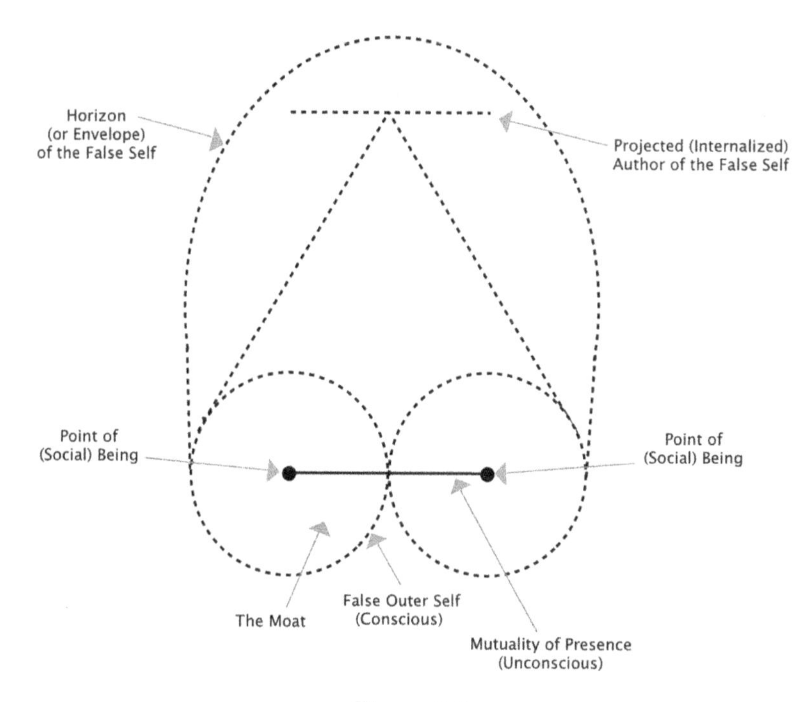

Figure 2.2

the child taking in to his self the authoritative adult that completes his social identification. For while the boy must struggle just as much as the girl with the lacking nature of the social self that is formed through alienated recognition, what we see so clearly in boys is the voice of the adult within the boy coming to install within him his (false) sense of social completion, and his moral stricture that the way he has been recognized is who he really is (even though it is not), and who others really should be insofar as he projects onto others the command of his own alienation.

Thus as the boy—as any child, male or female—"becomes" his or her alienation into adulthood, his or her experience is lived as an ontological schism: Each of us can sense ourselves as a true presence, as *here*, but we can manifest ourselves social only through our alienated "personality" which we actually experience as *there*, as outside-of-ourselves. If we return to the newscaster, we can recall that his gestures are slightly behind, because he is unconsciously enacting himself through his role while thinking and believing he is being himself. But although this schism is revealed most clearly in a somewhat caricatured form like that of the newscaster, we all suffer it precisely to the degree that our social-spiritual circumstances have denied us recognition of the presence that we really are. We are in hiding without knowing it until some social circumstance makes it possible for us to truly encounter another, others. And when an experience of authentic mutual recognition does occur, we spontaneously emerge into mutual presence in a way that reveals to us for the first time the schism that had previously enveloped us.

Here again an example may be of help. In 1989 when the Loma Priete earthquake struck San Francisco, the Bay Bridge partially collapsed, traffic lights failed to work at intersections, power was out for days all over the Bay Area. The forms that had been holding together the everyday "system," or that had been channeling the flows of that system, suddenly collapsed, creating a kind of free space which, when coupled with the genuine fear and need for mutual aid that this event generated, allowed people to risk coming out of hiding. On street corners, small groups of people (one of which I was a part of) watched the news on battery-powered televisions. And in my little group we saw a woman newscaster burst into tears and burst into presence, just as we all interacted animatedly with each other about what suddenly became our *present* situation. Instead of experiencing others and the world at a distance across the moat of our separation, the normal withdrawnness of our collective presence dissolved into a great outburst of presence manifested as concern about how to address our natural disaster. The normal detachment-sense of life taking place outside of us, including our own selves, and of peering out at this world from a spiritually imprisoned passive distance, dissolved into the joy of suddenly being *here* together. The city's mayor kept reassuring us as the first days passed that we would soon be back to normal, but the great secret knowledge of that earthquake was that we dreaded returning to normal, and suffered a collective loss when that reinstatement of the alienated system inevitably occurred after some two weeks.

Yet another example of this phenomenon of temporary dissolution of the alienated patterning of the system in response to a disaster took place in the two weeks following the World Trade Center bombing. Those of you who lived through that may remember the John Lennon-inspired telethon concert, and the transcendent performance by the Dixie Chicks of "I Believe in Love," a love emerging from our collective sense of awe at some of our humans having flown planes into and actually brought down in collapse those tallest of tall buildings, that as a species we had gone so far toward losing our minds, and that many of us responded heroically to save the injured as we shared a sudden loss that became truly "our" loss.

I give these examples to emphasize that the "movement" of social movements is certainly not the only way that our mutual presence can manifest itself, as there are other circumstances when the confluence arises of the prison-door of our system of alienation suddenly being thrown open, and our longing to emerge from that alienation suddenly becoming visible, through a circumstantial spark that could not be captured and tamed by our alienation in advance.

To return once again to the infant's process of becoming alienated, of being thrown into a floating outer self by his or her conditioning by others, we can see that yet a third ontological element of this outer self is that it cannot but seek to overcome its emptiness, or hollowness, or sense of being-lacking, by the paradoxical quest to become more of itself. Suppose that Johnny is recognized as "a good boy": He can sense through the shallowness of the sound of the words and the lack of being behind them that this is an image that he must try to be a kind of hologram without substance that he must somehow mould himself into. But since it is impossible to actually *be* a persona that is itself a lack of being (the insubstantial persona of a good boy recognized by the adult), he must begin a life-quest of trying to fill up his empty persona with "goodness," a task at which it is impossible to succeed. Thus to the extent that he now "tries to be good," he may in fact be praised by the adult, but he will never feel he actually *is* good because his entire effort cannot but take place on the slippery psychospiritual terrain of his outer self as a lack of being.

Thus the task of becoming the other that the other sees is a Sisyphean task, in which we all by our conditioning-in-alienation are condemned, we might say, to try to get a foothold in an outer self-gradient that has no substance because it is not sufficiently anchored to our actual presence, or to the presence of an actual present other. Since we are not recognized as the presence we actually are in our being, but are rather (mis)recognized as a reciprocal image of the other's own internalized imago, we can only try to perpetually inflate an absence of self that because it is a mere floating image of the self is doomed to deflation. In fact, the aspiration of the infant who is misrecognized and then tries to become his floating image, but whose image has a hole in it that prevents him or her from ever becoming this image, is to somehow become Perfect—a Perfect Other who would finally *be* the image that he or she has been cast into by the way he has been recognized into social existence.

The quest to become the Perfect Other, a consequence of the insubstantiality of the misrecognized self, is the equivalent in classical psychoanalysis of the ego's relationship to the Ego Ideal, but when we see this as a psychospiritual problem resulting from the alienation of social being from its own true relational presence to the other, we can see that it is not a personal challenge tormenting this or that individual as a psychological matter due to the particular qualities of a particular parent, but is rather a universal quality of social alienation itself. By our being cast out from our grounded presence to each other through the circulation of alienation, of the "rotation" of insubstantial otherness from one to another and across generations, we are condemned to chase our own tail, to try to become a perfect incarnation of what in truth lacks being, what cannot *be* at all.

The "Society of the Spectacle"

This description of the unmooring of the self from grounded presence in the creation of the "outer" self, and in the very split of inner from outer within the self, can be seen in its full social form in what Guy Debord and the Situationists famously called "the society of the spectacle." In his book by that name, Debord describes this society of the spectacle as a social world in which social relations that were formerly authentic and embodied have become, in effect, lost in mere "representations," and in which the human person, no longer in touch with his or her true self, passively identifies with the surrounding image-world or spectacle as if it were a true, active force. But while Debord identifies the source of this absorption of authentic human relations into the spectacle, following Marx, as a consequence of the alienation of human labor and of social relations themselves resulting from the dominance of the commodity form within the capitalist economy, we can see from my description here that this collective fascination with the "outer world" is actually simply an expression of the original alienation of self from other and the displacement of authentic mutual presence into a socially compulsory relationship of unmoored outer selves.

Just as the individual social person suffering under the requirement of the denial of desire experiences him-/herself as trapped in a lacking outer self, and just as this very insubstantiality of the social self leads him or her to continually seek to become a more perfect "other" in order to fill up "outerly" the self that is actually lacking in grounded presence, so also social persons collectively mis-identify their social existence with a kind of inflatable collective imago that they are always trying to "fill up" with hallucinatory meaning. Insofar as each person is "outer" and therefore lacking in presence, he or she projects this very same outerness and lack onto the experienced "world out there," to which a false realness is attributed. And this imago out there is the spectacle that holds everyone in thrall. Insofar as true social relations lack presence, to that extent the false social relations are repeatedly infused with a collective heightening, such that each person becomes enthralled by the fetishism and then elevation of the outer appearance. Hitler calls for "War!"; the "German people" are enthralled by their outer Nazi-hood and the Nuremberg rallies and the gigantism of the swastikas; and then suddenly 10 million Germans are dead and they become conscious, briefly, of the alienation that had enveloped them.

Thus when we say that we live in a media-dominated society, what we actually mean is that we as social beings have collectively given over our collective reciprocal presence to a watched world that has the quality of being outer to us, or outside of us, and that is enthralling in exactly the way that narcissism makes our own image enthralling at the personal level. The very same impulse that impels us, in the absence of true social relations, to puff up and make more perfect our "otherness" or outer self in narcissism also leads us to perceive the collective life of the group as a kind of collective self-spectacle that is also trying to make itself *exist* by the same kind of self inflation. This very collective process is directly revealed every night on "the news" when the newscaster speaks to us first (relating to us "one-to-one") about, for example, Donald Trump's latest "presidential campaign interview" "out there" and then cuts to a segment of the interview which we—the newscaster, and us—watch enthrallingly together. In this process, we first establish our mutuality as "watchers together" and then we turn to the clip and do the actual watching of the larger than life image of a person (Donald Trump "playing himself"), in which the object of the viewing becomes the spectacle to which we give ourselves over in enthrallment. In this example, Donald Trump is experienced as one aspect of the totality of the spectacle outside of us, to which we as absent presences are appended. Of course Trump is also alienated from his own outer self, and is a watcher of it just as we are, perpetually trying to make it "bigger," to inflate it, insofar as it is narcissistically a compulsory receptacle of his social desire, toward becoming a Perfect Other that will finally "deserve" authentic recognition through true mutuality, through love.

And yet all of the above having been said, we must remember that our authentic, grounded co-presence always co-exists with our alienated "outer" and ungrounded self-other enactments, and in most cases, it is that continuing silent presence that holds us together and provides each of us and the world with hope. The silent pull of the desire for mutual recognition, and the aspiration for that recognition to occur in the social world unfolding in front of us, co-determines every face-to-face interaction. If our conditioned alienation is a "co-efficient of adversity," to use Sartre's phrase, and if that alienation continually deflects us from fully encountering one another as mutual presence, the everpresent pull for mutual recognition is also a co-efficient, a co-efficient of hope that tethers us to each other as much as our legacy of our fear of each other separates us.

Relationship to Heidegger, Sartre, Lacan, and Psychoanalytic Theory as a Whole

It may be helpful, as a conclusion to this chapter, to link the above description of alienated social being with other related formulations that have influenced me—and specifically to compare and contrast my views with the related views of others.

Heidegger

With regard to my description of the newscaster, and the throwing of the infant into an artificial persona that in all of us prepares the way for our repetition of an absent outer self that exists in continual conflict with the pull for authentic mutual recognition of what would be grounded presence to and with the other, we can compare and contrast Heidegger's description in *Being and Time* of what he calls "the they-self." Consider the following passage from the section entitled "The Everyday Being-One's-Self and the 'They'" (the German word "Dasein" is used to mean "Being there" and is roughly a synonym for consciousness-in-the-world):

> Dasein, as everyday Being-with-one-another stands in subjection to others. It itself *is* not; its Being has been taken away by the others. . . . These others, moreover, are not definite others. On the contrary, any other can represent them. . . . The 'who' is not this one, not that one, not oneself. . . . The 'who' is the neuter, the 'they' . . .
>
> . . . In utilizing public means of transport, and in making use of information services such as the newspaper, every other is like the next. This Being-with-one-another dissolves one's own Dasein completely into the kind of Being of 'the others,' in such a way, indeed, that the others, as distinguishable and explicit, vanish more and more. In this inconspicuousness and unascertainability, the real dictatorship of the "they" is unfolded. We take pleasure and enjoy ourselves as *they* take pleasure; we read, see, and judge about literature and art as *they* see and judge . . . we find shocking what *they* find shocking . . .
>
> Everyone is the other, and no one is himself. The "they," which supplies the answer to the question of the "who" of everyday Dasein, is the "nobody" to whom every Dasein has already surrendered itself in Being-among-one-another.
>
> (pp. 164–166)

Heidegger is here describing the flight of each human being from his or her authenticity as a presence in the world into an adaptation of a false self that is absent, a "nobody." Elsewhere in *Being and Time* he describes this as a "fallenness" into "anonymity," by which he means that human beings tend to lose touch with their authentic human presence and flee into what I have called a persona, like that of the newscaster, which is not anchored to that presence but is in flight from it. His use of the term "the they" means to refer to the adoption of a way of presenting oneself and speaking that is not truly coming from one's own center, but is rather a flight into trying to "be" like everyone else. Yet because this "everyone else" is actually nowhere, Heidegger says, "Everyone is the Other and no one is himself."

For Heidegger, this tendency to evade one's own authentic human presence by adopting a kind of deferred pseudo-presence that is constantly trying to be "like the others" is a kind of moral failure, a potential of Being itself in which consciousness fails to grasp and claim its own authenticity and to ease what he calls the "burden" of that authenticity by becoming like the "nobody" that is "everyone else." In one respect, this view is identical with my description of the infant being cast from his or her presence into the precursor of the newscaster-self, in which we come to adopt an outer persona to which we attach the word "I" but which is in fact not truly expressive of our grounded presence-in-the-world.

However, what Heidegger does not grasp, in my view, is that this adoption of a false outer persona that is like what the other at first projects, and then expects, is the result of a socially coercive process of alienation growing out of our intergenerational legacy of fear of the other. He also does not grasp that this displacement of the relation of self and other into a relation of "otherness," of reciprocal relatively hollowed-out or empty personas, is passed on one to the other as a denial of the desire for true mutual recognition and functions to enforce the denial of mutual presence, for fear of being seen for the vulnerability that one really is. Thus at a deep level, Heidegger does not grasp or have empathy for the fact that we do long to fully recognize one another but nevertheless, because we have each been "recognized into social existence" by others who have felt compelled to deny that deep longing, cannot but reproduce within our own socially recognized selves the absent quality that protects us from what we ourselves most desire.

Heidegger's way of seeing the same artificial quality that I describe in the false self reflected his own revulsion at what he regarded as the fallen state of post-World War I Germany during the Weimar Republic. And because he saw this fallen state as a failure of Dasein, or consciousness-in-the-world, to live up to itself, his work became thoroughly reconcilable with the rise of Nazism. His later embrace of the "Fuhrer-principle" reflected his belief that if the German person were able to fully encounter the presence of a great leader as an Other manifesting authenticity of Being, he or she would recover from his or her fallenness into "the they" and become authentic him- or herself.

My description of the deflection into alienation in this chapter understands the phenomenon of alienation as a social process in which we misrecognize each other, while silently claiming implicitly that this recognition is both genuine and compulsory. It is entirely a social process, passed on from one person to another, and from one generation to another. And because our co-creation of an artificial self-other "outer" world is subtended or undergirded by a longing for mutual recognition that would transcend our alienation from ourselves and each other, the overcoming of alienation requires a psychospiritual social healing, rather than Heidegger's individual, moral recovery. As I have suggested, this psychospiritual social healing emerges in social movements, and in other redemptive moments within the existing world, in which we can spontaneously come to recognize each other's fully present humanity through a ricochet into social existence and experience of this presence itself. For this transformative process to actually change the world, it must carry forward the struggle for social justice, as the moral expression of the realization of our capacity for love, for the creating of what Martin Luther King Jr. called the Beloved Community.

Sartre

In *Being and Nothingness*, Jean-Paul Sartre puts forward a view similar to Heidegger's, characterizing what I have been calling the false self, or persona, or artificial outer self, as an intentional project of consciousness to exist in "bad faith" in relation to the other. By acting as he or she believes others want him or her to act and pretending he or she "is" this person, the individual carries out a flight from his or her own freedom and attributes a false necessity to the carrying out of his or her role that is a flight from his/her true being as a "for-itself," a free consciousness. Here is Sartre's famous description of the waiter in a café, which certainly enabled me to see my newscaster with new eyes, or more accurately, to name what I was seeing rather than be merely rendered uneasy by what I was seeing without being able to name it:

> Let us consider this waiter in the café. His movement is quick and forward, a little too precise, a little too rapid. He comes toward patrons with a step a little too quick. He bends forward a little too eagerly; his voice, his eyes express an interest a little too solicitous for the order of his customer. Finally there he returns, trying to imitate in his walk the inflexible stiffness of some kind of automaton while carrying his tray with the recklessness of a tightrope-walker by putting it in a perpetually unstable, perpetually broken equilibrium which he perpetually reestablishes by a light movement of the arm and hand. . . . He applies himself to chaining his movements as if they were mechanisms, the one regulating the other. . . . He is playing. . . . But what is he playing? We need not watch long before we can explain it: he is playing at *being* a waiter in a café.
>
> (pp. 101–102)

Whereas for Heidegger, this kind of "disburdenment" of one's authentic being by adopting a role supposedly dictated by others is a falling into the they-self, the self that consciousness succumbs to inauthentically and that is everywhere elsewhere, for Sartre the waiter is trying to give himself the pseudo-substantiality of "waiterness" by acting as if he really is a waiter rather than a free consciousness who chooses his self-manifestations, including how he waits tables. His "bad faith" is revealed in his denying that his movements are a product of his own choices, and presenting them to the other instead as if he simply *were* the waiter, as if the representation of himself as a waiter were "real." The distinction between Heidegger and Sartre is that performing the way "they" expect is for Heidegger a falling away from authentic Being, whereas for Sartre, at least the early Sartre, it is a flight from freedom into a kind of false thinghood.

Sartre modified these views in his later work *Critique of Dialectical Reason*, in which he tried to integrate his earlier existentialism, with its emphasis on the individual's freedom, the freedom of the "for-itself," with a Marxism that would affirm the power of social and economic conditions in decisively shaping human interactions. Seen through the lens of this later integration, Sartre would understand the waiter and the customer as always already caught up in a network of reciprocities mediated by "worked matter," by the power of the exigencies of the material world interacting with human needs under conditions of material scarcity to decisively shape how humans could be, or to use a beautiful phrase of Sartre's, how humans can "exist themselves" (the word "exist" here being used in an active, transitive sense). In place of his earlier "bad faith," Sartre would have later characterized the waiter as trapped in the social separation of what he called "seriality," a condition of mutual distance in which everyone is made other than himself or herself by the alienating pressures of the capitalist economic system. The waiter becomes alienated from himself not through his own bad faith, but because he is cast by socio-economic circumstances into a mode of passive functioning—what Sartre calls "passive activity"—that involves the carrying out of rote functions under conditions in which his own true humanity is superfluous. For the later Sartre, the waiter is rendered "other" to himself and "other" to others by the separation from others inflicted on him by the competitive capitalist market.

In his earlier work, Sartre's ideas correspond to Heidegger's to the extent that both understand the failure to be who one really is as a moral failing, a failure of authenticity. And to that extent, the early Sartre's view, like Heidegger's, fails to grasp the inherently social character of the adoption of an outer persona presented to others as if it were who one really is. My description in this chapter was meant to show that each of us must be as we are recognized by others, and if we are "recognized into social existence" by others who themselves are unable to manifest their true presence, who have internalized a fear of the other that prevents their being present in this way, then we too have no choice but to become in our outer aspect the social person whom the other sees. Thus the waiter's ontological challenge is not to recover his freedom (understood as a potential within him) as an individual, but rather to find a way to be healed into mutual presence through a healing recognition by other social beings. The waiter does not adopt his mechanical persona as a false self pretending to be real in an isolated present moment, but rather expresses the conditioning of his entire life from his earliest encounters with others, a conditioning in which his socially recognized self has been thrown into separation from his true embodied presence and has been held in this position throughout his life, only to be filled up with the content of "waiterness" when he takes and tries to carry out this particular job. And this is not his "fault"—if he were given the opportunity to recover his true presence through having that presence sufficiently recognized by others, the waiter would recover that presence spontaneously, as waiters sometimes do when they become part of the upsurge of collective being that arises in labor struggles, even sometimes simply in the empowering effort of a group of waiters to form a union. Of course it is rare that one such experience will override the fear of the other that has saturated anyone's entire conditioning, and a sustained psychospiritual transformation of communal relations, of relations with really existing other people, is required to fully support the emergence and integration into the social self of "presence" in the sense that I am using the term. But the access to one's otherwise unconscious longing to be in a relation of authentic mutual presence with others can be "recognized into existence" initially by even small acts of resistance that break through the patterning and reproduction of alienation that otherwise coercively encloses us in what I have called the "moat" that separates us from others, from the other "waiters" who surround us.

This last point reveals what I see as the critical shortcoming of Sartre's later work in the *Critique*, insofar as Sartre there locates the possibility of a social recovery of being in a simple breakthrough of this type. For the later Sartre, the social separation of "seriality," in which masses of people are scattered out into an infinite series of other-directed, alienated relationships by their objective relationship to the means of production and the relations of production, can be initially overcome by the emergence of the group into "fusion" through rebellion and revolt (his example is the seizure of the Bastille during the French Revolution, in which the poor (the sans-culottes) who had been languishing in seriality emerge into a "fused group" through taking collective action against the system). My direct experience of emerging into the social movements of the 1960s has shown this description of collective recovery to be accurate, but because the description limits its horizon to a hot moment of revolt against existing "objective conditions," it fails to see that the origin of our alienation is in our "rotating" misrecognition by others and the fear of the other that underlies and sustains this. As we will see in forthcoming chapters, it is this rotation of social alienation that actually creates and reproduces the economic system rather than the converse. And therefore, what is truly needed to overcome our alienation must be located in the intersubjective world rather than in the objective world, as we alleviate the internalized fear of the other through a sustained psychospiritual activism in which we nurture and become capable of sustaining our capacity to become present to others as they concomitantly seek to become present to us. Seizing the Bastille may indeed be a possible first moment of this collective recovery, but it will devolve into the blood-soaked Terror unless we attend to the legacy of fear of the other which is the true source of our collective spiritual suffering. Transforming so-called objective economic relationships will not produce the actual sustained mutuality of presence that such a transformation aspires to without a psychospiritual strategy that elicits from each of us the capacity to sustain the authentic mutual recognition that is only ignited in the formation of Sartre's group-in-fusion.

Lacan

Jacques Lacan, the French Freudian psychoanalyst, also developed ideas that sought to capture the process by which the person becomes alienated from his or her social self, in which a gap is inserted between the desiring subject and the way that the subject apprehends himself or herself as a conditioned social person in relations with others. But Lacan wrote in opposition to Sartre and in so doing, in my view, made something like the opposite error from Sartre, placing too much weight on the alienating effects of the encounter with the other (utterly rejecting Sartre's idea of individual freedom) and finding insufficient hope in the continuing force of human presence that always transcends the way that presence has been misrecognized.

In his short essay "The mirror-stage as formative of the function of the I as revealed in psychoanalytic experience," Lacan takes the position that the infant first comes to apprehend himself (Lacan uses the male gender pronoun, so I will in this discussion) as an image outside of himself in his perception of himself in the mirror at the age of 18 months. In this essay he asserts that the infant first grasps himself as he appears to the other through his own mirror-image, that he actually apprehends his image in the mirror and then (mistakenly) "identifies" with this image as who he "is." This attachment to what Lacan calls "the specular image" serves to alienate the infant from his actual instinctual desire (for Lacan a kind of "pulsion" out toward the world emanating from "the id") and the specular image becomes a kind of empty precursor of the "social I," which will forever identify itself following the mirror-stage with "the desire of the other" (*Ecrits*, p. 58). Thus Lacan says this deflection into the mirror-image "situates the agency of the ego, before its social determination, in a fictional direction" (*Ecrits*, p. 2) that will become the foundation of a permanent misrecognition of the ego as equivalent to himself as a real person. Oddly, Lacan attributes this tendency toward alienation in a biological, organic "insufficiency" in human reality, as if the infant cannot establish any relation to his surrounding reality except through the false or misrecognized manifestation of the imago in the mirror:

> These reflections lead me to recognize in the spatial captation manifested in the mirror-stage, even before the social dialectic, the effect in man of an organic insufficiency in his natural reality . . . a real specific prematurity of birth in man. . . . The mirror-stage whose internal thrust is precipitated from insufficiency to anticipation, and which manufactures for the subject, caught up in the lure of spatial identification, the succession of phantasies . . . to the assumption of the armour of an alienating identity, which will mark with its rigid structure the subject's entire mental development.
>
> (*Ecrits*, p. 4)

To this description Lacan adds that this "deflection of the specular I into the social I . . . decisively tips the whole of human knowledge into mediatization through the desire of the other" (*Ecrits*, p. 5), in which the person links his own desire to the chasing of a narcissistic image-for-the-other, an alienated image that can never be realized beyond permanent "anticipation."

Translated into a more straightforward form, Lacan is in effect saying that the infant first apprehends himself as an image in the mirror, that this image is a kind of empty mental reflection of self that is not the infant's real self, that this initial seen-in-the-mirror image becomes the initial form of the social image that one seeks in the gaze of the other, and as a result we live out a permanent alienation in which the image-that-we-are-for-the-other is mistaken for real existence.

Whereas the problem with Heidegger and the early Sartre is a failure to give sufficient force to the alienating effects of socialization in the formation of the false self, in effect attributing too much autonomy to the Being of the individual person in overcoming his loss of presence, Lacan effaces the presence of the person altogether except as an instinctual organism. In suggesting that the infant *wholly* identifies with his alienating image (except for the unconscious desire of the id, and at odds with this unconscious desire), Lacan fails to give sufficient weight to the continuing desire for genuine mutual recognition that each of us continues to feel and act on in every encounter. While focusing in much of his other writing on the unrealized strivings of the imaginary and the symbolic aspects of life that follow upon the mirror-stage and the transposition of the initial "specular I" into the "social I," he appears to treat what he calls the Real as something utterly inaccessible to consciousness, like and in defense of Freud's idea of the instinct-driven id (or "it"). And also like Freud, who renders social alienation inevitable by making the ego/superego complex a compromise response to unrealizable instinctual demands, Lacan also renders social alienation inevitable by describing the very being of the "I" as an ungrounded effect of how the "I" mis-sees itself and is mis-seen by the other.[3]

Although influenced by Lacan's quite powerful descriptions of the way that we all can be captured in empty mirror-images of the self that we then seek to "fill up" by pursuing the completion and idealization of these images in response to our "desire for the desire of the other," my ideas more optimistically affirm the co-presence of our authentic relational social being, always going beyond this alienation, always seeking in every encounter with others to see the other and be seen by the other for who we really are in our soul, in our heart of hearts. Furthermore, this continuing co-presence that we feel and will feel toward one another even under the most alienating circumstances is not outside of consciousness, but is known to us as the intuitive ground of our very existence. Amidst the significations of language and the congeries of the images of self which inundate and alienate us, we nonetheless reach out toward the other from the center of our social being in all our human interactions, so that co-presence and flight from that co-presence at all times co-exist. To say that we "know" this transcendent desire for mutual recognition is to say that we intentionally act on it without being able to directly access this knowledge in reflective awareness or linguistic significations (for example in these very sentences, I am appealing to the reservoir of presence and longing in you, in words through which I extend myself toward your Being through and past our respective conditioned personalities).

This intuited ground of our openhearted and always longing collective social being is actually what holds the world together in spite of the radical self-other disturbances reflected on a large scale in wars and in everyday life in the infinite small ways that we lose ourselves in our images of self and demean others by casting them into images that fail to recognize their authentic humanity. We do mistakenly identify ourselves with the way that we are seen by the other, and we do mistakenly project artificial and empty imagos onto others in our own present lives and as we give birth to and raise the next generations. But at the same time, we continually extend ourselves toward the other, seeking the authentic mutual recognition that would dissolve the inherited images that separate and alienate us.

Psychoanalytic Theory as a Whole

How then should my ideas be seen in relation to the vast body of work produced by psychoanalysis as a whole and even more broadly, in the field of psychology generally? So much has been written over the last hundred years that analyzes the complexity of psychological dynamics as they are lived out in the particularity of individual and family lives. Are the ideas that I am presenting rejecting or challenging these ideas, or if not, how are my ideas related to this vast and complex literature?

To answer this question we must make a kind of translation between the concepts and way of seeing expressed in psychoanalysis (and depth psychology generally) and the concepts that I am offering in this book. I have been trying to illuminate the desire for mutual recognition, as well as the distortions in our social being that result from the failure to realize this desire, as aspects of our common experience that are directly accessible to us through phenomenological description, through taking a kind of phenomenological x-ray of our experience itself. When I describe the internalization of a "false" self that we experience as "outer" to our withdrawn being, I am claiming we all actually experience this "outerness" in the course of our conditioning and in then living in the world. And I am offering examples, like that of the newscaster, that I hope are evocative of the experience itself to make the experience recognizable to you, in you yourself.

Psychoanalysis, on the other hand, tends to posit concepts about the person that attribute motivational forces to the person that are not themselves "experiential" in this sense (although they have rough experiential correlates)–such as instincts, drives, needs–and concepts about the person's "mind" that mediate the interaction between these attributed motivational forces and "the world"–with both "the mind" and "the world" also being concepts that are not themselves phenomenologically descriptive. Thus the person in some sense "has" "a mind" that in some sense contains an ego, a superego, and perhaps other attributed entity-like features that coalesce to form "intrapsychic structures" that direct the person's experience of the so-called outside world, including his or her relationships with others, sometimes conceived as "objects" of instinctual desires or needs (for example, in the large literature on "Object Relations" theory). Within psychoanalysis and depth psychology generally, there are many schools of thought including the Freudian school, the school of ego psychology, self psychology, attachment theory, control-mastery theory, intersubjectivity theory, and so on, that all make use of different attributed concepts about the person conceived as a kind of entity at a distance or "subject" in order to explain or account for what the person experiences and how he or she behaves in the world.

And where do the theoretical concepts of psychoanalysis come from? They are drawn from the problems in living that psychoanalytic patients or clients have, which are characterized as "symptoms" of a disorder that is measured against a posited normal state. Thus if a patient is very critical of himself or others, he might be said to have a strict superego, and a treatment process might try to help the patient to realize that his father was overly critical of him, that this was not necessary or required by reality, and might lead him to gradually develop a more "normal" superego. Or a patient who is very insecure might in therapy reflect on the childhood circumstances that brought this weakness in her "ego" about and might, through therapy, try to strengthen her "ego-functioning" so that her ego would then function normally. Or to use a concept prominent in present-day psychoanalytic therapy, she might be thought to be suffering from an attachment disorder owing to childhood abandonment and the therapy might be oriented toward helping her to better trust her "attachment" to others, to developing a normal sense of attachment. The key point is that all of these theoretical concepts understand the patient's difficulties in living in relation to an ideal norm that is drawn from the theorist's (or therapist's) sense of what is normal, appropriate, or adaptive. And because the psychoanalytic theorist or therapist also makes these normative concepts (like "the superego," or "the ego," or "the object relation," or "the need for attachment") attributes of the person—like the properties of an object—the psychoanalytic theorist unconsciously equates the normal functioning of the person with "the nature of reality," with what is and ought to be. Instead of illuminating the Being of the person through evocative phenomenological description of the person's actual lived experience, of the person's being-in-the-world as a relational presence-with-others, psychoanalysis *posits* the being of the person through the attribution of normative concepts to him or her that are made thing-like or are reified, and then "crams" the person's lived experience into the functioning of these concepts ("Once he relaxed his superego, he began having better relations with others."). And the result of this is that the suffering of the patient, and also what would constitute relief from that suffering, is measured in relation to what we might call the normal level of social alienation, or the normal functioning of the world of the false self that is in conflict with the longing for mutual recognition that transcends it. This is to say that psychoanalytic theory as a whole and much of psychology generally *unconsciously collude* in the false self's effort to represent itself "as if it were real" by assimilating often genuine and profound psychological insight to a framework that equates the (predominantly) false world with the real world.[4]

If psychoanalysis's often profound insights were freed from their own conceptual dependency on attributed, reified normative concepts, and if these insights were able to reveal themselves as illuminations of social experience as I have been describing social desire and the denial of that desire in the book's first two chapters, then psychology itself and the tens of thousands of therapists working in the field could better assist us in liberating ourselves from our own alienation. This socially redemptive reunderstanding would begin with the awareness that the suffering that psychoanalysis seeks to understand is the result of *a failure of mutual recognition*, through which we are thrown from a *here* in which we would become fully present to each other and into a *there* where we experience ourselves as outside of ourselves in the "self" that we sense we must become for the other, while at the same time remaining for the most part withdrawn in our being from the true and more fully realized social presence that we nevertheless continue to long for, to desire. To the extent that our authentic mutuality of presence is thus deflected into a reciprocity of images of self and other removed from the immediacy of true mutual recognition, to that extent a wide variety of problems in living result, many of which are well described in the psychoanalytic and psychological literature. If I cannot become fully present to my father in a relation of true mutual recognition, my response to the pain of not being so seen and confirmed and not being able to see and confirm him may lead me to develop split images of a good idealized "father" and a bad and rejecting "father" (both self-preservative distortions of my father as an actual person, distortions which psychoanalysis might show make use of the defense of splitting to preserve the good image from the undermining effects of the bad image while also splitting my internal emotional register into a "loving" affect (toward the ideal image) and a cordoned-off angry and vengeful affect toward the bad, rejecting image). I may develop "hysterical" or obsessive-compulsive symptoms of various kinds as a way of coping with my internal conflicts of image and emotion and with the dynamic interaction between these remembered (or internalized) conflicting images and my continuing desire to see and be seen in a genuine way by my real father, the man before me. But the main point I am making is that the features of my psychological suffering, whatever they are, are the result of my having been "thrown," away from the here of mutuality of presence, which is the ground of true love and the completion of our social being, and into an image-space in which my grounded present relation to my father is decisively subordinated to a reciprocity of images that are both preserved in my memory as an imaginary social realm in which I am forced to exist, and are enacted repeatedly in my actual relation to my father, and then in my relation with others whom I must experience on the basis of my earlier, original experience of my father (depending on the actual role of my father in my life, the ameliorating influence of my mother or other adults, siblings, or friends, and the general quality-of-being present in my social surround).

This is all to say that existing psychoanalytic theory and other forms of depth psychology and psychological insight can and should be understood as resulting from the displacement of authentic and grounding mutual recognition into a false self-other matrix that creates the imaginary realm of what psychoanalysis calls "intrapsychic" life. In relationship with my father who has been among the first social beings to "recognize me into existence" but who has (of course inadvertently) thrown me into a self outside my self and failed in part to fully recognize me in my Being, I enact and then re-enact as a remembered conflicted social relation, the me-for-father that has been transmitted to me comprised of a false or outer "seen" self, subtended by the residual love that remains my true relationship to him, and also a denied desiring residual Being that continues to seek authentic contact with him. To cope with, or more precisely to exist, the social conflict that this double-reality creates for me, I may develop a wide range of compensatory split images of my father that I also enact my self in relation to, creating a social situation which I carry over as my memory of "what the other is like" to my relations to all subsequent other people whom I encounter. In other words, what psychoanalysis and other depth-psychological theories call "mental" illnesses of "the individual" I am here redescribing as remembered and re-enacted original social relations which have in common the co-existence of a dominant false self resulting from a failure of recognition and a background, unconscious present Being that continues to desire authentic mutual recognition and the emergence into presence-with-the-other, with others, that would result from it.

If it is true that psychological conflict and suffering results principally from a failure of recognition of this kind, then it follows that psychotherapy, to be effective, must be "disalienating"; it is the authentic presence of the therapist that gradually helps to heal the fear of the other in the client or patient by gradually eliciting the client's or patient's psychospiritual presence. This is to say that "interpretation" of childhood trauma or other factors in itself does not heal, even when it is true. Only the radiance of presence as it may be manifested in the therapist and may be carried into and through the "reliving-process" of interpretation can begin to transform someone else's life. And even then, psychotherapy is decisively limited by its occurring episodically (i.e. once a week) in a private office separated from a world that is otherwise saturated with reinforcement of the alienation of any client's or patient's conditioning.

Although psychoanalytic thinking and psychotherapy itself can be a transformative vocation, it can only be so as a part of a larger effort to transform the wider social world within which it is but a partial, episodic intervention. The measure of how much difference any intervention can make in the life of another is how much the extension of human presence actually can be made manifest in its whole social context. The point of this chapter has been to sketch out the qualitative nature of the social alienation underlying psychospiritual suffering, whatever the particular content in any single person's life. That qualitative and painful experience of separation can only be overcome if the gravity of social presence emergent in the entire social environment is sufficient to bring forth the desire for mutual recognition that is otherwise sealed up in our loyalty to the images that have conditioned us, and have made us believe that allegiance to these images is the price of social membership, the price of what social connection there is in the face of the other's distance and flight.

Notes

1 In the examples I give of women's concern about their "looks" and of men internalizing and enacting their authoritative personas, I am making use of gender stereotypes to try to capture in a way that you can recognize what the "outerness" of the outer self actually feels like (in the case of many women) and how the commandingness of enacted authority appears in many men. But these splits in the self exist across genders precisely because they are ontological manifestations of alienation itself–what occurs in everyone when the desire for mutual recognition is denied through personas that intend to immunize us against the vulnerability of truly becoming present. When we dissolve the moat and become present to each other, we have no need to present and manage our "outer" selves (our "looks," for example) or to command compliance with outer role-performances in ourselves or others.

2 We can see that when the child takes in the adult's authoritative voice and thereby completes his or her social relation in his or her mind–as an intrapsychic, imaginary social relation in which both child and adult are a reciprocity of images–the child actually takes in the adult's own alienation, which manifests precisely the same "authoritarian" self-other character. To the extent that the parent misrecognizes the child as an "outer" version of him-/herself, it is based on the parent's own alienation, which reflects the same division between a floating seen "outer" self and an authoritative persona that is imagined to be the "author" of that otherwise floating and ungrounded outer self.

This is the phenomenological basis in experience of Freud's point that the superego of the child is modelled not on the ego of the parent but rather the parent's superego. In Freud's theory also, the person is not actually *here* as a present grounded being who has been recognized as actually *here* by the other, but is rather living out social images of self and other in which authority for the false-self complex that connects them "in the mind" is continually deferred backwards to prior generations, in theory to the beginning of time. The child says in effect, "I model my author not on *you* (because I am not fully in connection with a real you), but on your author" in a kind of infinite regress of non-presence. And so it must be, since the alienated social self is precisely not present *here* but is always *there*, somewhere else, which is to say, nowhere.

3 Freud and Lacan each render social alienation inevitable by presenting theories of the person that take what I show to be effects of relational non-recognition of each person by the other and picturing those effects as "ontological," as aspects of the very being of the person. In this chapter, I have shown that the fundamental desire of social being is the desire for mutual recognition, a social need emanating from the center of every person's being and realized or not fully realized through encounter with actual other human beings. When Freud posits his theory of id, ego, and superego, he a) presents a non-social fundamental "instinctual drive" at the heart of the person (emanating from the id or "it"), and b) presents the totality of a person's consciousness as a compromise effect of the instinctual drive's encounter with other persons and the world. This description renders the human person as a separate "individual" in his or her very being, transposing what I have described as the withdrawn presence of the person in a socially alienated environment into an inevitable aspect of a depersonalized "id" that can in its inherent nature never be fully realized in social relations. Even more, c) by presenting the ego as an inherently lacking compromise between the demands of the id and the restrictions of the world, Freud renders all of human consciousness as "lacking" in its very nature, rather than as suffering what I have shown to be a gap between the desire for mutual recognition and the social self that has not been fully recognized. And finally, d) the creation of the superego, which in Freud is a modification of the ego that the ego gives itself to create an authority to monitor itself so as not to dangerously express the wishes of the id, takes an aspect of the false self–the creation of a projected authority by the false self to try to give itself a ground that it otherwise cannot find–and makes that aspect an inherent structure of consciousness, rather than something that can be transcended through true mutual recognition. And a last and important point, taken as a whole, Freud's theoretical construct of id-ego-superego then simply makes ontological–as aspects of the very nature of being–what is actually an expression of the internalization of the false-self complex in an alienated social relation, in an unrealized relational context of the family in an alienated world.

In a similar vein, Lacan presents the very formation of the ego . . . the specular I that becomes a social I–as "already alienated" in the sense that misrecognition of its Real desire is inherent in its very makeup. From the very outset of his or her existence, the person is presented as lost in his or her image-for-the-other . . . and this "lack" in this image is presented as part of the structure of being itself. As in Freud, there is no inherently social or relational ground of social being; social being comes into existence only after the Real–emanating from the desire of the id–encounters the other through the mediation of the image-for-the-other. The constant attempt to inflate this image in futile pursuit of what Lacan calls the desire of the other, rather than being seen as a consequence of the alienated nature of the false self's lack of ground and consequent preoccupation with inflation of itself as a mere image, is presented as if this were simply the way the ego inherently is, inherently lacking, inherently "anticipating."

Both Freud and Lacan lack a truly social understanding of the person. Both identify Being itself . . . social being . . . with its alienated manifestation. And this alienated manifestation of distorted interhuman recognition is presented as inevitable, as ontological, and simply the way things are. In ontologizing alienation through the very theoretical constructs they use to describe human consciousness and desire in relation to the ego, Freud and Lacan actually participate in co-creating the precise illusion that the false self seeks to project: namely, to represent itself "as if it were real" and therefore unable to be revealed as false.

4 There is a significant recent literature on the importance of relationship in psychoanalysis, arguing that the self is inherently relational rather than an "individual" in the sense of existing separately from others. Some of this literature describes the self as inherently intersubjective and analyzes the development of the person through his or her developing encounters with others from infancy onwards (Daniel Stern); others employ language similar to the language I use, emphasizing the child's need for the achievement of mutual recognition (Jessica Benjamin). However, this literature as a whole, to the extent that I am familiar with it, shares with traditional psychoanalysis the tendency to see the person as a subject and to see relations with the other as intersubjective relations between two subjects posited as apart from each other, rather than as immediately co-present. While this more recent literature is an advance over traditional psychoanalysis's focus on the individual psyche in isolation, it appears to retain the difficulty of positing as ideal a normative state in which subjects "recognize" each other across what I have been calling the moat, rather than dissolving the moat altogether in the elevation of social being that is the radiant mutuality of presence. That requires a kind of "revolution" of the psychospiritual field as a whole rather than a proper psychological balance between two persons in which each subject would "recognize the other as an equivalent center of experience" (Benjamin, "Recognition and Destruction: An Outline of Intersubjectivity," *Psyche Matters*, 1995, p. 1). Nothing I say should be taken to minimize the importance of this work in advancing the effort to overcome the individualism in psychoanalytic theory and in liberal society generally.

Works Cited

Benjamin, Jessica. "Recognition and Destruction: An Outline of Intersubjectivity." *Like Subjects, Love Objects: Essays on Recognition and Sexual Difference*. Yale University Press, New Haven, CT, 1995.

Debord, Guy. *The Society of the Spectacle*. Translated by Donald Nicholson-Smith, Zone Books, New York, NY, 1994.

Dixie Chicks. "I Believe in Love." *America: A Tribute to Heroes*. Interscope, Santa Monica, CA, 2001.

Heidegger, Martin. *Being and Time*. Translated by John Macquarrie and Edward Robinson, Harper & Row, 7th ed., New York, NY, 1962.

Lacan, Jacques. "The Mirror Stage as Formation of the Function of the I as Revealed in Psychoanalytic Experience." *Ecrits*. Tavistock Publications Limited, New York, NY, 1977.

Sartre, Jean-Paul. *Being and Nothingness*. Translated by Hazel E. Barnes, Philosophical Library, Inc., New York, NY, 1956.

Sartre, Jean-Paul. *Critique of Dialectical Reason*. Translated by New Left Books, Verso, New York, NY, 1984.

Chapter 3

Humiliation, Authority, Hierarchy

We have not yet accounted for the "fear of the other" that inspires us to deny our desire for authentic connection with others and to place a moat between ourselves and the other that obscures and denies this desire. The adult alienates the child by "recognizing him (or her) into existence" through the casting of an alienating self-other net over the relationship, and the child of necessity internalizes this distancing persona and re-externalizes it in becoming what we might call his or her social-I. But what, then, is the adult, and then the child, afraid of? What underlies alienation?

Let me begin with the simplest of examples. If we walk down any street, we pass each other with what we might at first think are "blank" gazes, as if we were entirely disconnected monads. But more careful attention shows us that passing someone, anyone, seems to require that we avert our gaze from the other and resist the temptation to seek the recognition of the other. Although each of us does seek to empty our eyes of presence and turn them into ocular globes visible from the outside only, in reality what we do manifest to each other is an aversive presence—we attempt to become "blank" or absent, but the very work of attempting to be so reveals our residual presence, that we are really "in there" *resisting a pull* toward the other, toward each other. This is made evident by the fact that if we do each permit the slightest recognition of each other, we *must* accompany that glancing blow by a slight nod, usually the slightest possible nod so as not to endanger our position as decisively, intentionally at a distance, as "not in relation to you."

That pull that we are resisting is the desire for mutual recognition, and the aversive maneuver is the denial of that desire—we simultaneously evade the other's recognition and deny our own desire to recognize the other in a unitary reciprocity that would affirm our social bond. And we cement our (always unsuccessful) effort at disconnection or total separation by the meta-claim that we are being "who we really are," separated. Thus if I were to try to break through this mutual distance by simply looking warmly at the other without quickly averting my gaze, I sense that I would be violating an agreed-upon existential boundary marking not just the space between us but the agreed-upon requirement of mutual aversion.

But suppose I do attempt this actual recognition of the other's whole humanity, not in an exaggerated gesture but in a genuine extension of my presence toward the other. In order to extend myself in this way, I have no choice but to become vulnerable; I have, so to speak, abandoned the aversive maneuvers that were allowing me to deny my desire for mutual recognition, and revealed my desire by my extension of presence outward toward the other. But what am I vulnerable to that I was not as vulnerable to while averting my presence? I am vulnerable to non-recognition by the other, usually by an intensification of the other's aversion (as opposed to an actual rebuff, which would make the other more vulnerable to revealing an in-dwelling presence that he or she is seeking to deny the existence of).

Thus my fear—the fear that colors my entire encounter with the other—is a fear of "ontological" humiliation, of humiliation of my very being, that I know I would suffer if I were to extend myself toward the other in a plentitude of vulnerability and the other were to reject that extension by maintaining his or her non-recognition of me in return. The anticipated humiliation is a result of the imbalance of vulnerability, in which I cross the moat and in so doing momentarily dissolve it, only to be left "out there with the other" in a way that the other not only does not reciprocate, but in a way that also allows the other to reinforce his or her denial. So long as we are "balanced in aversion," we both conspire to mute our mutual risk of humiliation, but as soon as one of us "lets down our guard" by dissolving that guard in becoming present, he or she becomes vulnerable to a humiliating imbalance, placing his or her entire being out there for the other to utterly demean by failing to recognize it.

The power of this fear of non-recognition cannot be underestimated. It is not a mere psychological detail, or some common-sense fact about being strangers. On the contrary, the impulse to reveal one's being by extending it toward the other recalls for all of us our original alienation, our original longing from birth to be seen by the other in a way that fully recognizes our humanity and our longing to simultaneously affirm our recognition of the other in the same way. And the risk of non-recognition recalls for all of us the pain of what we have had to sacrifice for becoming our social selves, for our very social existence. So while the sting of non-reciprocation of an extension of our being on the street is not traumatic in itself, it is traumatic insofar as it makes manifest in being what had been denied, insofar as it raises to an echo a longing that has been denied and sealed off from consciousness in a patterned or structured way across the whole of our existence. Indeed, our capacity to take the risk of revealing our desire to the other is itself dependent on having been so affirmed by another or by others in one's life, through an especially loving family relationship or environment perhaps, or through participation in a social movement . . . because we can only intentionally extend ourselves, with our own agency, if we have been so recognized in our existence as social beings. If we have been given the blessing of "movement" out toward each other, the movement of coming into connection, that memory creates a capacity of and remains a possibility for our everyday social presence, but not otherwise.

Thus street life in periods of what we might call non-movement consists of a flow of collectively-monitored balanced aversion—"balanced" because we are always silently negotiating together a reciprocal distance that without this negotiation could at any moment "tilt overboard" under the pressure of the desire for mutual recognition itself, and "collectively monitored" because the tension created in balancing this desire with the denial of this desire must always be scrutinized "together," through a kind of collective unconscious attention, to maintain our reciprocal distance. To use Sartre's often-used term in the *Critique of Dialectical Reason*, we are always "totalizing" the street together, measuring our manner of distancing (for example, in how far apart we are walking) in relation to what we are perpetually co-creating as normal on the street. And the effect of this collectively-monitored balanced aversion is palpable to all of us in the *despiritualization* of the street, in the flatness and even deadness of our reciprocal being-together as we idly glance in passing shop windows or push our baby carriages eyes more or less straight ahead and in general pursue our seemingly important destinations, the importance of which is primarily, in most circumstances, to "seem busy" or, better, to seem destined in a definite direction that can displace our being-present in the moment, at risk of humiliation, onto a putative urgent future task that denies that risk.

Although normally we do not experience this despiritualization of the street because it is rendered unconscious by the conscious association of normality with collective denial, it does become almost astonishingly visible when a social movement does arise that allows us to release our desire for true mutual connection with each other. Then, as was the case during roughly the years 1965–1974, a ricochet of mutual recognition may occur in which we actually pull each other out of our mutual distance, solve the riddle of mutual vulnerability, and more or less spontaneously "break on through" the barrier of our reciprocal denial of desire.

At these moments of respiritualization of the street, the collective deadness gives way, like an ice break, to a wonderful, radiant joy that is utterly palpable but invisible. Collectively-monitored balanced aversion gives way to a quite sudden rotation of connection and mutual affirmation of one another's presence. The bodies relax, the collective vigilance abates, the destinations lose their urgent character, and we emerge into each other's company, relieved at our suddenly being-here and being alive, instead of determinedly not being-here and having to be muted and withdrawn. Photographs from the (rising period of) the 60s actually reveal the radiance that I am here describing—the openness of people's smiles, the relaxation of their bodies, the ontological fullness of the entire psychospiritual field captured as a kind of halo even by a still lens. And in the case of the 60s, it was because of this rotating opening-up-into-mutual-presence that so many things happened all at once—say, the civil rights movement, the women's movement, the gay and lesbian movement, the environmental movement, the creating of millions of non-profits, the explosion of new more collective experiments in living from the abandonment of conventional family-and-career choices laid out as channels by prior generations to the growth of communal forms of living, in the expansion of government programs for the poor, the liberalization of Supreme Court decisions led by even a Republican Chief Justice (Earl Warren), and the appearance of warmth and a beginning discourse of love even in the voice of a major presidential candidate (Bobby Kennedy) who had only a few years earlier been a legislative enforcer for J. Edgar Hoover. This same outbreak of opening-up enabled the extraordinary transformation of music, from the bubble-gum rock of the late 50s, early 60s to Cream, the Doors, Jimmy Hendrix, and from the early Beatles of "I Want to Hold Your Hand" to "Eleanor Rigby" and "Here Comes the Sun" and so many other songs of great depth, insight, and beauty. Indeed, in "Penny Lane" the liberatory transformation of the street itself is captured by the very joy and compassion with which a Liverpool street scene from the Beatles' childhood is re-experienced through a present moment in the late 60s, in which the hidden longing and beauty of the "lane" has become visible in later life.

Yet this description of the extended opening-up of the 60s must not lead us to underestimate the true spiritual suffering that resulted from the subsequent ebbing-away of mutual recognition and the gradual retreat of our sense of vulnerability and presence that gradually pooled us back up within our cellophane barriers. As I showed in my earlier book *The Bank Teller* (see Chapter 8: "Clinton and the Id"), the Reagan Revolution was actually the culmination of a revolt by the collective superego against the longing of the collective id as that id became no longer able to sustain its vulnerability. And the pain of the loss of each other resulting from that historical shortcoming haunts us still, however unconscious we may be of its effects, a pain far deeper than the sting I referred to that results from a mere mistaken extension of our being in a street encounter. As I showed in *Another Way of Seeing* (see Chapter 10: "'Yes We Can'?"), we recently endured a repetition of this kind of pain in the first years following the election of Barack Obama in 2008, an election in which large numbers of people rotatingly recognized each other into "Hope" through the mediation of Obama's own televised symbolic (as an African-American) and actual presence, only to have that hope disappointed by Obama's (and our) inability to see how to sustain and reciprocate it against the force of collective denial that sought to rapidly close the opening this hope itself had created. The conversion of "Yes We Can" into "No We Can't" involved a collective and widespread experience of the humiliation that had been risked by the vulnerability of hoping-together, a pain that shook us to our origins and spurred the emergence of the rage of the Tea Party and what we so perfectly call "the forces of reaction."

I will return to the critical importance of the collective process by which we burst past our fear of humiliation by the other's non-recognition and encounter each other in a respiritualized social space, and in particular how to sustain that opening up of social space through a new kind of self-conscious spiritual activism, but for now I draw attention to the breakthrough experience to show how it reveals what is normally concealed, how it makes manifest what is normally denied and not accessible to our conscious awareness. We will return in Chapter 9 to the importance of building out of these "outbreaks" of mutual recognition a "parallel universe" within the existing culture of denial, a co-existing relatively liberated social space in which we can continue to experience each other as loving and connected beings-in-relationship while we seek to both continue our transformation of enclosure of the "system" around us and prevent that counter-movement of enclosure from once again swallowing us up. But for now we must continue to name the elaboration of that system as a rotating reciprocal denial of desire as it monitors and sustains itself in the service of the fear of the other that haunts it and drives it forward in a reeling, outside-of-itself fashion.

From the Street, to the Role, to the Hierarchy

I began my description of risk of humiliation as the core of our fear of the other with everyday life on the street because the experience of being on the street is so accessible to all of us. By the way we live out this reciprocal fear on the street, we create each other as "strangers," which is to say we render each other "strange" by the act of mutual distancing itself. We do not begin estranged and then come to our wariness of each other; rather we bring with us our conditioned wariness undergirded by the anticipation of humiliation, and out of that "construct" treat each other as mutually estranged. During a period of rising social movement when masses of people are mobilized within a common transformative project, people do not experience each other as strangers when they pass each other on the streets, but rather as probable co-creators of a new and comradely public space. Thus the stranger him- or herself is an everyday mutual projection of a withdrawn being colored by fear of recognition, or more precisely by having to hold in check with vigilance the conflict between the desire for mutual recognition and the felt, learned need to deny and conceal that desire.

Now take the precise condition of this everyday withdrawnness on the street and extend it to how we live this experience with the others with whom we regularly live and interact with in a patterned fashion, at home and at work. I have already shown in the previous chapter how the child develops his or her social self through how he or she is "recognized into existence" by the adults who condition him or her. And in that description I emphasized how the child's social self becomes "outer" or "false" insofar as he or she is not fully seen for who he or she is in his or her being. But in its earliest forms, this self is not fully formed as a social "I," but is rather a kind of unformed mould or un-filled-in moat that will acquire content as the child is absorbed into the rotating patternings that we call social institutions. I say that these routinized manifestations of collective being are "rotating patternings" because in spite of our everyday use of the term, there is no such actual entity as a "social institution." The concept of the social institution is actually a reification, or conceptual solidification, of a moving psychospiritual field that is perpetually being created and also being dissolved by those who constitute it out of the co-determinations of their desire for mutual recognition and their efforts to cabin that desire within authorized manifestations of the self, or really the self-in-relation. The idea that this moving, conflicted psychospiritual field has the solidity of a thing, the "institution," expresses our attempt in everyday language to give to our own defensive and fear-saturated creations a fixed character that would seal off their vulnerability to dissolution.

Now if we follow ourselves from our withdrawnness on the street into our workplace, we can see that we can support our withdrawn and guarded or wary positions at work by the adoption and replication of a multiplicity of roles (although this multiplicity is always fused into the unity of one's way of being-at-work). So, for example, if we imagine I have walked down the street passing various "strangers" in my withdrawn and wary state, and I now come into my workplace where I am a "waiter" to continue with Sartre's superb characterization in *Being and Nothingness* from the last chapter, I must convert my withdrawn street-self into a new self-at-work who retains my essential distance from others but yet is integrated with them in a patterned and regular way. I (and everyone else) accomplish this by "filling" the alienated mould of the false self, the mould always subsisting within me since the creation of my misrecognized "I," with the learned patterning of being-a-waiter. Once again, Sartre's description:

> Let us consider this waiter in the café. His movement is quick and forward, a little too precise, a little too rapid. He comes toward patrons with a step a little too quick. He bends forward a little too eagerly; his voice, his eyes express an interest a little too solicitous for the order of his customer. Finally there he returns, trying to imitate in his walk the inflexible stiffness of some kind of automaton while carrying his tray with the recklessness of a tightrope-walker by putting it in a perpetually unstable, perpetually broken equilibrium which he perpetually reestablishes by a light movement of the arm and hand. . . . He applies himself to chaining his movements as if they were mechanisms, the one regulating the other. . . . He is playing. . . . But what is he playing? We need not watch long before we can explain it: he is playing at *being* a waiter in a café.
>
> (*Being and Nothingness*, pp. 101–102)

If I now put myself in this waiter's place and identify compassionately with what I am now describing as social alienation from a withdrawn longing for authentic connection, I would describe myself as patterning my outer appearance so as to simultaneously integrate me with the other waiters and shield me from the risk of humiliation. This I accomplish by introjecting all the mannerisms of the waiter and then externalizing those mannerisms as an outer performance, a performance that both connects me in an outer, relatively artificial way with the other waiters and conceals my true being within. Thus I fill the alienated conditioned, socialized, self-mould subsisting since childhood with waiterness as an other-directed patterning required for the current moment, for my being-at-work. I am in reality just as essentially withdrawn as I had been on the street a little while before (subject to an important qualification I shall come to in a moment), but I am now "convivial" about it in the manner of a waiter with other waiters.

But here is the qualification: Although the stranger and the waiter are both constructed out of the conflict between desire and fear that I have described, in my role as waiter I can actually partially realize my desire for connection to others through the medium of my own alienation. Or to be more precise, my desire for authentic mutual recognition is itself realized in part through the very forms of my alienated social recognition, insofar as these "roles" as I have been calling them are the actual carriers, within the culture as a whole, of what social connection there is. Although I sometimes am describing the desiring self and the fearful, alienated self as if they were opposing or entirely distinct aspects of our social being, they are always lived as *co-determinations* of the present moment. Thus the "stranger" who averts our gaze on the street simultaneously recognizes us in that very aversion—his presence remains "there" and recognizes me in the very act of pulling himself away. In the same way, the comradeship of the fellow waiters transmits a reciprocal cathexis of recognition that is mediated through the very artificiality that Sartre describes; a social recognition takes place, but we could say that because the desire for mutual recognition that energizes it is transmitted in denied form, it is blocked and contained at the surface of the interaction. It is the co-existence of this erotic connection with its containment in an alienated form that establishes the paradox of the false self, and, as I have said earlier, provides a continual hope of transcendence and transformation.

On the other hand, because the erotic (or binding) dimension of the adoption of the waiter-role is linked to what I am calling a false appearance or "outer" performance, it circulates among the waiters as a kind of *collective narcissism*: this erotic pleasure-at-the-surface of being-a-waiter is drawn always from, in Lacan's formulation, my desire for the desire of the other, my attachment to my own image as I seek to adapt my image to what the other appears to desire. Thus each waiter gains an erotic substitute gratification from the rotating mirror-image, as each conforms his or her social persona to what the others appear to desire, and also actually do desire insofar as each exhausts a portion of his or her libidinal energy in what social recognition the group can actually provide. This means that collectively the group exists as a rotating pleasure-at-the-surface enveloping a collective longing for an authentic mutuality of presence that cannot be realized, of course, at this surface. The waiters therefore replicate in the alienated work setting the conditioning-in-alienation of the family, in which the child originally becomes attached to and "cathects" in narcissism the "outer" self by which he has been "recognized into existence" by the adult. But to again state the critical shortcoming of Lacan's formulations: the dialectic of self-and-other reciprocity also transcends at every moment the alienation from mutual presence suffered through the reciprocation of images, and carries forward in each person and in the collective as a whole the hope of salvation in a true, beloved community, a hope known at a felt but unconscious level by all who live out their alienation from this hope.

Now let me return to how the "social institution" of the café is constructed as a rotating patterning. Suppose I arrive at work for the first time after walking down the street, passing strangers in balanced aversion, and so forth. How do I know how to "be" the waiter that Sartre describes? Obviously, I must learn the outer way of being, the synthesis of mannerisms of what we might call pseudo-presence, from the other waiters. But I am not at all like an alien who has arrived from another planet with no idea how to accomplish this modification of my self. On the contrary, I have grown up in the same world as my fellow waiters, been prepared in the same culture to speak the same language with the same general balance of connotation and denotation, of idiom and inflections of meaning. Also, to the extent that the waiters are male like the person being described by Sartre, I share a common history of rotating patternings that has produced being-a-male, or what we call fixedly masculine "identity," within the culture. And even more, I have learned through walking and other movement styles, and through sports of a certain shared kind, and through an infinity of other nuances of my conditioning, how to manifest my limited presence through patterned modes of motility—to "walk like a man in 2017." This is what I mean by the fact that in integrating myself into the workplace, I must synthesize a "multiplicity" of roles into a new unity . . . and *all* of these roles drawn from the totality of my conditioned history embody the unstable conflict between desire and fear—for example, the constrained and somewhat rigid bodily manifestations of patriarchy that must limit the way a male waiter carries a tray and relates to customers. Thus I as a new waiter can learn my waiter-role relatively quickly by performing the synthesis required, as all the other waiters otherwise quite like me and living at this historical time have already done. I can fairly quickly, through synthesizing intuition, "fill up" my "holographic" mould that is so to speak ready for any role's content with the role required of a waiter.

As I take this waiter-role in by enacted gestures and movements, accompanied by the meta-message that "this is who I really am," I immediately externalize it as a manifestation of my "withness" with the others, which, by enactment, establishes me as with them and not with them at the same time. I am with them, but not as a fully present being, but as "another waiter," inflected by my unique history and conditioning, and by my desire to transcend my separation (although this is transmitted only in denied form, so that it is not visible to the others, although they do experience it just as I do their desire for this same transcendent reciprocity). And when I externalize this waiter-role in this way, I pass it on; I "rotate" it back out into the social field, which then permits it to be internalized and re-externalized by the others. Thus to the extent that the café itself is created by the waiters, they rotate the café into existence perpetually by a near-instantaneous passing-around of their collective being—in the case of Sartre's example, it is the collective being of the waiters in late 1930s–early 1940s Paris, perhaps incorporating a mood in the pre-war years of lightness and performance that was seeking to deny the fear of imminent war with Germany. The rotating patterning of Sartre's café is very different in form from, say, waiters in San Francisco where I live now.

Just as quantum physics has shown that entities science had previously perceived as objects can actually be dissolved into waves and particles, so we can see in the case of the café that what we had previously perceived as an institution can actually be dissolved into a rapidly moving rotating patterning that carries the intention to both connect and separate those who create it, to establish the waiters as at once "with" one another and withdrawn and protected against each other's deeper, authentic recognition. The rotation of this kind of outer-directedness or otherness is therefore lively but hollow, a rotation of a surface unconsciously but anxiously guarding itself from the vulnerability within it. If we introduce into our description the other actors in the café—the customers, the suited maître d' (who makes himself like the other maître d's in the same period and vicinity), the signifying style of the menus and signage, and so on—we approach the vast moving, rotating energy that is the café itself.

Thus although the café appears to our thought to be a kind of entity, it is in reality, as I say, being brought into being by its very rapid prereflective rotations and being partially dissolved by the introduction of the desiring or transcendent impulse into every rotation. This is why the waiters are not Stepford waiters—their authentic presence continually surpasses their own collective attempts to contain it—and so "waiterness" is itself continually being modified, absorbing new manifestations of presence that are "captured" and co-opted by the protective rotation of the waiters' collective externalization.

Thus when we view it under this phenomenological microscope, we can see that the café is actually an unstable moving field, and it is so in a way that is inadequate to the task of protecting the gathering from its vulnerability to humiliation. Rather than having the security and fixity of an institution, the café, insofar as it is a collective alienated from itself, is more like a spinning top that tends at every moment toward falling over. To focus again on the waiters, how are the waiters in their rotating patterning able to keep themselves from falling over—that is, how are they to "cement" their rotating patterning sufficiently to hold their alienation in place against the threat that the longing for transcendent mutuality (and the concomitant threat of humiliation by non-reciprocity) poses for it?

The answer to this is that the café as a rotating patterning gives itself the modification of a *hierarchy*, an imaginary top-down ordering, whose purpose and function is to monitor and enforce the security of the group's alienation from itself. A hierarchy as I am using the term has nothing to do with one person being able to tell another what to do, but rather with a collective modification of consciousness itself. For each person who is delivering over his or her being to the waitering role, perpetually internalizing its contours and synthesizing and re-externalizing these contours as a way of being, knows that the group's alienation is perpetually destabilized by the desire that transcends it and must be guarded against. And so the group spontaneously and in its very being grasps that to secure itself against that risk, it must reflectively watch itself and install a normative order on top of itself that it—as a nexus of alienated persons in flight from themselves—can exist as "underneath." The new waiter thus defers to the more senior waiter, that waiter to the line manager (perhaps the maître d'), the line manager to the on-site boss, the on-site boss to the owner. By *deference* once again I am not referring to "doing what you're told," but rather to pretending to be "under" another who is "above" you and who is charged with monitoring and enforcing the group's alienated unity. If a waiter does not "act like a waiter," he or she will be corrected by the hierarchy; but more important, everyone *does* act like a waiter by deferring through the very being of their role itself to someone above them whom the group has created and charged with authority for cementing the group's alienation from itself.

This imaginary nature of the hierarchy, of *all* hierarchies, is seen most easily if you imagine waiters playing their roles in a café without a hierarchy. You will see that to the degree that the waiter role is "false" in the manner I have been describing, we cannot even think of a gathering of waiters without someone being "in charge," because the gathering's very "decapitated" nature means that it lacks any ground to stand on. The gathering must create an author, or author-ity, to ground itself and sustain itself as "real," and to permit each waiter to carry himself off as "who he really is" in his waiter role. However unfamiliar this characterization of a hierarchy as a modification of collective consciousness may be, I would point out in passing that since Freud it has been taken for granted in psychoanalysis when describing the intrapsychic life of the individual: It was Freud himself who pointed out that the ego gives itself the modification of the superego to protect the ego against the wishes of the id, although what he was here describing was a deference internal to consciousness. However, in the context of this book, I would say that he was unknowingly describing the alienation of the individual person conceived in isolation from his lived reality. If we introduce him or her back into the actual psychospiritual field of his or her social world, we can see that he or she is situated within an alienated rotating patterning that projects and then internalizes an imaginary top-down ordering, characterized by collective deference to authority, to guard itself against its own collective longing that perpetually escapes its role-boundaries. Within Freud's frame of reference, that social reality is the *family* and thus what he is actually describing in his theory of the superego is the collective internalization of hierarchy as an "observing" and monitoring modification of social consciousness within the actual surrounding social world of the family (with its inherited alienated role-system). What I am here describing is precisely the same process as it is enacted and internalized in the workplace. Thus what Freud was (unknowingly) describing was the origin of alienation within the family as a rotating patterning of mutual distancing (although longing to transcend itself), a process which is carried forward in later settings suffering from the same reciprocal separation and the same artificiality of collective self-manifestations.

An aside: Nothing I am writing should be understood to mean that "real power" is not exercised in the workplace. Those in control of workplaces—the owner, the on-site boss, the line manager, and so on—do have and of course do exercise the power to hire and fire, and if someone is fired, the power of these owners of the means of production and their representatives will be supported by government officials capable of physical force if necessary. And these real social relations are encoded and legitimated in the law. But unlike my views in my youth when I believed this threat of force was "behind" and causing the alienation that I have described, I now see this relationship the other way around . . . and in fact, this is one of the key points of this book. That is to say, it is the fear of the other that causes the real power relations rather than the converse; and it is this fear, underlain by the fear of humiliation, that is the driving force in reproducing society's injustices and inequalities. To this point I will return in Chapter 8.

Thus the most precise way to account for the hierarchy is to say that it is the means by which an alienated group secures itself against the fear of the other that haunts it, and the group brings this hierarchy to itself through a series of human gazes spread "upward" within itself. The hierarchy is characterized by a distribution of authority and deference, in which a few enact authority to monitor and enforce the group's behavioral code, while the majority enact the deference of "underneathness" to achieve the same end. Violations of what we might call the code of alienation, in which stabilizing the patterning of contained fear of the other is the group's objective, will be corrected by the collective as a whole, through "peer pressure" and even if necessary through State officials, who are participants in the society-wide participation in the alienated system-as-a-whole.

To synthesize the points made thus far: Each newborn child is born seeking the transparency and mutual presence of authentic mutual recognition. But the adults whom the child encounters pass onto the child a fear of the other carried forward from past generations into the present one, which requires that the child develop a false "outer" self that forms the basis of the child's social "I." This misrecognition is coercive because to be a social being means that one must become who one is recognized as, and that recognition, even though it is a misrecognition, establishes for every child what social connection there is. Becoming-alienated is thus a condition of social membership. While initially the child's alienated social self is something like a mould without content, a kind of "specular I" that precedes the "social I" as Lacan puts it, the elaboration of social interaction (supported by the signifying power of language but also by the totality of society's roles that are intuited in our being prior to their signification) gradually fills this mould with the content of the multiplicity of roles that are unified in the child's sense of him- or herself in his or her social existence. The reciprocity of roles pervading the growing adult's world contains and masks, from both self and other, the deep inner longing for mutual recognition while guarding both self and other against a vulnerability to each other, and a risk of humiliation, that from each person's isolated vantage point, feels too painful to even become conscious of. The alienated network of roles thus formed monitors and enforces itself through the collective installation within itself of an imaginary hierarchy, and through this hierarchy seeks to deny the collective fear of the other and seal off the inner desire to "break on through to the other side" as the Doors put it. In social movements and other extraordinary moments, such breakthroughs do occur, but we have not yet figured out how to sustain them by sustaining the psychospiritual field that can support a loving world.

Works Cited

The Doors. "Break on Through (To the Other Side)." *The Doors.* Elektra, Hollywood, CA, 1967.

Freud, Sigmund. *The Ego and the Id.* W.W. Norton & Company, New York, NY, 1990.

Gabel, Peter. *Another Way of Seeing.* Quid Pro, LLC, New Orleans, LA, 2013.

Gabel, Peter. "Clinton and the Id." *The Bank Teller and Other Essays on the Politics of Meaning.* Acada Books, San Francisco, CA, 2000.

Lacan, Jacques. *Ecrits.* Tavistock Publications Limited, New York, NY, 1977.

Sartre, Jean-Paul. *Being and Nothingness.* Translated by Hazel E. Barnes, Philosophical Library, Inc., New York, NY, 1956.

Sartre, Jean-Paul. *Critique of Dialectical Reason.* Translated by New Left Books, Verso, New York, NY, 1984.

Chapter 4

The Imaginary Community

The Family, The Nation, and "Race"

When we think of the social world "from the outside," which is the normal way that the social sciences have thus far understood and interpreted it, it is not a mystery to account for the way small groups, like families and kinship groups, add themselves together to form larger social and political collectives with which its inhabitants then identify as a "we" or "us." Kinship groups, clans, tribes, villages, townships, city-states, and eventually nations all seem natural developments based on geographical proximity, division of labor, commonality of language, intermarriage, mutual protection from outside physical threats, and the like. Depending on the narrative approach taken, thinking "from the outside" in this way can produce enormously sophisticated analyses that link multiplicities of objective factors, such as changes in technology or growth in population, to changes in group life and developments in group identities, including the formation of economic groups like classes and the formation of political groups like nations. Because of the basic assumption that this kind of "outside" view of the social world is an accurate and sufficient way to interpret the phenomena so described, most such thinking proceeds as if referring to a collective being like "the American People" is unproblematic. The American people were added up originally from kinship groups and clans, mostly long ago in Europe, eventually were absorbed into nation-states, merged from various locations during and after the colonization of the New World, wrote the Declaration of Independence and Constitution, and formed the nation we live in today.

But if we approach what "the American people" is from the inside, from within our collective consciousness trying to describe an aspect of itself, the whole nature of the inquiry assumes a different cast. The word-sound "American" seems to signify something—some group feeling—outside of me that I am supposed to be a part of, and yet as I sit here in my office looking out the window, I do not quite feel a part of it; I feel it might be a hallucination. I can certainly start naming qualities I associate with "me" that seem to be aspects of my Americanness—my way of speaking, my jeans, my somewhat relaxed posture, perhaps my taste in music—but there is still a gap between any number of such qualities and the felt sense that I *am* American in the way that I *am* my own presence. This precise existential gap is the place to begin to recover the meaning of national identity "from the inside" and to understand the relationship of this "identity" to the conflict between desire and fear that has occupied my discussion thus far.

Because we live in a world in which the desire for authentic mutual recognition is reciprocally denied, casting us into the spiritual prison of mutual distance and withdrawnness, our existence lacks the social ground that mutual recognition would provide. Of course as I have said repeatedly we are not entirely cut off from this ground because it is present in denied form as the transcendent impulse toward the other that animates each encounter as its "co-determination": We desire each other but deny that we desire it on pain of the extinction of what connection there is. Thus, we are tied together by the spiritual bond that unites us and defines our existence as inherently social beings, but because of the rotation of reciprocal denial of that very bond, we "float" in each other's presence rather than exist fully in that presence as the ground of our being.

We have seen that this contradictory push and pull of existence colored by the conflict between the desire for and fear of the other leads to the development of a false or "outer" self which presents itself as "who I really am" and both defines and makes compulsory the visible world. But the pooling up of desire in separate units that we call "individuals" and the unmoored or unanchored quality of the rotation of outer selves that characterizes the entire social world in its negative or denying aspect leads to a felt need to generate substitute forms of communal identity through which we can feel connected to each other in a substitute, imaginary way.

Consider the most basic group in which this imaginary quality of our group identity is most well-recognized: the family. Psychoanalysis and family systems theory has long recognized that children develop an idealized image of their families that involves splitting off and denying "bad" aspects of their parents in order to preserve a good, idealized sense, that this splitting and idealization are even essential to the child's fundamental sense of social security, however personally harmful this denial of aspects of the child's reality may be to the child and, eventually, to his or her children intergenerationally. Much of psychotherapy may involve the gradual and delicate letting-in of these "bad" denied elements of childhood and family life to relieve to some extent the suffering of the adult patient who initially cannot admit these traumatic memories. In the context of the theory that I am presenting in this book, we can see that the core problem described in this perspective is that the child has been "thrown" into a false self as the price of social membership in his or her family of origin, that this false self has placed the child at an infinite and painful distance from the parents that are the very source of the child's love and sense of social existence itself, and that therefore, the child develops an idea of "the good family" that is both unconsciously compelled by the parents and defends the child against the absence of connection that actually haunts the family relationships. To the extent that therapy is a positive influence on thawing out and transforming this frozen original dynamic, the therapist is able to transmit a more authentic presence and sense of recognition to the adult patient that may allow a partial letting-go of and surpassing of these original, pathological convictions.

Thus the imago of the family is an idealized meta-image that legitimizes the family's latticework of false selves and defends the family's members against the desire for authentic mutual recognition that would, if suddenly released, be frightening, like an earthquake in relation to the stable earth. The defensive function of the idealization of the image is carried out by transmitting itself as compulsory, as "the ideal family who we really are" in a precisely homologous way to the transmission of the false self's claim manifested in each person's persona or role that "this is who I really am." While the existential reciprocity of artificiality carries within itself the meta-claim that the rotation of artificiality is also "real," the idea and imago of the family cements this otherwise invisible insistence on what we might call the reality of the artificial, through the medium of a reified meta-sign: through the word-sound (or in some cases written glyph) "the family" and the reflected image that is signified by it. Of course, it must also be reiterated that in spite of all I have just written, the family also expresses a real ideal to the degree the true desire for mutual recognition, for the mutuality of love and true sight, transcends its own alienation: Even in very painful self-replicating family dynamics, the family longs for itself, and therefore, the idea of the family remains, as I have been saying "co-determined" by the desire for and fear of the other that co-constitutes it. Families really do love each other at the same time that they are the incubators of alienation for each new generation.

We see all these features of the role of the imaginary group across the landscape of the social world, understood "from the inside" rather than the outside. Thus the waiters at the café who endure and reproduce the alienated social relations I described in the last chapter also have an allegiance to "the café" as a reflected image and idea–indeed, I have often been struck by the way a new bank teller at a bank, to use an example I often use, will refer to the bank as "we" (as when my local recently hired bank teller said to me, "we issue free checks to depositors who maintain a minimum balance"). In reality, the bank teller is enacting a series of role-performances and has but the slightest connection to the other tellers, the managers, the vice presidents, the board and stockholders, and yet she (in this case) can almost immediately identify with an imaginary "we" in order to affirm a substitute sense of "withness" that covers the absence that is actually his or her alienated condition as a worker in the bank–employment may offer the relief of a substitute community compared with the floating disconnect of unemployment. And in the professions, those engaged in a particular profession often "proudly" refer to a collective imago when a lawyer or doctor says "we lawyers" or "we doctors," providing an imaginary invocation of pseudo-recognition that barely masks its own hollow core. The lawyer who says "we lawyers" to preface a description of thinking a certain way or acting a certain way does not actually experience him- or herself as in a community of true mutuality, but rather makes reference to an imaginary "we" in order to back up a professional characteristic with a proud collective status, which invokes and conveys a slightly elevated, imaginary sense of withness. The assertion of presence conveys the absence within it.

But precisely because the isolated, withdrawn person within the alienated matrix does not feel grounded in a true relation of mutual recognition with others, precisely because social life as a whole lacks *presence*, the group must establish a unity across all the partial group imagos generated within every local setting such as families, workplaces, professional associations, teams, and so forth, and also to account to itself how this overarching unity is politically constituted. In a world more fully manifesting and embodying love and mutual recognition, our self-understanding would carry within itself our relation to our ancestors and embody a narrative of our really existing presence as a community across historical time. And to the extent that this collective manifestation of our universal social essence will take an infinite number of particular historical forms, each historical community will narrate a unique particular history of the unfolding of our universal presence in time: What a beautiful vision!

But in our existing world still so haunted by its own alienation and absence of connection, the narrative of how we are constituted as "together" is inevitably in significant part imaginary in nature, and as a collective defense against an inner absence too painful to become conscious of, inevitably requires that we "pledge allegiance" to its virtually tangible reality.

Thus we come to the role of nationalism, that synthesis of all partial group formations in our current historical period through which social consciousness narrates to itself how "we" came into being and who "we" are as an entire group. Because the desire for mutual recognition exerts an unceasing pressure on the alienated ego or false self and *must* realize itself in the imaginary precisely to the extent that it is prohibited by the other from doing so in reality, each "citizen" as a withdrawn being catapults him- or herself into an imaginary, idealized community which at once provides a sense of substitute connection (or we could say substitute mutual recognition), and denies that this connection in truth is repressed: "I *am* an American." Because of its imaginary and therefore unreal (in its alienated aspect) nature, each person's sense of being-American is inherently insecure and unstable, and for that reason must perpetually aggrandize itself, in the same way that, as I showed in the last chapter, the false self itself is beset by the grandiose impulse to become the Perfect Other. Whether one can be proud of being an American is of necessity constantly in doubt (because one actually is *not* "American" as a true presence with others), and therefore, the we-image that is signified by the Americanness affirmation must constantly demand, as I have said, pledged allegiance, flags that cannot touch the ground, songs and anthems, pride-enhancing rituals (like the bombers which fly over stadiums on baseball's opening day each season as described in my essay "Patriotism at the Ballpark" (see Chapter 17 in *Another Way of Seeing*), bumper stickers (like "These colors don't bleed," which, of course, reveals the fear that they might bleed and the risk of humiliation that the threat of such bleeding symbolizes) . . . all collective enactments of an exaggerated affirmation that "we" really do exist, exaggerated precisely because of the immanent or secret knowledge that *we* in actuality do not exist.

Thus in its alienated aspect, national identity is a puffed-up outer cloaking-in-an-image-of-unity of our actual mutual withdrawnness and separation. And because this imaginary unity must account for itself in time just as we ourselves know we exist in time, the imago of the we-image is accompanied by an imaginary narrative that tells the story of how this "we" came into existence. In reality, in our alienated aspect "we" do not yet exist except in a complex dialectic of movement toward each other and toward mutual recognition (in social movements and on other special occasions) and away from each other (in the anti-movement inertial flows of rotating patternings characterized primarily by fear of the other). This is the story of our real existence as a real "we," and I will return to the working out of this praxis and process in historical dynamics in Chapter 5. But in the narrative establishing the false reality of the imaginary "we," an idealized tableau is sketched out that is then layered over our real existential history and must be "believed in" as our shared story of the origin and perfection of the we.

As I showed in my essay "Founding Father Knows Best" (see Chapter 15, *The Bank Teller*), the story of America involves an original moment in which a group of clairvoyant and larger-than-life figures emerged from a pre-existing colonized mass to bring us all together as "We the People" through the creation of sanctified documents that "we" then democratically ratified and have hereafter been willingly governed by. Now of course this description is not a pure hallucination—actual historical events did occur that roughly correspond to this narrative. But in its imaginary, substitutive aspect, these actual events merely provide the figurative ground for the compensatory fantasy supporting the creation of the we-image, and these actual events give this we-image narrative legitimacy. The quality of "belief" that is invested by reciprocally isolated and withdrawn citizens in the narrative is what reveals its imaginary character. Thus, although the group of men referred to in the story of the founding of the nation were mainly in their late 20s and 30s, we treat them as "fathers" and each subsequent generation must convene a group of specially trained robed figures who sit upon an elevated bench in a hushed and sanctified room and are charged with divining these fathers' intent in order for us really existing beings to know how we are authorized to act toward each other. The images of these founding fathers are carved into mountainsides, and appear on cereal boxes (as in, in one case, " 'Total' Brings You James Madison" followed by a photo of Madison). And while there is room in "the law" for debate about what the intent of the founding fathers really was, the strictures of the belief-system require that we bow down to whatever interpretation of their original intent prevails in each generation.

It is important to note here that the substance of what we have the founding fathers "intend" in the construction of the we-image is itself a constitutive component of the image. First of all, we must take note of the fact that the founding fathers' intent is the basis of what we call "the law," which in its symbolic aspect conveys the quality of compulsoriness that is associated with "belief" in the we-image. It is true that the law also exists as a mass of statutes, court decisions, and everyday legal practices, but these everyday manifestations of law are, so to speak, backed up by the imaginary character of "the law" corresponding in quality to something like pronouncements by Zeus from Mount Olympus. In the American we-image, a weighty aura permeates the collective cultural idea that "the Founding Fathers' Intent is The Law," but this very imaginary, or even hallucinatory, character of the idea is masked by the utterly routine activity of Supreme Court Justices debating in prosaic terms what this intent actually was or is in relation to a particular legal case. To illustrate: It might be considered absurd or even preposterous for a reasonable person today to care what the 21-year-old Alexander Hamilton would have thought some 250 years ago about whether a gay couple can get married today, but in the Supreme Court debate on the subject that took place prior to *Obergefell v. Hodges*, the absurdity of the inquiry did not enter anyone's mind, simply because we have given ourselves over to allegiance to the we-image in which that inquiry is necessary to maintaining the integrity of the image itself, in which, as I have said and everyone actually pretends to think, "the Founding Fathers' Intent is The Law."

In addition to the correlation of the founding fathers' intent with the binding character of "the law" for all subsequent generations, the we-image itself presupposes that the "we" in which we "are" is a collection of "individuals" floating in an ahistorical and abstract space with no inherent ontological bond uniting and grounding us as social beings. While in reality we are always *here* in a real intersubjective, psychospiritual, historical field enmeshed in actual social relations however conflicted and alienated and however saturated with desire and longing as well as with fear and distancing, in the we-image world of "the Law" we are relieved of the anxiety generated by our real existence by being catapulted into a world of disconnected monads outside of embodied time and space, all of whom are free and equal. Thus the "we" that we are each one of and in relation to functions to at once deny and defend us against our awareness of our desire for mutual recognition, to actually prohibit that awareness as violative of "the Law," and at the same time provides a substitute imaginary community in which we "are" together realizing in a utopian way the desired qualities of freedom and equality, for ourselves and for all.

Finally, it is important to emphasize the we-image's authoritarian character, in the sense that it locates each of us as "underneath" the founding fathers in psycho-historical space, and as passive receptacles of their will and intent. Through seeking to carry out their intent as citizens within the image, we deny our own agency as present beings. And we do this precisely in order *not to be present,* in order to collude in the service of the denial of our own present desire for mutual recognition with the apparent necessity, for our own sense of social belonging, of deferring to the false or "outer" recognition that we have received from others in the course of our conditioning. Thus the imaginary narrative of "the nation" co-exists in collective consciousness alongside our direct experience of alienation itself: Insofar as the existential life-world is lived out as a terrain of fear of the other and of our own desire to surpass the constraints of the other's misrecognizing conditioning, we also co-create an imaginary world that a) provides us with a substitute imaginary experience of community, b) reinforces the necessity of alienated life, c) locates this alienated life in an ideal history, and d) ontologizes our experience of the pain of social separation and recharacterizes it as a "good" gathering of free and equal individuals.

Idealization of the Imaginary Community and Demonization of the Other

The power of our attachment to imaginary communities like those symbolized in "the nation" are revealed by an absurdity inherent in the recurrent propagation of wars. For if you were inclined to react to my above description by thinking it was an exaggeration, I would remind you of the tens of millions if not hundreds of millions of human beings that have been killed in only the last century because people have felt their imaginary group was "under attack" or that "our interests" were threatened. The absurd element revealed by this fact is that which side of these wars one was or is on depends solely on where you were born. For example, if you were born and then conditioned within the group that thought of itself as North Vietnamese, you would have been on the side of the North Vietnamese in the Vietnam War, whereas if you were conditioned within America and its historical narrative, you would have been (or at least would have been expected to have been) on the side of the United States. It is of course possible that your participation in a social movement in either country would have freed you from social dependency on the alienated network of your birth, but no such social movement has yet emerged that has successfully understood and fully transcended the power the fear-dominated heritage that has produced the alienated networks out of which the "nation-states" are imagined, made coercive, and are sustained.

Another manifestation of this same absurdity that, when we experience it fully can create something like the experience of nausea that Sartre wrote of in his first novel, is the very popular 2014 Oscar-nominated *American Sniper*. The movie is allegedly a true story about a man who is a sniper in the Iraq War and who kills some 150 other human beings. In the movie, the man who is represented in the film clearly "believes in" the realness of the American imaginary narrative—he sees "our country" under attack on 9/11 and joins the army, becomes a sniper, and eventually wins many medals for killing men, women, and children, much of which we witness during the film. Unless the viewer "believes in" the American narrative, someone attending this film watches and knows he or she is watching a mass murderer shoot and kill many people from a rooftop. While the public understanding of the character in the film—as I say, a real person—has been to treat the protagonist as a kind of national hero and to react to the film as about a national hero, once we drop back from the imaginary world of "us" against "them" we realize, sitting there in the audience, that we are simply watching a calculating mass murderer killing people while those around you are, in effect, cheering him on or at least sympathizing with the "necessity" of what he is doing. My point isn't that the character "is" a mass murderer; it is that it is absurd to see and participate as a viewer in what is taking place if one has awakened from the imaginary world within which the action acquires narrative intelligibility and legitimacy. It is an experience of the absurd to sit in a theater and realize "I am sitting here with several hundred people who are psychologically participating in a mass murder of men, women, and children and do not realize it because of how they are imagining what they are seeing."

Like the false self itself, the collectively believed-in imago of the imaginary community, of Americanness, incorporates within itself the rule that it cannot be disbelieved in by others, and the patriot is always on the alert for the slightest signs of disbelief. Imbued with unconscious knowledge of its false or imaginary character, the patriot behaves like the pod-people in the film *Invasion of the Body Snatchers*, keenly attuned to any signs of disloyalty to the imago's proud validity. As I have said, the validity of the imago reveals itself to be in question or even doubt by the simple fact that the believers in it must constantly idealize it as if to puff it up from imminent potential deflation, but more is required to repeat a public ritualized enactment of the necessity of the validity of the belief—namely, the creation of corresponding negative imagos whose goal is to dissolve the imago itself. We call the bearers of these negative projections "enemies," and in fact, real wars do occur as carryings out of these public enactments, but the fundamental dynamic underlying theme is the repeated effort to invent and then ward off threats from imagined threatening others who might undermine the "realness" of the belief-system. Thus the constitution of the American image as a believed-in substitute community includes both the idealization of the image and the creation of the threats to it that provide repeated occasions to publicly demonstrate the realness of the believed-in image and the compulsoriness of allegiance to it.

And what is the actual threat? It is not, as the quality of belief would make it appear, that the we-image of Americanness will be tarnished in itself, but rather that the fear of humiliation by the other, by others, will be revealed through dissolution of the imago that is defending us against the awareness of our actual reciprocal vulnerability. And when I say that "we" will be humiliated, I am not speaking of being humiliated by our "enemy" since this enemy has no real existence and is merely the result of a collective projection of threateningness onto a negatively colored image of a group-other. I am rather speaking of fear of humiliation by *the person standing next to us*, or by our family members or fellow waiters or bank tellers—that is, by any really existing human who is capable of actually seeing and recognizing us as we really are through our false or outer selves. The illusion created as part of "believing" in the image is that the threat comes from the blacks, or the Jews, or the gays, or the immigrants, or the potentially infinite number of groups that the negative projection can and has been cast onto, but this is a displacement of the actual experienced threat, which is always from the nearest real person. Because the desire for authentic mutual recognition exerts its pressure continually on every interaction with the other, both from within the person and within the other whom the person encounters, every person becomes the agent of the other's potential humiliation, as the one who will seduce us into revealing our vulnerability and longing for connection and then will fail to recognize us in return, will see us as ridiculous. In real social relations, the possibility of extending ourselves to each other in this genuine way is dependent on having been experienced in this way by an other already—our desire does not just "pop out" but of ontological necessity conforms to its prior conditioning, including the aspect of that conditioning that transmits that compliance with it is the price of what social connection there is. But unconsciously, we do at all times seek to transcend that limitation, and that very impulse perpetually re-creates the actual threat to which all our defensive maneuvers are perpetually responding to. Thus, during the Cold War, the patriotic American demonized and felt constantly threatened by "the Russians" in his or her conscious mind, which is to say from within his or her conditioning including his or her belief in being "part of America," but in reality, the person in his or her true existence lived with withdrawn presence, adapting to all the outer roles of the 1950s, mediating all his or her social relations through those roles, isolated and in fear of the others around him or her. The repeated invocation of "the Russians" displaced that fear onto a projected other and displaced his or her own fear of humiliation by the actual other into fear that America might be under attack. Repeated public enactments of America protecting itself against the Russians (and "mediations" of those enactments through the media) were that historical moment's channel for the fear of being humiliated by the person next to you.

Although actual physical self-defense is occasionally a true basis for wars, as was in part the truth of World War II (although only if we overlook the historical origins of that war in prior humiliations of the self-imagos of "the German people" and "the Japanese people"), most wars are outbreaks of reciprocal idealizations of "we" and demonizations of "them." To the extent that social collectives are alienated and characterized predominantly by fear of the other, they cannot but reconstruct out of their reciprocal vulnerability their respective, defensive us-and-them images and historical narratives, saturated on both sides with idealization and demonization. With the psychospiritual equivalent of a magnetic pull, each side repeatedly scans the horizon for threats to its imaginary integrity and repeatedly locks on to some other who will, like a dance partner, serve as a counterpart to a physical war enacting a kind of psychospiritual panic. For example, as I write these words, "America" is preoccupied with whether Iran will be allowed to develop a nuclear weapon and there are a range of social activities going on in both countries designed to accentuate the threat of war. Thirty years ago Iran's spokesperson (the Ayatollah Khomeini) called America "the Great Satan"; America's spokesperson (Ronald Reagan) called Iran part of "the Axis of Evil," and this legacy of images—though relatively uninvoked and really invisible for many years—is again being called upon to heighten the threat which each side presents to the other. As part of this process, the news media increasingly reports on events as if of course we all agree and take for granted that Iran is our enemy and poses a threat to "us," and the Iranian news media does the same. The anxiety generated by fear of the other—*by fear of the person next to everyone*—in both actual communities seeks out with magnetic pull such opportunities for reciprocal projections of this kind, occasionally locking on to each other for a few decades (or only a few years or in some cases centuries), occasionally breaking out in actual mass killings, and then receding to relative quiescence. War itself, when it "breaks out," is no more than the fully realized public enactment of the fear of the other already saturating both groups and provides an opportunity for a period to "act out" the protection of and securing of the withdrawn self. As I have said, which side one is on is just dependent on the accident of birth, although partisans on both sides "pretend" that virtue is the reason for allegiance.

White Racism: Why Racists Are Racist

It is an obvious fact, roundly decried in today's world, that it is wrong to hate blacks or Latinos or Jews, or to support white supremacy. But almost no one attends to why racists are racist beyond denouncing their racism as evil and wrong. The description I have given of the formation of imaginary community as a vehicle for substitute connection in the service of denial of the fear of the other does help to reveal racism's source in Being itself. The fissure of race is an imaginary characteristic suited to the marking of difference (especially through variations in skin color, although always incorporating other features) and therefore ideal for use as a kind of helium for idealization on the one side and xenon for demonization on the other.

Although the historical and sociological factors that may lead to the choice of racism as a strategy for defense of the withdrawn self depends on particular historical and social circumstances, the ontological basis of racism conforms to what I have so far said. The Ku Klux Klan member suffers from an absence of recognition of his or her authentic humanity, and without that ground of mutual presence, inevitably lives in fear of his or her own desire and the desire of the other for that very mutuality, which has been coercively denied in the course of his or her own conditioning. Entering the world as a loving being seeking authentic connection with all other beings—seeking "eye contact"—he or she has in fact been recognized and made social by a gaze denying that loving impulse and making "pride at being white" one aspect of the source of what connection there is, a substitute connection erotically charged through the medium of the false or outer self. The element of "pride" (at "being white," which amounts to having pinkish outer skin) reveals the fear of humiliation emanating from the racist's actual withdrawn presence. And therefore, the white person must constantly be "inflating" the empty suit, the outer persona haunted by its own absence, within which he or she is gaining his or her sense of being connected to others. In racism, skin color, along with other physical features, is made use of to link one's own outer self (and inner hollowness) with an entire imaginary group, imaginary because no one within the group is actually experiencing the other as a Thou, as a true channel of mutual recognition of one another's humanity. Instead, the "white" group uses an external characteristic to apprehend itself as "together" and guard itself against a humiliating longing too threatening to experience in oneself or to allow to be seen by the other.

Because the pride of the white self is not anchored in true recognition but is rather merely the inflation of an outer characteristic that exists on a slippery slope of nothingness, it must create an other who threatens it and against whom it can leverage itself "up." Obviously in the case of skin color, this other must be a non-white color from which white can be differentiated, and in American history, black, brown, red, and yellow have all been selected. However, the African-American community has been singled out as the primary vessel for projection of collective demonization, because being "black" fused with that community's enslavement, and enslavement of the other cannot be carried out without use of a feature or features to distinguish the enslaved from the enslaver. Since the slaveholder knows ontologically, in his or her very Being, that his enslavement is illegitimate and is based on the elevation to superiority of a false self within a false group, the slaveholder must deny this knowledge and attribute a reified (meaning here fixed and unchallengeable or "factual") validity to the feature chosen to legitimize the slavery. That very denial produces an intensified level of ontological guilt that in turn intensifies the racism which functions to deny it.

So the "whites," to create and sustain their own imaginary "white" group, project a negatively charged "blackness" onto African-Americans, which they (the "whites") then use as the vehicle for the idealization of their own whiteness as the basis of their own sense of connection to each other. Since this whiteness creates only an imaginary sense of withness, since it is haunted by the absence (or lack of true presence) at the heart of it, it must constantly prop itself up by creating for itself the threat of "blackness," which threat it must continually ward off. "Whiteness," because it is "nothing" in the sense that it lacks any weight of mutual presence, can never relax–it is always under threat of collapsing in its own nothingness, generating a perpetual need for persecution of the black threat. The white slavemaster must keep *whipping* the "black" slave in order to support his own feeling of whiteness, which he experiences as lacking, but as the only source of connection (or identity with others) that he has.

The Southern codes, which used fractional distinctions to define who was white and who was black, are one example of the obsessive-compulsive work of the imaginary group creating and managing the creation of a threat to itself, here through its legislatures, to constitute itself as racially superior. A well-known example of the same pathological psychospiritual phenomenon was Heinrich Himmler's Posen address, delivered in 1943 to his SS troops in the name of "the German people," quoted as follows by Alice Miller in *For Your Own Good*:

> The wealth which they [the Jews] had, we have taken from them. I have issued a strict command . . . that this wealth is as a matter of course to be delivered in its entirety to the Reich. We have taken none of it for ourselves. Individuals who have violated this principle will be punished according to an order which I issued at the beginning and which warns: Anyone who takes so much as a mark shall die. A certain number of SS men—not very many—disobeyed this order and they will die, without mercy. We had the moral right, we had the duty to our own people, to kill this people that wanted to kill us. But we have no right to enrich ourselves by so much as a fur, a watch, a mark, or a cigarette, or anything else. In the last analysis, because we exterminated a bacillus we don't want to be infected by it and die. I shall never stand by and watch even the slightest spot of rot develop or establish itself here. Wherever it appears, we shall burn it out together. By and large, however, we can say that we have performed this most difficult task out of love for our people. And we have suffered no harm from it in our inner self, in our soul, in our character.
>
> (p. 79)

This quote shows perfectly an inner absence hallucinating its own compensatory fusion with "our people" by obsessively working off the threat created by a "bacillus" which might "infect it" if any of its property were appropriated into "our people's" imaginary group unity. The imaginary connection of the German people and the threat to it from the Jews are created simultaneously, just as whiteness is constructed and maintained in its pure idealization only by the construction of the blackness which poses a constant threat to it. When Himmler uses the word "we" repeatedly throughout this paragraph, he is referring not to his real relations with his listeners, but with a hallucinated projected unity shared with his listeners which he must strive to keep pure in order to keep it from dissolving under the weight of their own knowledge of its merely imaginary nature, an awareness which "the slightest spot of rot" (symbolized by the taking by a Nazi of a single Jewish cigarette or coin) can raise into awareness.

Here we come to a key point. In the case of both the white racist and the Nazi, the virulence of racist hatred and obsessional thought appears to result from the level of intensity of the threat to the imaginary unity, to "our people" whether articulated as "the German people," "the Aryan race," or the "white race." And if we focus on the example of the Nazis, it was in fact the case that the formation of the Nazi party, the rise of Hitler, and the hyper-cathexis of "inflated-balloon" patriotism that was Nazism emerged from the humiliation of "the German people" following World War I, resulting from multiple factors including the Versailles treaty and its supposed humiliating treatment of the defeated Germans, but also including the Russian revolution and the rise of the communist party in Germany which threatened to fracture German unity with its vision of class conflict, and including also the "deflated-balloon" patriotism of the Weimar Republic with its lack of strong national vision and leadership and its supposedly decadent and narcissistic cabaret culture. As Hermann Goering himself said at his own trial at Nuremberg after the war, the virulence of Nazism was necessary to reverse this humiliation of the German people and restore German pride. However, we can now see that while this kind of description is accurate enough from a historical and sociological standpoint, from an ontological standpoint the true threat of humiliation is not to "the German people," which is in any case an imaginary and substitutive entity, but rather to the vulnerable withdrawn selves which are in a state of mutual fear and separation and which create what we might call the nationalist bubble around themselves in the first place. The threat posed by the Jews or the blacks is not actually to the "Germans" or the "whites," respectively, but to the universal and fragile souls who are concealing themselves and sealing themselves off in these artificial unities in the first place.

Seen in its true ontological dimension, nationalist identifications can therefore normally exist in what we might call non-virulent form so long as the nation-state is stable along with the alienated social relations that produce and for the most part require a collective belief in the shared imaginary unity. But when upheavals occur that threaten that shared experience of "withness," as was the case with Germany after World War I, the virulence of the identification and the projected threat inevitably intensifies because the vulnerability of the withdrawn self to being seen in all its vulnerability, in all its true longing for authentic mutual recognition by and with the other, is proportionally heightened at the same time. What the Nazi really fears, in other words, is that he will be revealed as the vulnerable child that he actually is, innocently seeking the love of the other, and that he will be utterly repudiated, rejected, and despised for having revealed that very longing, that beautiful longing that all we humans share.

Thus neither the Germans nor the Jews, neither the whites nor the blacks, should ever be mistaken for real entities within the idealization/demonization matrix—in every case, they are internalized and projected artificial unities that are imposed on actual human beings who are in truth simply universal presences seeking the recognition of the other and the realization of a social universe based on loving reciprocity. Of course terrible evil can be committed in the service of denying this truth as the holocaust and slavery show, but we must always resist the impulse to ourselves dehumanize those who carry this evil out. Instead, we must recover the distortions in their experience from the inside through intuition and empathy, and we must invent psychospiritual modes of public intervention that actually address the pathological and pathogenic alienation within which these social actors are immersed.

Thus it is not sufficient, if we actually wish to end racism, to make discrimination illegal or even fight against discrimination in all its forms because for the racist, too much is at stake to give up discrimination. In the case of the white working-class member of the Ku Klux Klan, materially impoverished and demeaned all his life as "less than" in the wider culture, cut off from any social force that would recognize him and hold him in natural esteem for his true self, his "whiteness" is, from the point of view of his lived experience, indispensable to his very existence. If we understand that he gains his sense of "withness" through co-creating that whiteness as substitute community, we can see that from his point of view he cannot give up demonizing the threats to it on which his identity itself depends unless a real-we offers him a way out—for example, a restorative justice circle in which he experiences himself recognized as fully human and worthy of love and affirmation and respect, or less ambitiously, a wider social movement that invites him to become part of a universal, idealistic world grounded in empathy and mutuality (with meaningful work, universal health care, social security, family support, opportunities for communitarian participation in co-creating the social world). While those attached to the most pathological and virulent forms of artificial group unity are likely to be among the last to be reached by a psychospiritual movement with these elements because they are the most defended against "letting down" the defenses they exist inside of, it remains possible that some of them would be so reached, and more important, it is likely that many fewer people would be drawn to a pathological world like that of the Nazis or the Klan if such a movement were to radiate its presence across the wider culture.

Nationalism as an Expression of Authentic Community

For all that I have said here about the pathological aspect of the imaginary community as an aspect of social alienation, we must always recall that the description remains partial because at every moment social reality is co-constituted by, or co-determined by, the transcendent desire for mutual recognition co-existing in everyone with the fear of that very impulse. To the degree that we are trapped in the spiritual prison of reciprocally-enforced isolation, to the extent that we are enveloped by a social milieu in which the rotation of "otherness" leads to the collective withdrawal of our true mutuality of presence, to that extent all of the pathological features of imaginary group unities are dominant in the culture. In today's United States, for example, conservatives have been able to sustain their large following for almost forty years since the first election of Ronald Reagan by appealing to an idealized image of God, America, and the family, imagos of imaginary unity which are represented as always being under threat from an enemy (today Iran and Russia, among others; thirty years ago "the liberals" and the ACLU). By continually invoking both the idealization of these images of community and the battle against the threats to the "perfection" of these images, conservatives have spoken to the longing for mutual recognition immanent within a dispersed and isolated people and offered an imaginary form of it which serves both to provide a substitute sense of community and to prevent such an authentic community from actually coming into existence.

But whenever social movements are able to arise in which authentic mutual recognition does become possible, religion, nationalism, and other manifestations of the new group-in-emergence acquire a real basis. Whatever the historical and social causes that pre-condition the emergence of such liberatory movements, the "movement" itself always emerges in a ricochet of recognition across social space—in fact, that very ricochet is what actually "moves" in a movement, a turning of social being itself outward from its withdrawn and trapped location and into a growingly radiant and new ground of common existence. At such moments, the pre-existing, conditioned forms of identity may undergo a reversal of meaning, as when Fidel Castro and his fellow rebels, for example, could "reclaim" Cuba as an evocation of national community from the dictator Fulgencio Batista. In a period of just a year, both Castro and Batista held the title "President of Cuba," but the meaning of that phrase underwent a kind of ontological reversal during the revolutionary transition: In Batista's regime, the title signified an imaginary ordering with the president "on top" of a passive dispersal of withdrawn selves contained within an imaginary hierarchy and falsely unified in an image of a nation; as the revolutionary movement overwhelmed that prior scattering of reciprocal solitudes in the ricochet into existence of the emergent revolutionary group, the idea of Cuba became a real expression of the new authentic community and Castro's title became a true incarnation of his leadership of and symbolic embodiment of the new group-in-emergence. It is the base of real social relations, in other words, that determines the degree of authenticity of the way the social relations are represented in reflective discourse. And of course this redemptive capacity exists not only for names and titles but other symbols of the group's (authentic or imaginary) unity as well: A flag may be a symbolic object that an isolated people stand around to pledge their allegiance to in the service of the denial of their actual desire for true contact, or it may be in transformative historical moments a mediation in a symbolic object of an emerging authentic community of mutual presence, sometimes among millions of people.

Even in periods in which alienation "outweighs" authenticity in the rotations of cultural life, symbols of national unity are never wholly vehicles for the imaginary and reinforcements of the false group. To refer again to the United States today, there remains an authentic impulse to some aspects of patriotism that is carried forward from generative historical moments when these cultural manifestations expressed an authentic meaning emanating from their genuinely connected social base—for example, the moral conviction that we quietly feel in supporting the progressive liberatory meanings of freedom of speech or civil rights or other forms of social progress that emerged from their respective historical movements, or other positive aspects of the culture that in their generative origins provided channels for our authentic communitarian impulses, like rock 'n' roll. All of these aspects of our collective life can retain their link to the creation of a world that would actually realize our desire for mutual recognition, at the same time that these very same aspects of our cultural life can be intended to and actually do serve to reinforce our separation (as when freedom of speech is used to rationalize unlimited corporate campaign contributions, or civil rights are used to defend merely equality of opportunity to compete in the marketplace, or rock 'n' roll music becomes a co-opted and anti-spiritual rhythmic distraction from psychospiritual pain). We must always remember that the co-existence of desire for authentic connection with the other and the fear of the other co-exist across the culture; each gains ascendency at different moments in the spiral of our real (as opposed to our imaginary) collective history; and this very doubleness of our social reality means that reflective identifications like "America" are never carriers of a singular negative or alienated meaning. Our analysis of the effects of alienation must always be leavened by our awareness of the boxed-in social longing—that permanent potentiality of hope—that seeks at every moment to transcend our alienation, and that has transcended our alienation in those historical desire-realizing movements of the past which are never wholly repressed in the present.

Works Cited

American Sniper. Directed by Clint Eastwood, performance by Bradley Cooper, Village Roadshow Pictures, Los Angeles, CA, 2015.

Bowen, Murray. *Family Therapy in Clinical Practice*. Jason Aronson Inc., Lanham, MD, 1985.

Gabel, Peter. "Founding Father Knows Best." *The Bank Teller and Other Essays on the Politics of Meaning*. Acada Books, San Francisco, CA, 2000.

Gabel, Peter. "Patriotism at the Ballpark." *Another Way of Seeing*. Quid Pro, LLC, New Orleans, LA, 2013.

Goering, Hermann. Nuremberg, Germany: International Military Tribunal, 1945. *Hearing of Hermann Goering*. Cornell University Law Library, Ithaca, New York, NY.

Invasion of the Body Snatchers. Directed by Don Siegel, Walter Wanger Productions, United States, 1956.

Lacan, Jaques. *Ecrits*. Tavistock Publications Limited, New York, NY, 1977.

Miller, Alice. *For Your Own Good: Hidden Cruelty in Child-Rearing and the Roots of Violence*. Translated by Hildegarde and Hunter Hannum, Farrar, Straus and Giroux, New York, NY, 1980.

Obergefell v. Hodges. 576 US _ (2015).

Sartre, Jean-Paul. *Nausea*. Translated by Lloyd Alexander, New Directions, New York, NY, 1964.

Chapter 5

Language, Thought, Ideology

When a child learns language, he or she actually makes the sounds that the parental adult makes based on a *prior* apprehension of the parental adult's meaning. I learned this truth when Lisa and I were raising our son Sam, now a grown man. From birth (or prenatally), Sam immediately began to experience us experiencing him, began to take in his sense of our love for him and also the limitations we have been conditioned unconsciously to place on that love, but also the total surround of human relations that form our culture and the conflict within that surround between the desire for mutual recognition and the fear that in part contains it. Sam absorbed all of this intuitively and, of course, pre-linguistically, as the possible psychospiritual field of his own coming-into-being as a social person. As every parent knows, this vast intuitive flow of mutuality is saturated with the mutual understanding that the German phenomenologists call *verstehen*, which is to say that the meaning of all human interactions and the symbolic world that mediates and encodes those interactions are instantly comprehended by the newly born infant without being interpreted reflectively. Thus if a parent is cold and anxious in the first few days after a baby is born, the baby will start to be anxious and cold because he or she understands in his or her being that this complex mixture of presence and absence is a condition of the connection (although the baby and young child exudes a transcendental authenticity and desire that will pull for a long time on the parent's withdrawn self-regulation). Or to give another common example drawn from Sam's history, the child will understand, will comprehend, the social requirement of gender long before he knows through language that he is a "boy," and this is so even if he initially likes to wear dresses and is actively supported by his parents in doing so; from the surrounding world he will soon shun the "outer appearance" of girls because he simply grasps, through the vibes of the socio-psychospiritual field into which he is more or less instantly integrated, that he cannot otherwise gain a stable and "good" recognition as a social person in the social world into which he has been thrown.

Thus the transmission of social meaning in all its complexity is conveyed to and understood intuitively by the child before he or she begins to use language: Being is prior to thought. To be clear, the adult's use of language is of course an important part of what the child understands at the level of connotative sound without him or her being able to interpret the "what" of what is being said; the intention in the sound itself conveys meaning before the sounds are understood as significations. And it is on the basis of this prior intuition of the world of the adult's meanings that the child will gradually, after about a year of listening and experiencing the sensual totality of parental self-expression including spoken language, begin to make the same sounds the parent makes to make these previously understood meanings visible in reflection. This is why children, once they start to realize they can make the same sounds the parent makes, learn language so remarkably quickly: Their global comprehension of the meaning(s) of the entire intersubjective, interactional field has already laid down the terrain-to-be-signified so that to become a speaker of language they only need to make the signifying sounds that reveal it. Language thus reveals already understood meaning, and creates a new ground of mutuality on which the child can stand with the others in his or her world, a kind of second level of reciprocity built entirely on the first. Language adds to the child's sense of withness by allowing him or her to make sounds together with others that make visible the already understood meanings.

But this is not and cannot be an unmixed blessing because the limitations on mutual recognition present in the social-psychospiritual field are carried within the connotations of the sounds themselves as well as through the denotative signs of the language. When I was in my 20s, I took peyote for the first time with two friends while we were at the racetrack because we thought it would be a fun place to have a mind-altering experience, but as the drug started to affect us, we instantly realized that we had made a mistake—that the racetrack was actually a ghastly manifestation of many forms of social alienation in something of the way this same congeries of distortion is conveyed in the amusement park scenes in Alfred Hitchcock's "Strangers on a Train" or Orson Welles's film "The Third Man." So the three of us hurriedly left the racetrack and went back to my apartment, where we turned on the radio, which was playing Bach's second double-violin concerto. Almost immediately the three of us began crying at the extraordinary beauty of the music, sharing the relief we experienced as the beautiful sounds of the violins evoked a kind of healing communion among us. But when a human voice came on to tell us in words of a station break, we each became painfully aware of the loss we suffered as the music gave way to the monotone of the speaker, and as the evocative sounds of the violins were interrupted by the informational sounds contained in the verbal announcement. What was suddenly revealed to us and what I remember so well more than forty years later was the connotative power of language as a limiting terrain of social being, the mere hearing of which served to rob us (temporarily) of the communion of being we had felt so deeply a moment before.

This is to say that the connotation of discourse expresses precisely the "level of alienation" transmitted in the pre-discursive psychospiritual field out of which language emerges. As Sartre has emphasized in his critique of those semioticians who treat language as a text, as a kind of dissociated field of signs to be analyzed from the outside, language is always *spoken*—and so it can only express what the speaker is capable of uttering through the limits and potentialities of his or her social conditioning. This means that the participants in a culture signify *how they exist* (or, better, *who they are*) in what they say—their words are backed up by intentions comprehended *through* their language that transmit the blend of desire for and fear of the other that I have been describing up to this point. And to the extent that fear of the other colors the psychospiritual field constituting the cultural environment, to that extent the inhibition on intersubjective connection saturating that psychospiritual field also saturates the meanings of their spoken language. Their collective being (their "who") grounds the meanings of the discourse they are able to share (their "what"). Or to say this more simply, through language we only illuminate what we want to be seen.

This realization helps us to understand the meaning of the important idea of "reification" as that idea is used in Marxist and neo-Marxist theory. Reification means literally making something into a thing, a "res" in Latin, but its meaning in analyses of culture describes the way that we take an existing cultural reality as if it had a fixed character, transforming a contingent reality created by human beings into something that appears to be natural and given, as simply "the way things are." I recall the following example from a phenomenon I witnessed following the second election of Ronald Reagan in 1984. After having been part of the social movements of the 1960s when I had experienced the palpable reality of social change through my participation in the shared experience of the "parallel universe" of the 60s counterculture (which lasted far longer than the 60s and perhaps still has not been completely extinguished), I was in 1984 astonished to see a new generation of young people coming into their 20s and beginning to head off to Wall Street to work in the stock market. Whereas those of us living "in" the counterculture had sensed at least the intimation of living in a new world that would dissolve collective "belief" in the received institutions of the society that we had inherited, I suddenly realized that as our movements were abating, this new generation was "re-believing" in these inherited institutions and reattributing to these institutions a fixed character, as if they were simply "there." Whereas to me under the influence of the transcendent world coming into being through the movements of which I was a part, the stock market had come to acquire a phantasmagoric and comic character, a massive gambling operation whose comical essence had been perfectly captured by Abbie Hoffman when he famously dropped dollar bills from the visitor's balcony above the actual market floor onto the traders below, to this new generation this "stock market" was once again being taken seriously as if it were a kind of "real thing," at which one got a job and to which one might devote his or her actual life, often his or her whole life. To this new generation, the stock market had become reified as simply a fact of the society, a completely normal source of wealth and value that one should if possible to seek to append oneself to, an institution which these young people, enthusiastic in their suits and increasingly dresses or pantsuits, were experiencing as a thing, as simply a given aspect of the world.

Thus reification is a quality of experience rather than an aspect of language as such, a way of seeing the world as if it were two-dimensional instead of three-dimensional. And when we "believe in" existing reality in this fixed character way, we render ourselves passive and make the world active, as if the institutions of the existing cultural reality are simply recruiting us to become part of the "real world" that "they" are creating and re-creating. For Marx, reification was the result of what he called the fetishism of commodities through which the true social relations shaped by the material, productive relations of the capitalist system come to be masked by the relationships of exchange of goods and services, including human labor, as they are simply being repetitively bought and sold within the capitalist marketplace, such that the value of everything and everyone appears to be "created by the market." And Marx linked his conception of reification to the alienation of labor, in which the worker becomes a mere cog in the machine, reduced to performing mechanical functions valued not as "sensuous labor" directed toward realizing a socially useful product embodying his or her own meaningful intentions, but rather as mere "labor-power" contributing to the creation of a product whose purpose the worker has no meaningful and creative relationship to (because the product is assembled by the capitalist production process and obtains its value primarily through its exchange-value in the market). Marx understands the process of reification, or to use his word the process of "fetishism," as resulting from the divorcing of the worker from the product of his or her labor, which creates in the worker the self-experience that he or she is a mere function of a system outside of him- or herself.

The limitation of Marx's description, however, is that it locates both the problem of the alienation of labor and the resolution of this problem in the process of material production rather than in the intersubjective, psychospiritual alienation of self from other that produces and reproduces the material production process in the first place. We are blocked from experiencing the dehumanizing character of the hierarchies of capitalist production or of the competitive, profit-driven, money-valuing marketplace not by the form of production as such, but by our felt need to deny our desire for mutual recognition and our fear of ontological humiliation by others if we reveal who we truly are and what we truly long for. Thus the worker who is disconnected from, alienated from, the product of his or her labor is *already* enveloped in a milieu of experiential isolation and social separation, hardened by his or her own conditioning to pledge a kind of existential allegiance to the world as it is because that world, he or she has learned over the course of his or her life from birth, is the condition of social membership. The worker "fetishizes" the commodity form, to use Marxist language, not because he or she is cut off from the creation and use of the product of his or her labor, but because he or she has no experiential intersubjective channel out of the inevitability of his or her reduction of him-/herself to a mere function of the system, alienated from him-/herself and alienated from the other. The solution to the worker's problem is not a reorganization of the production process as such from capitalism to socialism, but a disalienation of the psychospiritual field through the movement of collective intersubjective action through which he or she could come to realize his or her desire for authentic human connection, for mutual recognition. He or she needs to become part of the creation of a spiritually redemptive socialism, not a mere reorganization of the economic system in its material aspect.

Relocating this analysis in relation to what I have already written in prior chapters, we can see that the flattening-out of the world that occurs in reification, or in the collective reifying of experience, is actually a projection onto the world of the denial of desire in the service of fear of the other. Just as the false self involves the throwing up of an artificial persona that presents itself as real to the other to avoid an anticipated humiliation by the other, in the service of maintaining the withdrawal of the authentic longing to become fully vulnerable to the other through mutual recognition, so also the world itself is frozen in its falsehood, "made into a thing" in the service of collective repression of (or more precisely denial of) intersubjective desire. Seen through this lens, an institution like the stock market is actually a temporal, psychospiritual flow of "rotating otherness," a nexus of relationships of intersubjectively-linked alienated beings, apprehended as if it were a thing, as if it were "real," as an "it" without depth, or as a fetishized pseudo-object. This reification of the "outside world" and its institutions is not something projected and internalized by each individual as such, but rather by the entire group collectively insofar as the group is, to use Sartre's word, "serialized," which is to say present to itself as a rotating denial of desire that has the effect of scattering the group into the reciprocal self-experience of being isolated individuals. Each person co-creates the freezing reification with all the others insofar as each is "other to each other and other to him- or herself." Or if we regard the same collective phenomenon from the point of view of each person's ontological desire for authentic mutual recognition, in reification each person withdraws his or her authentic being from the other because each other person around him or her, which collectively comprise "everyone" or "they," appears to be withdrawing his or her being as well.

In this sense, reification is a conspiracy of collective experience in which a collective attributes to the world a frozen character, a thing-like character, because there appears to be no way out, no intersubjective channel that could allow the true longing in each person to (spontaneously) emerge, or burst forth. Only in the context of a social movement as a movement of collective social being does the group recover itself, and through a reciprocal ricochet, does each person become at least partly able to experience the purely contingent, non-necessary character of the surrounding world and its institutions. At such moments of liquefying movement, the surrounding world starts to lose its character as an "outside" world, as each individual begins to transcend his or her reciprocally enforced passivity. A brief example may again be of help. Mario Savio, a leader of Berkeley's Free Speech movement in the 1960s, once told my friend and fellow Free Speech movement activist Michael Lerner that only when he began to participate in the upsurge of street demonstrations in Berkeley in 1964 did he really realize that the sidewalks had not always been there. By emerging into the street with others in such a rising moment, he suddenly overcame the sense that the sidewalk was a fixed thing and simply "there" alongside the street. Along with his own being liberated by the reciprocity of the rotation of social movement, the sidewalk itself recovered its true temporal character, as a temporary material creation of human beings and creative human labor.

This is all to say that through reification, the "worldhood of the world" (*Being and Time*, p. 91), the world as it is projected in collective experience, is already flattened and frozen in our collective alienated experience before language and what we might call the arrival of ideology. When we start to speak collectively about the world, that which we collectively reveal is therefore the world that we already experience as thing-like, as a ubiquity of thing-like institutions, processes, routines, and role-playing false selves, all of which are intuited by us pre-reflectively and prior to language as a kind of existential hologram. Of course to repeat myself, this is not a world of Stepford Wives or Body Snatchers because at every moment the desire for mutual recognition tries to break out and is blocked from doing so, and in this sense reification itself is a constant *work* of the group rather than being a passive condition, a work to contain a desire that is constantly breaking out and being contained by the collective "superego" subjecting it to what Foucault called disciplinary observation. And to qualify what I am saying in one other way, I am not literally speaking about the experience of young children first learning language because the enclosure of the child's experience, the "recruitment" of the young child to reified experience, is a gradual process of corralling the young child's imagination that as many psychologists, including Harry Stack Sullivan and Lacan, have shown expresses itself in early language as well. But what I am saying is that for the community generally, language describes a world that has already been restricted in our experience by what we might call "fear of presence" which manifests itself in language as the intention to be passive, which is to say, absent. When my newscaster says "the stock market went up today," he is using his false self to signify that an institution experienced as outside of himself has in his experience performed an action, like a machine, and he transmits to the rest of us the necessity of experiencing the event in the same way, insofar as his false self represents itself as if it were real and insofar as the world being described is "real"—which is to say flat, or frozen, or reified—in the same way.

Discourse, as it is learned, "nests" in this pre-existing psychospiritual field. And by learning to speak the world that we have already reified, we so to speak seal it off at a second level of consciousness, at the level of self-consciousness, or reflection. In our understanding, or verstehen, we already know that the socially conditioned world that we experience and feel compelled to append ourselves to is "false" but this awareness is suppressed, or dissociated from consciousness, in the early formation of the false self. With the help of language, this very dissociation is supported by the selective illumination that language itself intends, or that we ourselves intend in language. To the extent that we intend, through what we allow to be reflected in language, to stabilize our own "appendage" to the inherited social world, to that extent we *illuminate* the world-as-alienated and we *place in the shade* the world as contingent and saturated with transcendent desire and longing. And on the other hand, to the extent that we intend to break open this concealment, to use language with the force of presence to break on through the other side—as I am trying to do in writing this book, and as is beautifully done in the best of poetic expression and song—to that extent we use language to illuminate the shaded world and may enable the normally unsaid to be heard and the reification of the alienated world to be lifted.

Ideology

Ideology is the attempt by consciousness to seal into permanence the alienated world by a discursive nesting that pre-reflectively apprehends the alienated world and then represents it as if it *ought* to be the way it "is" in reified form. Ideology is compelled into existence by the fact that the world as it "is" in reified form is constantly subject to challenge by the intersubjective desire that it is suppressing. Thus ideology at once affirms what "is" as if it were a simple eternal fact and illuminates that "is" as if it ought to be so. And in addition, ideology as a continual work of creation constantly absorbs into itself the challenge being put to it by the force of the desire, or presence, that is attempting (usually unconsciously) to dissolve ideology's attempt at hegemony or dominant sway. To be precise, the force of desire, or collective presence, is continually trying to dissolve the totality of the alienated "world" as a reified enclosure because desire, or the reality of mutual presence, perpetually overflows our collective attempt to contain it, and this means that ideology must perpetually co-opt into itself this continual challenge to its "hegemony of illumination." To give the simplest of real-world examples, when The Doors recorded "Light My Fire" in 1967, alienated consciousness immediately sought to re-present that same song in muzak form as an utterly defanged and non-transcendent Buick commercial. The ontological purpose of the commercial was not to sell Buicks, but rather to neutralize the force of desire released into the movement through the song by absorbing the song into the collective denial of desire that is, in part, the Buick market. Of course the manifest content of the commercial was in fact to sell more Buicks, but the deeper meaning of the Buick market is found in the allegiance of all those who constitute it (including the advertisers, the sellers, the prospective buyers) to the fear of the other that undergirds the rotating otherness that actually constitutes the market at an ontological level. Thus the Buick commercial as ideology stated that the power of the Doors is not at odds with the social separation of the alienated world but can be reconciled with it, and will be so reconciled, and ought to be so reconciled: The message is that the fire in Light My Fire "cannot singe a sleeve" as Yeats put it in his poem "Byzantium" (*The Yeats Reader*, p. 104).

Ideology as a whole is the work by consciousness of the absorption of desire into social alienation in the service of desire's denial of itself.

Let us now see the way that ideology nests upon the alienated fabric of the entire society in order to sustain its alienated character through the legitimation of that alienation. I will use The Law as an example, but ideology saturates all of the discourses in alienated society insofar as the discourses intend to legitimize the world-as-alienated against the world as longed for. Therefore, while we could begin with the ideological dimension of science, or psychology, or medicine, or philosophy, I will begin with The Law because it is the most explicitly legitimating of the status quo and because it plays the special role of stating "as law" who human beings are and how we are bound to each other.

As I indicated in my earlier description of nationalism, The Law is a manifestation of ideology insofar as it purports to represent the group as a whole to itself through the prism of a we-image by which the group was supposedly constituted at some time in the past. Because the group is in reality "unconstituted" to the degree that we are everywhere (in significant part) separated by fear of the other, I described this we-image as a kind of collective hallucination formed into a narrative about "Founding Fathers" who created us in 1789 and whose intent or will we are still, out of collective duty, following. The manifestation of this hallucination is elaborated through the totality of what we call the legal system, an actual network of social roles and linguistic significations (the rules and principles of "the law") that are repeatedly enacted and uttered, respectively, to incant the collective hallucination into existence. To repeat myself, when I say that this process of incantation involves a nesting, what I mean is that the alienated network of social relations has been transmitted and understood intuitively prior to the creation of legal ideology in reflection, as an invisible hierarchization of authority generated out of our reciprocal artificiality seeking to police itself and manifest itself as "real." The hierarchy pre-exists "the law" and is seeking to cement the hierarchy and give it the character of law.

Thus, to draw down ideology upon itself, alienated consciousness first apprehends the network of social relations in which it is itself caught up as:

a) A network of "infinite" social separation
b) Which is itself reified or thing-like in the sense of having a pseudo-substantial or "is" character

c) Which is lacking in presence and is therefore experienced as "out there," or as a projection imagined to be outside of consciousness itself which alienated consciousness is in effect watching, like a movie
d) Which because it is in fact insubstantial and lacking in presence to itself must be supported by a hierarchical authority that provides it with a false ground, a hierarchical authority (or "author") which each participant in the imaginary network is underneath
e) Has a narrative historical content that is specific to the mythos of the era in which the ideology is created or elaborated over time

With the exception of (e) above, we can recognize that this list of pre-reflective phenomenological elements is simply a replication of the elements of the false-self system described earlier in this book, but projected out and applied to society as a whole as a projection. Thus from the point of view of my own alienation and withdrawnness as a fearful human being, I see myself in terms of what normal psychology calls my ego, my "I," which is not my actual presence, but is rather my reflected image more or less deposited in me via my conditioning. When I seek to participate in ideology, I "hallucinate" on the basis of this alienation from self a projection of the entire network of social relations that forms the group. In this projected network that we call "society," we all are floating in space "out there" just as I myself feel I am floating outside myself. In contemporary thought, or the contemporary version of The Law, we project that "we" are all "free and equal citizens," a mere mental picture of a world "out there" of disconnected monads, decreed to be so by God or Nature (a "natural rights theory") or by the Founding Fathers (whose own authority can derive either from a natural rights theory or a positivist theory of the origin of our democratic community). To the extent that my alienated consciousness wishes to and intends to "believe in" the realness of my false self or ego, to that extent it must posit that the Founding Fathers are "above" me in a hierarchical ordering, and I am underneath them and am "following" them. And I must posit that this world out there, is thing-like in the sense of being "real" rather than merely hallucinated and made up—obviously, an ideology cannot "work" in the service of legitimation of our alienation unless it is believed in as if it were an accurate description of the real world, just as I myself experience my socially recognized self as being real in order to guard my true presence from becoming vulnerable to humiliation by becoming conscious of itself. Thus in sum, in creating ideology, I first apprehend the "whole world" as a projected imago of ontologically separated actors in a hierarchical ordering that makes them "undeniably" real (or gives them a thing-like or fixed character), and I then envelop this pre-reflectively apprehended "world" in a narrative content that is the content of the shared belief-system that I have learned in the course of my conditioning. In this way, I come to "believe" that I am one of a group of free and equal citizens who exists under the authority of Founding Fathers and their present interpreters who are judges or legislators and whose will (or intent) I must seek to divine to discover how I am "allowed" to behave, which is to say, how I am allowed to be.

Let me say as an aside here that it is difficult for us to see such a belief-system when we are in effect "inside of it" and it is so much a part of our cultural common sense that we ourselves, even in reading a text like this one, experience it as a realistic normative description of the society. It is difficult to relate to the idea that such a perspective that seems so commonsensical is actually imaginary and a kind of hallucination. But we do not at all have this difficulty if we think about earlier historical periods when those alive at the time "believed in" quite different narratives. For example, a mere 500 years ago, most people "believed" as a matter of common sense in the "natural" character of the feudal hierarchies, the divine right of kings, the fusion of church and state, and the demonic nature of crime. Most people "believed" that the feudal lord really was "higher" than the serf, that in fact the multiple gradations of the feudal hierarchy were "real," and that the way they were allowed to be, to exist as social beings, was dictated by their place in this hierarchy. Or to be precise, they collectively, unconsciously, *pretended* to believe this insofar as they participated in the shared conspiracy of collective denial of their own frightening desire to become fully present. And they did this through giving a fixed character to their alienated social reality . . . although they continually rebelled against and sought to transcend that reality and recover their collective presence just as we ourselves do. But the point I am making here is that we have no difficulty at all today seeing that the feudal hierarchy, with its multiple gradations, was actually an imaginary projection. A very good way to be able to begin to see the imaginary nature of the ideology of our own historical period is to realize that had we existed 500 years ago, we would have (insofar as we were alienated) "believed in" the feudal hierarchy as if it were real. In a future more empathic and communal world, our descendants will, I hope, be able to look back upon our time and perceive the fear-based character of our own ideology, its imaginary hold on us, and the defensive function that it performed for us, just as we now see the imaginary creations of those who existed in earlier historical periods.

But you may say at this point, what is wrong with saying we are all free and equal citizens? Why is that a hallucination? The answer to this is that *we* only actually exist in the psychospiritual field of our existential intersubjectivity—or more, we do not really exist "in" that field but we actively exist the field itself as an intersubjective life-world of living social being. While the words freedom and equality convey important metaphorical qualities of what our collective life aspires to in its lived dimension as we seek to realize our social being in a plenitude of authentic mutual recognition, the *concepts* of freedom and equality within present-day legal ideology are assimilated to a projective imago of an abstract "society" "out there" of socially separated "citizens of the United States." When we think and talk "in" legal ideology, we take as real the imaginary world of this collection of separated, abstracted, free, and equal citizens and think and speak as if each of us were "one of" these imaginary figures. And when we do so, we are hallucinating, since this imaginary world does not really exist, does not describe our grounded and actually real intersubjective, collective existence. And one day in the future, human beings will look back at the imaginary tableau that we embraced as our real envelopment and see it precisely as we now see the prior belief of humans past in the feudal hierarchies, in the validity of the gradations of the vassalage, of the importance of condescension as a lordly quality, and of the humble fealty of the serfs.

But what then is the relationship of the important metaphorical truth of the ideas of freedom and equality to the imaginary conceptualizations of these ideas in legal ideology, in the imaginary tableau? The answer here is that the force of the social movements against feudal society actually brought into evolutionary awareness, through the liberatory action of the mutual recognition enfolded within the force of the movement itself, the intuition of true freedom and equality as manifestations of unalienated life—and this may be why in the context of the French Revolution these ideas were coupled with the idea of "fraternity." But in the confrontation between desire for and fear of the other that these movements engendered, liberal political thought sought to absorb the authentic meanings of freedom and equality, then being carried by the social movement, into a new liberal imaginary that would defang the transcendental meaning of these ideas by assimilating them into an abstract ideological world-picture that would legitimize and secure the boundaries of our alienation, just as the Buick commercial assimilated into itself "Light My Fire." Ideology actually works, and does its work, by this assimilation of the transcendent into the anti-transcendent, and in this instance by fusing the liberatory meaning of freedom and equality with the alienated meaning. Thus in present-day legal ideology, "in" the imaginary tableau of the world of free and equal citizens "out there," freedom and equality are interpreted to justify and to be the very basis of our alienated capitalist society. And since what I am describing here is an ontological struggle, we cannot advance our movement by simply getting our lawyers to argue with the Supreme Court over the meaning of words: The capacity for social change derives from the life-force of the ricochet of mutual recognition generated by the movement of resistance to the surrounding alienation, and that life-force is the fuel for any transformation of the meaning of legal discourse.

If we now seek to synthesize the elements of legal ideology, of "The Law," that alienated consciousness draws down upon itself so that it can nest on and legitimize the alienated matrix of social relations that our consciousness denominates "our society," we can sift out the following elements (elements which appear in parallel ways in non-legal ideologies as well):

First, in thinking legally from within the current conditioned consciousness, in engaging in "legal reasoning," the thinker "stands back." What this means is he or she withdraws her authentic presence from the present moment in whatever room or other social space he or she is in, and from this withdrawn standpoint seeks to think "about" the world, understood here as "our society." He or she then apprehends "the society" as a vast reciprocity of rotating otherness, as if conditioned reality were all of reality. In the case of natural science, this same method of approaching phenomena can be well-described as involving *distanciation* by an observer and *objectification* of the phenomena observed. In the case of legal thought, since we are speaking of thought apprehending the ostensibly human universe of "our society," the legal thinker also adopts the stance of an observer in withdrawing his or her presence and "standing back," but apprehends the phenomena observed, the phenomena to be "thought about," as human beings in what we might call flattened out spatialized motion. In other words, in the first movement of legal thought, the thinker, without being aware of so doing, goes "inside" his or her head and imagines and projects a social field made up of human-entities-in-motion. Whereas in the natural sciences, these moving entities would be called particles, in the legal world, they will come to be called parties.

The most important aspect of this first moment of legal thought is the thinker's withdrawal of or suspension of his or her own presence and the erasure of any interiority in the being of the actors in the social field. This is equally true in the case of both feudal and liberal ideology because the central point about ideological thought is not its content, but rather the fact that it is motivated by the intention to legitimate the status quo—here understood as the inert world of blocked connection that is characterized by the denial of erotic energy, the energy of true mutual recognition. Thus in the feudal period, the initial apprehension of the social field when thinking legally is characterized by what we might call roles-in-relation, whereas in the liberal period, the social field is characterized by roles-in-disconnection, but the essential similarity is that the actors in the social field in both cases are grasped as external to their true selves, which is what I mean above by human-entities-in-motion. This is to say that the alienation of social being that occurs through the envelopment of the role-based false selves, fueled by desire that is the basis of all human energy but also denying that desire on pain of the extinction of what connection there is, is also characteristic of the way the social field is apprehended by the thinker who is attempting to "make legal" this alienated field. Animated by the intention to legitimate the alienated world and "make it the law," he or she withdraws his or her own presence from thought and projects out a fixed world of passive actors who may be apprehended as relational (the feudal period) or disconnected (the liberal period).

Once the social field has been pre-conceptually apprehended in this reifying, spiritually flattening way, the thinker then draws down images upon the actors that are signified and transmitted or communicated through concepts. Social being itself is ontological and transhistorical—but the manner in which social being is made manifest is historical, and the images and signifying concepts of ideology receive their content from the historical narrative that makes up the world we tell ourselves that we are "in." So, for example, the thinker in feudal times who seeks to legalize feudal relations—to fix them in the law—draws down upon him- or herself and his or her community the image of the feudal lord as a figure immanently in relation to his serfs and other vassals, and owing them duties and receiving service from them, as attributed qualities of what we might call their "legal being." In his lived reality, the feudal lord is simply playing the role of being the lord; his true being as a desiring social person utterly transcends this role and in truth, he seeks to be recognized in his true being by the others in his world. But like our newscaster, insofar as he is alienated he feels compelled to act like a "lord," to enact gestures like a lord, to manifest condescension toward his vassals, and to otherwise exist his social life in accordance with the conditioning that has enveloped him since birth. And insofar as this conditioning is colored by fear of the other, he will be motivated to *insist that his role is real* and participate in the imaginary world that gives his role and the feudal world of images hierarchical authority. It is the totality of that world that will be drawn down upon the alienated social field by the legitimating intention of the feudal legal thinker and signified by the legal concepts of the times.

In the case of the feudal legal world of reifying images, projected by the legal thinker onto that twelfth-century social milieu, the skewing of social being into a network of alienating images generates, out of collective flight from true mutuality of presence, the supernatural authority of God, the transmission to the king of divine right, the transmission to the lord of that divinity establishing the "natural" place of the lord "above" his vassals, and all the relations of fealty and obligation that flow from that divinity. In other words, the displacement of authentic mutuality of presence into a relationship of images, which is lived out as alienation moment to moment, is apprehended as a fixed exteriority of human-entities-in-motion and then conceptualized as hierarchically legitimized legal relations with both connotative elements (the qualities of condescension and deference) and denotative elements (the list of rights and duties of the role-playing social actors, of land tenure (a social relation mediated through land), and of hereditaments).

In today's legal world, whose images and concepts were invented between 300 and 500 years ago and which achieved a full breakthrough away from the feudal period with the liberal political revolutions of the late eighteenth century, the very same social alienation, or the alienation of social being from itself, is represented in a different way. As I have said, the initial apprehension of the human-entities-in-motion, grasped with a legitimating intention by the withdrawn observer who, fearful of the person next to him or her seeks to secure the inevitability of the fear-saturated conditioned world through making it "the law," is an apprehension of disconnected monads, or more accurately roles-in-disconnection. Instead of entities floating in relation, the human-entities-in-motion are apprehended as floating without bonds. The liberal-legal thinker then draws down upon this world of false selves without interiority the images and concepts narratively appropriate to our era. Those are that each floating disconnected monad is a "free and equal citizen" whose obligations to others are established democratically through legislation or through voluntary associations of various types (contracts, corporations). Yet as different as the liberal concepts are from the feudal concepts in terms of their connotative and denotative content, because they are also brought into social thought animated by a legitimating intention, because they both seek to legitimate an alienated social order and make their social orders "the law," the liberal order also must signify in images and concepts the imaginary community that unifies it and gives it authoritative legitimacy.

Thus, in the mental picture of the liberal-legal world, generated out of the displacement of authentic mutuality of presence in lived reality into a network of socially alienated roles, we have a new hierarchically ordered network of images and concepts that signify them: The Founding Fathers create the Constitution which creates the political collectives (States and Federal governments) which define the rights and duties of everyone to everyone. Thus, if in the midst of the alienated nexus that is the free market a seller delivers goods late to a buyer and the buyer sues for damages measured by the loss of the benefit of his or her bargain, the totality of the relation between "the parties" as understood through the prism of legal reasoning refers itself to the entire legal world stretching "up," ultimately, to the Founding Fathers and their "intent." As God bestowed divine right upon the king in the earlier imaginary depiction of "the world," so the Founding Fathers intended the creation of a federal system that left contract law to the states which judges elaborated through local common law which determines the duties of the buyer and seller. Marx pointed out in *Capital* that the concepts of buyer and seller are actually "character-masks" superimposed on what for him was a conditioned economic transaction—i.e. the "real" relation for Marx was the economic relation and the personae through which the commodity exchange was enacted were simply masks—but what Marx failed to see, I think, was that the mask of social roles in actuality covered over the alienated nature of the economic transaction rather than the transaction itself as a so-called objective activity. When we see the exchange of commodities as a displacement of authentic mutuality of presence into a reciprocity of performative roles, we can then see the attribution of a normative character to these roles in the law (i.e. the attribution of rights and duties to the roles) as a legitimation of an alienated social interaction.

The core intention of legal ideology then is that of social alienation trying to maintain itself by appropriating all social relations as fact-like—as reified external relations without interior mutuality of presence—and re-presenting those social relations back to consciousness through the prism of legitimating images and concepts as if the social relations thus conceived were "the law." In the case of liberal thought, the core relation of self and other applicable to "everyone" is the relation of disconnected monads, or roles-in-disconnection. Emerging from that core relation are the many generalized patternings of social life, grouped as economic relations (contracts and corporations), everyday civil obligations (torts), relationship to land and things (real and personal property), family life (domestic relations law), and so forth in a way that can be catalogued to "cover" the whole of the externalized social patternings of life. Through this legitimating prism of legal images, the norms of rotating otherness that characterize life in its alienated aspect are then encoded as general rules which signify the normal flow of these rotating patterns as establishing "the rights and duties of the parties" to each other. Each "application of a rule" transmits a simple narrative that reifies in legitimating form the alienated social norm—in my sale of good example, party A simply *is* a seller, and a seller *is* a social being that has a duty to deliver the goods on time, and if she fails to do so the norm of rotating otherness is reestablished over and over again in the social mind by holding her liable to the buyer through the "application of the rule." In the very same way that natural science apprehends its world as particles in exteriority whose laws are induced and then applied through an analytical reasoning that presupposes the exteriority of the natural world and then "narrates" how this world "operates" through the elaboration of its laws, so also the law of humans uses this same logical operation to tell our collective consciousness the narrative that the world *is* the rotating patterning of role-relations-in-exteriority that we attribute to it, that it *ought* to "operate" in accordance with what it *is* (conveyed through the normative attribution of rights and duties to the roles-in-relation), and that it is "the law" that it must do so. *Is* and *ought* are fused in the very way that the social world is conceptualized.

The elaboration of this legitimating narrative in every aspect of social life takes place through the repetition by "legal professionals"—lawyers, judges, Supreme Court Justices, professors, text writers, and their editors—of the legal narrative applied to every conceivable situation. We have seen the way that the waiter, as he arrives at work, seeks to "fill up" his false self with the rotating patternings of otherness that seem to be required of him to maintain what social connection there is at work in the café (while also, of course, always seeking to transcend that limitation in his connection with others). If the waiter misbehaves in some way, and if he is then excluded from the café as a social milieu (if he is fired), and if he or the person who excluded him brings a case to the legal professionals, "the law" will redescribe the social milieu itself as a reified legal milieu in which the excluding person is redescribed as "the employer" who is possessed of enumerated rights and duties drawn from the normal operation of the rotating patternings of alienated café life and the waiter is redescribed as "the employee" who is likewise possessed of these normative legal attributes. The person who writes the legal opinion deciding the case will represent back to social consciousness, to the social mind, what took place through a prism that represents as "the law" how normal alienated relations are supposed to be enacted, and "narrates to an outcome" how the case must be resolved in thought. The interiority of a complex human situation—the waiter entering into a community impelled by a desire for authentic connection with others yet saturated by a legacy of fear of the other that has led to certain patternings of false-self relations becoming compulsory on pain of excommunication—is represented as simply the enactment or the playing out of law-like employment relations in which the actors are seen from the outside, in their exteriority, as carriers in their very "legal being" of the norms of rotating patternings of otherness. Whatever "misbehavior" the waiter engaged in in the real existential world is represented and reappropriated in the reflection of the social mind as a reified narrative about the playing out of a legal version of the story that reinstates the legitimacy of the alienated patternings themselves. That is the very purpose of the case as ideology, as one of millions of ideological narrations back to the social mind of an inherently legitimating view of the inertness of the alienated aspect of the world.

Or to take another example from today's jurisprudence, should same-sex couples be "permitted" to marry? As if they were ascertaining a question of divine right, the Supreme Court Justices had to determine, through their lifetime of expertise in legal reasoning that required going to school for several years and practicing using the reasoning over and over again for their entire lives, whether "the Constitution," as sanctified by the Founding Fathers and as totemic embodiment of the Founding Fathers' intent, permits two people who were until very recently subject to imprisonment for engaging in sexual relations with each other to now "enter into" the special, very positive imagined state called matrimony. From the standpoint of the fear of the other that produces the rotations of alienation, we may first ask how social events could have been so altered in recent years that this requested modification of law could have gotten "heard" in the first place. The answer to this is that through the determination and courage of the gay liberation movement as a movement of social desire, the universal longing for mutual recognition has been able to exert its claim with such force upon the alienated matrix of denial enveloping it that its "call" upon the conscience of the alienated world could not be suppressed by simply "applying the law" that it was illegal to be gay. Please note that the law never changes because judges simply think in a new way, through a new and more progressive interpretation of words, since the words are signifiers in sound of congealed images that are themselves drawn from the ontological state of actual social relations. If the patternings of social relations are "frozen" in their alienated position, which in the case of sexual identity would mean frozen in such a way that the community of heterosexuals would feel the need to defensively cling to the compensatory internalized memory of sensual connection to others in a way that excludes others from having that same experience homosexually, then a judge purporting to represent this frozen situation would not be able to alter that frozen ground by a mere verbal interpretive leap. Rather, it is the movement's exertion of the desire for mutual recognition—the erotic longing at the heart of all human relations—that expresses itself here through the gay liberation movement that both challenges and also makes a "call of conscience" toward the defensive heterosexuality that opposes it . . . it is this sustained exertion that creates the conditions for a change in the law.

In the case of the gay liberation movement's struggle for marriage equality, the "call of desire," in making its claim for equal protection of the gay community under the Fourteenth Amendment, must displace itself into a "claim of right" so that it can "get into" the legal cognitive schema. As we have seen in today's liberal-legal world this means engaging in a kind of interpretive dialogue, within social consciousness, with the dominant culture's commitment to maintaining the law itself as a schema of alienated interpretation. And after an almost fifty-year struggle since the Stonewall uprising in 1969, in which this interplay between the movement of desire and the legal interpretation of that movement has been perpetually renegotiated, homosexuality was at first "permitted" within the law, through piecemeal legislative reform and eventually through judicial decision removing gay sexual love from the demeaned category "sodomy" (*Lawrence v. Texas*) and finally through a Constitutional decision by the highest court granting same-sex couples the right to "enter into" marriage (*Obergefell v. Hodges*). But the displacement of desire required for this gradual interpretive victory in the form of an expansion of rights within "the law" has involved a compromise between desire and alienation that gradually mutes the erotic dimension of desire. Thus the actual legal opinion by Anthony Kennedy deciding, by a 5–4 margin, that same-sex marriage must be permitted "under the Constitution," does so only by absorbing the gay liberation movement itself, by "interpretation," into the sanctity of traditional marriage. What began as a wild sexual revolt of desire against the heterosexist institutions of society that sought to contain it may be ending by an absorption of desire back into those very institutions. And if so, the radical effort of the gay liberation movement to free sexuality itself from its alienated constraints will have had to sacrifice itself at the altar of alienation for the sake of equality, an immensely important victory nonetheless in a world in which violence against gays, lesbians, and transgender people has been unrelenting and brutal for centuries.[1]

This story of the legalization of same-sex relationships provides us with a good micro-example of exactly how the liberal revolutions have and have not been socially progressive. For in my comparison of the parallel ways that the feudal and liberal-legal ideologies make their respective forms of social alienation "legal," I do not want to be understood as saying there is no difference between the two, that they are identical except for the fact that they employ different narratives of social relations each in their respective alienated forms. What the gay liberation example shows us is that we must separate the revolutionary impulse, expressing itself as an exertion of the desire for mutual recognition as an erotic force, from the transformation of legal forms and legal ideologies. The liberal revolt against feudalism as a total culture of (predominantly) social alienation that denies desire and displaces it into a collective false self of roles-in-relation was initially a movement of desire for authentic community—for liberty, equality, fraternity as embodiments of liberated human relationships expressing itself through centuries of resistance and revolt, and also as a "call of conscience" through the carapace, the alienated shell, that contained desire in its prior feudal form. The achievement of the long liberal struggle was the freeing of the individual person from the form in which his or her autonomy had been suppressed within the divinely legitimated and therefore supposedly natural feudal aristocracy, with Protestantism's revolt against the church, the early capitalist (merchant, small shopkeeper, burgher) revolt against the aristocracy, the rise of empiricism and revolt against metaphysically justified truth, the separation of church and state, and the rise of popular democracy all being manifestations of that long exertion of desire itself. But just as the labor movement's erotic, communal impulse was absorbed into a rights-claim for higher wages and safer working conditions alone, just as the civil rights movement's claim for a world based on love across our racial differences was absorbed into the equal right to compete in the marketplace to succeed as an isolated being, just as the women's movement's rebellion against patriarchal detached rationality became the equal right to participate in that very rationality, and just as the gay liberation movement is now being drawn toward the right to participate equally in erotically normalized institutions of the wider social order, so also liberalism's impulse toward liberation of the individual from social suffocation and denial in the feudal divinely-ordained "natural" role-system has been in part absorbed by the hierarchies and social separation of capitalist culture. And my point here is that once this transfiguration of the call of desire for authentic mutuality of presence occurs, once the fear of the other instilled in our collective memory reasserts itself through modification or even transformation of "the law," then the new ideology is repeatedly invoked in the service of legitimation of the alienated status quo rather than in the service of liberation from the rotating patternings of mutual distance and fear of the other that continues to divide us.

This book is based on the hope that we are becoming conscious of precisely this process, that the desire for mutual recognition is learning to *think* itself, to reflect itself to itself in consciousness, so that new legal forms can carry forward the longings of the heart so as to dissolve the fear that thus far has limited their (full) realization in the world.

Note

1 There is no necessary conflict between the longings of desire and legal culture, only between the longings of desire and the alienated conception of law that we have inherited from prior centuries. If legal culture were transformed to make manifest Martin Luther King's conception of justice as "love correcting that which revolts against love" (from his Address to the First Montgomery Improvement Association (MIA) Mass Meeting at Holt Street Baptist Church on Dec. 5, 1955, http://kingencyclopedia.stanford.edu/encyclopedia/documentsentry/mia_mass_meeting_at_holt_street_baptist_church/), then law would become an important arena for the realization of desire rather than an alienating, resisting force.

A hopeful emerging manifestation of this transformation is the restorative justice movement, which seeks to resolve social conflict at large and small levels through a relational circle process in which social healing rather than the vindication of individual rights is the objective. Unlike the detached, disembodied, analytical approach of existing legal reasoning, which is based on the liberal social image of a world of disconnected monads bumping into each other like atoms in opposition, restorative justice understands harm as an outcome of social distortion and seeks to address it through an empathic, intuitively-based social process emphasizing the taking of responsibility, apology, and forgiveness. South Africa's Truth and Reconciliation Commission, which under the social-spiritual leadership of Nelson Mandela and Bishop Desmond Tutu helped to elevate the community of South Africa out of the distorting legacy of racial apartheid without great violence, is the best example of restorative justice principles being employed on a large scale in the service of love correcting that which revolts against love.

Works Cited

The Doors. "Break on Through (To the Other Side)." *The Doors*. Elektra, Hollywood, CA, 1967.

The Doors. "Light My Fire." *The Doors*. Elektra, Hollywood, CA, 1967.

Foucault, Michel. *Discipline & Punish: The Birth of the Prison*. Translated by Alan Sheridan, Random House, New York, NY, 1977.

Heidegger, Martin. *Being and Time.* Translated by John Macquarrie and Edward Robinson, Harper & Row, 7th ed., New York, NY, 1962.

Lacan, Jaques. *Ecrits.* Tavistock Publications Limited, New York, NY, 1977.

Lawrence v. Texas. 539 US 558 (2003).

Marx, Karl. *Capital, Volume One: A Critique of Political Economy.* Translated by Samuel Moore and Edward Aveling, Progress Publishers, Moscow, USSR, 1887.

Marx, Karl. "Estranged Labor." *Economic and Philosophic Manuscripts of 1844.* Translated by Martin Mulligan, Progress Publishers, Moscow, USSR, 1932.

Obergefell v. Hodges. 576 US _ (2015).

Sartre, Jean-Paul. *Critique of Dialectical Reason.* Translated by New Left Books, Verso, New York, NY, 1984.

Sartre, Jean-Paul. "Replies to Structuralism." *Telos Journal*, Candor, NY, Fall 1971, pp. 110–114.

Strangers on a Train. Directed by Alfred Hitchcock, Transatlantic Pictures, United States, 1951.

Sullivan, Harry Stack. *The Interpersonal Theory of Psychiatry.* The William Alanson White Psychiatric Foundation, New York, NY, 1953.

The Third Man. Directed by Orson Welles, London Films, London, 1949.

Yeats, W. B. "Byzantium." *The Yeats Reader: A Portable Compendium of Poetry, Drama, and Prose.* Edited by Richard J. Finneran, Scribner Poetry, New York, NY, 1977.

Chapter 6

The Economic System as a Network of Alienated Reciprocities

Once we grasp the centrality of social alienation to the reproduction of the existing society, we must re-understand the economy and change our view of it. The economy comprises the practical organization of work we engage in collectively to satisfy our material needs for food, shelter, clothing, and other elements of our physical survival. But contrary to our normal way of describing this practical organization of work, including both production and distribution of material goods and other goods related to caring for the body (i.e. health care), we should now see this vast interconnected activity as the manifestation of a vast interconnected network of predominantly alienated social relations coercively reproducing "itself" through what I have been calling rotating patterns of otherness. The normal way of describing the economy is to stand outside these social relations and look "at" them from our own withdrawn presence, and then characterize the moving object thus observed as a "system," typically the capitalist system. This objectifying way of seeing erases the interiority of the vast network, and turns what are actually lived social relationships into a kind of moving thing. Once we realize that the system is not actually a thing, we see that it is also not a system: Its regularities are patterned and coercive but not "systematic" because the movement of the system is always subject to subjective tilting driven by the rebelling of the alienated self against the constraints that coercively shape and reproduce it. To "change the system," we do not need a wholesale objectified replacement of one set of objectified mechanisms with another (to give the simplest version of this, to replace capitalism with socialism with each being seen from the outside as a thing-like system), but rather we need to generate the creation of social processes that affirm the desire for mutual recognition and invent socio-economic processes that allow that desire to begin to realize itself in the practical organization of work upon the material world. Indeed, to think we can simply replace one economic system with another makes the error of thinking there is an objective "it," the "economic system," that creates social consciousness. The failures of almost all "really existing socialisms" including the Soviet Union, Eastern European communism, China's cultural revolution, even many worker collectives and 60s-inspired experiments in the West, reveal that changing the outside does not *of itself* change the inside, and that the interhuman distortions of capitalism must be healed and transcended rather than being eliminated by "replacement." At the same time, the re-description that I am offering shows that transformative possibilities always exist *within* the so-called system, to the extent that disalienation of the parts through the generation of mutuality of presence is coupled with transformation of the economic forms as carriers forward of this disalienating, elevating mutuality, prefiguring new more liberatory socio-economic possibilities. Of course, the success of these partial efforts will be greater the more that they can spread, horizontally and from the inside, in the way that turning over stones through surrounding those of one's opponent in a Go game is more effective depending on how widespread the impact is on the entire set of stones comprising the board as a whole.

Let us now examine more closely the distinction I am making between the normal, objectifying way of looking "at" the economy and the non-objectifying way of seeing socio-economic relations illuminated by the interiority of the social subjects co-creating them. Suppose we start by recalling my description earlier of the waiter arriving for work at the café. If we perceive the café "from the outside" as an "economic institution," we might say about it that it is organized for profit by a group of investors who invest capital in the purchase of the business and rental of the land or premises, that the café is overseen by a Board of Directors which may include the investors (or may not) who are expected (by law) to assure the café is properly run so as to maximize short-term profits, and that the café's operation is properly overseen by a managerial staff who hires and supervises the workers, including our waiter. Seen from the outside, the relationships of all of these social actors appear to be bound by corporate and contractual relationships based upon money, in the sense that the café is in competition with all surrounding cafés and must hold down its prices to retain customers and must hold down its wages to assure profit for the investors who might otherwise invest elsewhere, which in turn, in forcing the workers' wages down, places our waiter and all waiters and potential waiters in competition with each other. To those who think of the café as a moving object of parts bound by money, the café organized in this way is but one firm in a vast interrelated set of businesses ranging from little cafés to multinational corporations, all in competition with other like businesses, all functioning within the requirements of a capitalist market economy, all forced to seek to be profitable or go out of business with their workers thrown out on the street (absent temporary government assistance) and perhaps investors forced into bankruptcy (and eventually, to follow the logic of the system, to be thrown out onto the street). Whether one perceives "it" as good or bad, this vast "system" so perceived certainly appears to be objectively coercive and more powerful than other psychosocial and cultural forces in society, since whether one can eat or sleep indoors or otherwise have the tools to survive depends upon one's somehow making it in the universal market thus constructed.

But if we look at this same vast fabric of social relations from the inside, we see a qualitative psychospiritual field of interhuman dynamics, strangely mediated by pieces of paper with numbers on them (or in the absence of cash, by pieces of plastic with numbers on them, or increasingly by numbers alone on a mediating computer screen). The method we use to understand and develop knowledge about this vast fabric of socio-economic relations cannot be to start out by looking at it from a di-stance, but rather to go inside it by the use of intuition and empathy, through the wormhole of a consciousness of one of the actors. Let us take our waiter: We have already seen him enveloped in the contradictions of his childhood, divided into a conditioned, socially compelled false self and a transcendent, longing being seeking authentic mutual recognition with the other, with others, having navigated the "aversive presence" of the street and entering into the café to work, gradually adjusting to the rotating patterning of "otherness" that fuses the container of the false self with the role of being-a-waiter in the way that all the waiters unconsciously teach each other to do, so as to protect themselves against the vulnerability of authentic presence and direct sight, all overseen by the observing consciousness of the supervisor who makes sure all the waiters conduct themselves as normal waiters with the panache or style of this particular café, the supervisor him- or herself being overseen by a manager who in turn is overseen by the Board of Directors responsible to and fiduciaries of the investors. Please note that when we have empathically entered the consciousness of the waiter in this way, we will have abandoned the detachment that we used to see the café as part of an objectified "economic system" with its moving parts and we have begun to describe the same set of interhuman relations from the inside as they are actually lived by the social beings who constitute them.

Now if we stay with this interior description, let us try to gradually work up to an account of the café that is as "total" as the objectifying economic description. Can we reach in to these social relations so deeply that we can illuminate the entire psychospiritual field and make the same totalizing claim for our knowledge of it that the economist can claim by describing it as he or she does, from the outside? Let us recall first that the waiter has no choice but to conform to the waiter role (unless he has been liberated from his alienated conditioning by some other or others, via the counter-confirmation of some other experience of authentic recognition). The waiter conditioned within the flattening and repressive influence of the false self must behave in accordance with how the other waiters behave as a condition of what social connection there is. And this is equally so for all the social actors who constitute the café—the supervisor observing the waiters defers to the manager who defers to the Board who defer to the investors who all imagine themselves, through the medium of this hierarchy which "grounds" and disciplines the artificiality of the entire network of social roles thus constituted, to be "of the café." And even more: The wages paid to each worker and the interest or other return on capital paid to the investors are the medium of their separation—they serve to assure each other's material survival and also to keep each other at a distance, which is to say to preserve each other's disconnection and non-dependency on each other.

Now *in its alienated aspect* the café thus perceived, from the inside, is an artificial unity—one can imagine Peter Sellers or Charlie Chaplin playing a waiter and revealing through the exaggerations of comedy the robotic dimension of the waiter's normal role-playing, the deference to the boss which enacts the disciplinary hierarchy, the boss's superiority, what we might call the café as an imaginary entity that pretends to be, and believes itself to be, real. To the extent that one is trapped inside this alienated dynamic, one perceives everyone else "believing in" the café thus enacted and therefore, absent some liberating recognition by an other, each person in his or her isolation must come to believe in "it" him- or herself. You may think as you read this, "well that's not true; I can imagine just working there and doing what I am supposed to do but not believing in it," but actually that very reaction presupposes that you have the internal resources, which can be gained only from a liberating recognition by others, by at least one other, to exist as a social being outside the rotating patterning that is the enacted café. To the extent that you have been alienated from yourself and from others in the course of your conditioning, to that extent you must accept as real the social relations of the café as if they have substance, as if "this is the way things are," without being able to be conscious of their imaginary, alienated character. You may even be able to complain in private to your friends about your job's stressful and artificial character, but that will only itself enact an imaginary separation between "private life" where you can speak "underneath the system" to your friends and your "public" life at work where conformity appears compulsory—that very complaint about one's job "in private" elevates as an overwhelming or massive reality "in public" the "it" that is simply the reality of the café as a compulsory aspect of "the way things are."

To each actor in this alienated situation, in every alienated situation, all of the others appear to be behaving as if they accept as real the enactment of the roles of the false self and the actual existence of the hierarchy of authority and deference that appears, to the isolated person, to enforce it. As I have said, this hierarchy does not actually "exist" except as an imaginary projection that is then internalized and acted out by everyone and, through authority and deference, appears to be providing the ground for and then enforcing the ubiquity of the false self that would otherwise float unstably at the surface of everyone's being. But it nonetheless appears to each person in his or her isolation to be perfectly real in the sense that each person, in his or her isolation, experiences it unconsciously as artificial but consciously as the way things are. What cements each person in his or her isolation is that everyone else appears to accept the alienated network as the way things are, as "real," whereas in truth, this "everyone else" is actually *also* a series of isolated beings peering out at the same apparently real world. Thus the café, to the extent that it is the enactment of a reciprocity of false selves, looks like a kind of fixed entity to each actor who constitutes it in mutual isolation and peering out "at" it from his or her withdrawn presence. Unconsciously, I as the waiter long to recover my authentic being and emerge from my withdrawn state to manifest my true presence through a relation of I and Thou with others, but consciously, I have no choice but identify my "I" with the waiter role that I have assimilated to my false-self mould from earlier in life up to the present moment, with relatively routinized movements and gestures that are, so to speak, pretending to be me. Each other waiter sees this me as one of the others who appears to be "real," and so becomes like me to be in relationship "with" me, to socially *exist* with me, yet is in reality, in the unconscious truth of his or her being, peering out longingly, desiring to emerge into authentic mutual recognition from his or her withdrawn presence just as I am. Without realizing it, I become one of the imprisoning others to the other waiters, just as each of them does in relation to me, and because no one can help him- or herself from his or her isolated vantage point, we are all trapped by a circle of collective denial of desire. We form the patterning of rotating otherness that, because it is coercive and produces allegiance to a (somewhat) fixed pattern, can be characterized as a "system" if looked "at" from the outside.

This coercive, mutually enforcing rotating patterning of alienated reciprocities when it is grasped from the inside is what actually forms what we call the capitalist system when looked at from the outside. Everyone is assimilated to his or her false-self role, everyone participates in the hierarchies of mutual enforcement, everyone experiences him- or herself as "underneath" the thing-like ubiquity of the system, everyone experiences the depression and pathos of being unable to become fully present to the other, to become who he or she really is in his or her being. The sense of vitality and fully embodied realness can only occur in moments of collective resistance, which emerges from unconsciousness into consciousness, and into public visibility, only through the mutual liberation of social movement, perhaps through political action, perhaps through a workplace strike, perhaps through the simple act of collectively wearing a union button at work when, during an organizing drive, all the workers together "come out" and button up. Then "the system" partially dissolves before the marchers' or the workers' eyes, although of course this is only temporary in the absence of a great societal surge of social being which only occurs and spirals upward in a sustained fashion on rare occasions. The rest of the time the "capitalist system" holds itself in place through disciplinary self-observation on the part of everyone toward everyone else and toward one's self.

Now as I have said, we have no difficulty seeing this just as I have described it if we hurl ourselves back a thousand years to feudal England in 1100–if we see the king enter with his crown, and all the servants at court fall to their knees or bow in courtesy, or witness the haughtiness and kind condescension of "the Lord" toward his serfs. Yet insofar as these social relations were actually lived by the participants as present beings, they experienced their world thus constructed as "real" rather than merely enacted, because they too were each spiritually imprisoned by the mutuality of their alienation. Of course, each newborn child in 1100 was born as a plenitude of human presence seeking to give and receive completion through mutual recognition and love, but each was also, through the mutuality of separation, gradually conditioned to sacrifice this presence for membership in the feudal order, through coming to accept this order as if it really existed, as if it were real like a thing. Yet the reality of this existential human universe found its enforcement, like the present-day café and the present-day system as a whole, through the fact that each person in his or her isolation, separated by the ubiquity of fear of the other, peered out from his or her withdrawnness at a tableau that "everyone else" appeared to believe in as if it were real, as if the king really was "a king," the Lord really was "a Lord," the serf really a serf, as if all the dozens of intermediate identities of the vassalage constituted a real world outside, which was therefore internalized by each person in his or her isolation as also real "inside." To think that feudalism was an "economic system" (characterized, say, by the extraction of surplus value by the Lords from the serfs among other objective features), is to forget that the totality of its social relations were constructed from the inside in the mutually isolating reciprocal manner that I have described, and that the appearance of the fixed "system" results from the universal acceptance of the mutually projected, internalized rotating pattern of otherness enforced by the hierarchy that otherness itself constructs to enforce itself.

If we now bring ourselves back to the café of the present and return to the experience of our waiter, we can see that he is enveloped in precisely the same way, except that the owner-manager-employee relation has replaced the Lord-vassal-serf relation. And just as we could locate the social relations of one manorial complex "under feudalism" as co-constituting the feudal relations of England with every other such manorial complex, so we can see that our café exists with and competes with all other cafés in the ubiquity of separation that envelopes them all, and the café itself exists in a co-constituting way with the surrounding culture's networks of market relations co-participating in the owner-manager-employee "hallucination," for lack of a better way to characterize it. If we remember that the waiter will go home after work, passing "everyone else" on the street with a mutually aversive presence, and "watch the news," he will see the same pseudo-reality of "a world"—with newscasters, pontificating politicians, fantastical commercials—all appearing to insist to him in his isolation that this world is "the way things are," is real. To grasp how this matrix acquires what from the outside has the appearance of a system, we need only let ourselves grasp that everyone "in it" is the waiter, *everyone* peers out from his or her isolation at what appears to be the way things are and, therefore, co-constitutes that very appearance for everyone else.

What then is the place of strictly economic factors? How does the alienated character of these social relations integrate with the production and distribution of material goods and the circulation of currency, of money? The answer is that the collective satisfaction of our material needs is the indispensable, because necessary for survival and for life itself, channel through which our social alienation expresses itself, and the use of money or currency is (unconsciously) designed to carry out the satisfaction of our material needs in a manner that is shaped by our fear of each other, and that maintains our alienation, our universal separation. Thus when we walk into a supermarket, we *could* see simply a vast and beautiful shared effort to grow and distribute food for the collective well-being of everyone who participates in it—those who grow it, those who carry it to the market, those who place it on shelves, those who put the food in bags for us to carry home. And this way of seeing the market is both empirically accurate and, as I say, beautiful to behold. But because of the collectively withdrawn state through which the supermarket is in fact experienced and intermediated, the mutuality of presence thus manifested is collectively denied and the supermarket is collectively apprehended as a series of separated, discrete economic transactions mediated by money, pieces of paper with little numbers on the corners that we might, from our interior viewpoint, call units of alienation that are used and distributed to secure our rotating separation, our mutuality of distance. Through the supermarket understood as an "economic institution," *we feed each other at arm's length*, and absent our functional value for each other in mutual feeding, we treat each other as expendable. Thus do 20,000 children a day unnecessarily die of starvation around the world.

If we now move from the micro to the macro level, we can see that the economic logic that enriches some at the expense of others across the community is simply the logic of the necessity of mutual fear and distance seeking to maintain itself, with the wealthy seeking to "pool up" their control of land, machinery, housing, and food so as never to have to depend upon others for survival, and the poor having to endure whatever is left over to them for their material needs because they too–in their reciprocal isolation–perceive that this is simply their situation, that they have no choice. They too have been conditioned to believe, to *experience* as they peer out, that universal separation is the inevitable situation of humanity, that the imaginary hierarchies that envelop them are real, that they confront an external "system" that is impenetrable because everyone else represents it in their externalized collective being as if it were so. Similarly, the hierarchies of class grounded in fear of the other (by which I mean not fear of "the poor" but the fear on the part of the wealthy man or woman of *the person next to him- or herself* right there in the same room)–these hierarchies invented by fear of the humiliation of non-recognition express themselves through imaginary enactments (the head held a bit high, with emotion damped down to prevent an "explosion" or any revelation of the vulnerability of spontaneity) and draw down upon their intuited necessity the images and concepts of legitimating ideologies just as I showed in the previous chapter ("I deserve my wealth because of merit, or private property passed on to me through family inheritance, or the lack of initiative of others and their failure to better themselves"). Through this imagined and enacted hierarchy, the wealthy gain a sense of substitute connection or "withness" with others of their class, which, as we have seen always produces some form of demonization of the other which is imagined to threaten what we might call the wealthy false self, the pride of its "success" and its underlying terror of actually being seen through to the vulnerability of the true self within. Thus the class structure of the capitalist economy is in reality *the manifestation of alienation in necessity*, or simply the spiritually alienated way of collectively satisfying essential material needs. The material needs do not cause the social alienation in a ruthless objective competition for scarce resources, but rather the legacy of social alienation originating in fear of the other produces the class struggle over essential material resources.

What this means is that when we speak in economic terms about living in a competitive, capitalist system, we are in fact describing only an approximation of how social relations are lived out by really existing social beings who are in part (and mainly) alienated from themselves and each other, and in part trying in various ways to escape that mutually reinforcing spiritual prison. To the extent that we are actually trapped (because we inadvertently entrap each other), to that extent our collective behavior can be described as an objective-ish "capitalist system" if we take the position of standing outside ourselves and looking "at" ourselves objectively, as a moving object. And thus it is approximately accurate to say, for example, "if the Federal Reserve increases interest rates, investment of capital will be constricted and job numbers will go down," even though in reality it would be possible for the very same community of people who behave in accordance with this economic description to instead work cooperatively and feed and house each other more or less instantaneously (i.e. this could be arranged right now) through simply paying no attention to the blend of fear of the other, imaginary hierarchy as source of substitute identity, acceptance of money-numbers as interpersonal currency, and ideological beliefs that will, if believed in, make the description come true. Of course an escape from the prophecy of capital disinvestment and lower job numbers in fact cannot occur by wishing it to be so because it is through our movement toward each other, toward mutual recognition via a social change movement of some kind or possibly through the accident of a natural disaster or other revolutionary event, that we each gain the spontaneous strength to liberate each other from our respective positions within the alienated matrix that we call the capitalist system. Thus it is approximately accurate to characterize normal economic relations as a system because they cannot be appreciably affected by the acts of isolated persons or even isolated small groups, since these marginal actions must inevitably be swamped and swallowed up by the pattern of rotating otherness that seals each of us in rivulets of isolated functioning—thus it is actually the case almost every time that capital disinvestment will lead to a decline in job numbers and the predictable nature of this unconscious, cooperative pattern supports the characterization of the economic relations comprising the pattern as "systematic."

But what is important to see is that this system is not actually "objective" but only held in place, or maintained in its patterning, by the social force of the rotating mutual adaptation to the apparent necessity of the circle of collective denial of the desire for mutual recognition. This circle of collective denial can be partially dissolved or undermined by outbursts of intersubjective resistance that a) can occur with conscious intention if the theory I am putting forward is fully understood by a social movement becoming conscious of itself as a loving, healing force; and b) always *is* occurring with *unconscious* intention insofar as the id cannot be fully repressed by the ego/superego complex, or in my terms here, insofar as the desire for spontaneous authentic connection with others cannot be fully contained by the efforts of the fearful false self observing itself to deny that desire. Thus to take one example of the latter manifestation of unconscious intention, the sudden surprising appeal in the United States 2016 presidential campaign of Donald Trump, who comes out on stage with no handlers and does not bother with being "introduced" and favors the abolition of teleprompters, reflects a collective longing for "a world in which I could be spontaneous with others and through that really connect with others," however distorted and co-opting Trump's apparent spontaneity is; or to give an everyday economic example of the unconscious co-presence of desire in more exclusively economic matters, stocks often "go up" when investors more or less spontaneously exude collective enthusiasm over some imagined occurrence (like momentarily imagining "better relations with Russia" due to some blip in international relations), an occurrence that has nothing directly to do with material well-being, as realistic economic indicators may be pointed down.

Let me now conclude this section with a brief discussion of how the above intersubjective and psychospiritual characterization of the economy relates to Marxism and the vast literature comprising the Marxist critique of history, economy, and society. When Marx developed his historical-materialist analysis of the development of human societies in general and the rise of capitalism in particular, he proceeded by *materializing* the psychospiritual patternings of the relatively fixed, relatively entrapped social relations that he was studying. Thus he developed ideas like the theory of surplus value, the tendency of capital to expand and for the organic composition of capital to rise, the tendency of the rate of profit to fall, and the like as if he were analyzing laws of the system . . . when in reality he was describing (with whatever degree of accuracy his analytic description actually has) how the socially-produced rotation of otherness actually reproduces itself insofar as this rotation is alienated. Thus when Marx said that capitalist firms are pressed into competition with each other in a way that causes the rate of profit to fall owing to the relative decline of surplus value in relation to the sum of variable capital and constant capital, and when he developed a mathematical formula to predict and measure this falling rate of profit, he was without realizing it treating an approximate intersubjective patterning of alienated social relations, ordering itself hierarchically, as if it were a thing driven by materialist imperatives. It is true that what I am calling an intersubjective patterning does embody a mutually coercive process among the social actors who constitute it, and therefore the patterning is somewhat fixed, regular, and predictable; and it is also true that within its pattern, material goods are produced and distributed in a way that is mediated by money in such a way as to maintain the balance of fear of the other that is inherent in the reproduction of social separation. Although I am not an expert in such matters, it may well be true that within such a patterning when it is looked at from the outside through the flow of money (or capital) that mediates the pattern's relationships, the rate of profit may tend to fall. And when Marx argues that the tendency of the rate of profit to decline creates inherent problems, even "crises," for the pattern's continued smooth continuation, he may well be right again.

But whether Marx's claims are right or not from this "economic" or "systemic" perspective, what is important to see is that he has imposed this perspective on the world he describes; and to the extent that this social world is not actually a system so conceived, he has fundamentally mischaracterized it. From the social-spiritual point of view that I have been advocating, what Marx is describing as an economically-driven system is but an approximation of a pattern of mutual fear reproducing itself across social space, and the fundamental project is for us is to overcome the alienation that reinforces this fear rather than to revolutionize the capitalist means and relations of material production through a class struggle between capital and labor. The project of overcoming alienation absolutely entails at the same time dissolving class hierarchies of material production and creating something like a spiritual-socialist world, including a spiritual-socialist way of producing and sharing material goods to satisfy the world's material needs. But when Marx and those influenced by Marx argue that this process of transformation must and will take place through "contradictions inherent in the capitalist system" like the contradiction between the needs of capital and labor, they confuse their descriptions of economic processes with the underlying reality of those processes as lived effects of social alienation. This leads, among other mistaken perceptions, to

a) Failing to see multiple opportunities for social change within the rotation of alienation that may give rise to emancipatory social movement characterized by greater realization of the desire for mutual recognition
b) Overestimation of the likelihood of conflict between haves and have-nots over material inequality when the smooth functioning of alienating patterns can be maintained in a way that minimizes, through various forms of psychospiritual co-optation, the importance of this material inequality as a force for change
c) Attributing mistaken motivations to human beings within the overall social matrix, as in believing the capitalists and workers are primarily motivated by the struggle for material survival in a world of scarce resources, or by "economic self-interest," when in reality all social actors, whose collective reality is only partially captured by the concepts of "capitalists" and "workers," are motivated by both the fear of the other in the face of social alienation that produces the divorce between self-interest and the interests of the other, and who are also motivated by the countervailing desire to transcend the pattern of social separation that otherwise imprisons them
d) A mistaken belief that wars and other manifestations of social violence are explained by struggles over access to material resources, instead of by fear-saturated pathologies of alienated identity generated by the false self's terror of humiliation (although one effect of such fear-saturated group identities may well be seeking to take from others the material resources needed for one's own "identity group")
e) A mistaken belief that the solution to "the problems of capitalism" can be found in the creation of a new economic system that eliminates the supposed contradiction between capital and labor instead of realizing the centrality of a psychospiritual, social healing of the

legacy of fear of the other, one consequence of which will be the transcendence of the need to divide ourselves up into capitalists and workers

f) Following from e above, an overestimation of the benefits of new economic forms of equality and community (i.e. at its worst, the Workers' State) that obscures what it will really require to create the lived substance of equality and community, of a "beloved" community.

When we instead see our world as fully lived and brought into being by each of us in relation to the people next to us, and in relation to our sense of everyone else in relation to the people next to them, and of all of us in relation to all of us as that totality is grasped somewhat in this fashion (that is, as we each live our worlds *here* intuited outward to *there*), then we are free to shift our way of imagining change and improvement toward using our life force—which is to say our own desire—to generate new experiences of mutual recognition. We can abandon our relentless efforts to become little battering rams against some huge economic system outside of us while awaiting some future time when there will be a "revolution" that will replace the whole giant existing apparatus with a new and better one. And we can instead pursue organizing efforts grounded in soul-force, as Gandhi put it, and proceeding by ricochet that through the grace of social radiance, or what George Katsiaficas has called an "eros effect," can sometimes occur exponentially, at an almost lightning speed, as when decades of collective inertia and rotating passivity can galvanize into a movement-force almost overnight. As my friend and critical legal theorist Duncan Kennedy said at a Critical Legal Studies Conference in Minneapolis, MN, in 1982, "It's not about reform or revolution; it's about making the kettle boil," where the boiling water is the more-or-less spontaneous ricochet of what were socially separated atoms into a new interconnection and co-recognition that allows the liquid of "the system" to become and then gather steam, the steam of humans-in-love.

That conversion by ricochet is what we mean by social movement, and it carries within itself the new ground for the creation of a better world. This is not at all to say that reforms "within the system" like expanding health care or social security or workers' rights are unimportant—such reforms are good and very important ends in themselves and they are often the best available means of assuring us across our mutual distance that we are still connected and *here* for each other instead of being merely "out there in society." Nor is it to say that we do not ultimately need a "revolution," a fundamental transformation of the entire intersubjective, psychosocial field. But it is to say that the medium of actual change is in the interspace that connects us as a lived reality rather than in a hypostasized materialization of that lived reality conceived as "the economy"—a thing-like entity that we, as withdrawn presences, stand apart from and in awe of. To emerge into and act upon the interspace that connects us calls for an intuitively-sparked spiritual activism that produces and then carries within itself the mutuality of presence that both generates change and prefigures who and what we are changing into.

Works Cited

Katsiaficas, George. "The Eros Effect." *1989 American Sociological Association National Meetings in San Francisco*. 1989.

Rai, Dr. Ajay Shanker. *Gandhian Satyagraha: An Analytical and Critical Approach*. Concept Publishing, New Delhi, 2000.

Chapter 7

Politics as the Struggle Over Who "We" Are

On the Necessity of Building a Parallel Universe

It follows from everything I have written thus far that politics must involve a new coming-into-connection that partially dissolves the inertia of our conditioned selves in a newly emergent present moment. In the absence of such a coming-into-connection, each person seeking to affect the self-constitution of the group through the group's own authorized political process is of necessity a voice crying in the wilderness because insofar as the authorized political process is a congealment of the collective false self, the process *is* the wilderness. Like the "economic system," the political system is actually the objectified mental picture of the self-creation of "our society" that results from each person standing in his or her withdrawn space imagined to be "outside" the group looking down or back "at" the group as a ubiquity of separation and mutual distance. Thus instead of being *here* in direct relation to everyone else *here*, I imagine myself to be "out there" with all the others as others, a "citizen" among other citizens in the imaginary unity of a large group of socially constructed entities. Among them in my case are "Noe Valley," "San Francisco," "Democratic Party," "California," "the United States of America," a member of both the state and federal electorate, and so on until we name all the mentally-pictured entities received by each of us in the course of our conditioning. Now, of course all of these mentally-pictured entities have some residue of genuine and live social presence—I am not saying "California" is a totally imaginary entity inhabited by robots of which I am one, and I do like California because I feel freer here than I felt in my east coast childhood, and I like the loose flow and the liberal spirit of the place. The residue of genuine human community and mutuality gives the notion of California a residual political legitimacy for me to honestly say that I am a citizen of "it." But the mental picture of it, like that associated with the United States of America, is primarily a kind of externally imposed badge that is a part of the cement sealing me in my separation. To the degree that being a citizen of the State of California refers me back to my "place in the political process," to the extent that I actually stand outside my immediate presence-with-others and "think of myself" this way, I unawarely hurtle myself away from being here-with-others and reflect myself to myself as "there" in the world of socially separated citizens, as "one of the citizens of the State of California."

It is not possible to make social or political change "as a citizen of California" so conceived and so pictured because it is not possible to create presence out of an accumulation of absence. One *can* inflect the political process so conceived to the extent that the residue of genuine human connection remains—"we" can legalize marijuana this way for example, which may be a reaching out for a more real and communal world—but the changes so achieved must be limited to changes consistent with remaining pooled up in our mutual distance and separation. And it *is* possible to transform the meaning of being-a-Californian altogether and to radically transform the expressive meaning of citizenship so that "we" become a true community of mutual recognition, but this requires a coming-into-being of a new mutuality of presence that would actually dissolve the political process that we have inherited and place us on a new ontological ground. And while this kind of utopian hermeneutic redemption of received meanings, appealing to a transcendent idea of California or America, are conceivable (as I showed in my discussion in Chapter 4 of Castro's redemption of the meaning of "Cuba" from its meaning under Batista's dictatorship), such efforts are subject to the co-optation by the rotation of fear that lurks within them expressive of their heritage as mental carriers of collective absence, of collective non-presence and mutual distance. Van Jones's campaign to Rebuild the American Dream is an example of political action that seeks to transform the meaning of an alienated mental image legitimizing social separation based upon fear of the other (appealing to the image that "we" all share an "American" dream of a free society where you can succeed on your own merit and have a house in the suburbs with a white picket fence and become Dr. Welby with your wife and child coming to greet you lovingly after a long day at work) into a new image expressive of an actual solidaristic, communal world of free and socially-connected human beings. Such an effort at political change, though not doomed to failure, is a high-risk effort because it involves trying to appeal to people by using a familiar idealized image drawn from the world of the false self; yet that residual artificiality itself will tend to dilute and undermine any transformative potential. It is hard to get to heaven by dancing with the devil.

But the main point for us to grasp is that a transformative politics capable of generating social change requires an emergence into connection with each other, through a coming into mutual recognition, that dissolves the moat that otherwise separates us and allows us to rotate a new "we" into being out of what had been our rotating otherness, the patterning of our mutual withdrawnness. The official political narrative that we receive and internalize during the course of our conditioning masks our longing to bring this new and authentic political "we" into existence by telling us, from birth, that "we" already exist in our capacity as citizens of our country, with each of us being "one of the citizens." If we recall that acceptance of our false selves *as if they were real* has been a condition since birth of our very social membership, since we have all been "recognized into existence" as social beings by becoming (in part) the person recognized by the others who introduced us to the inherited world, we can see that allegiance to the idea that each of us is part of a "we" insofar as we are all citizens of the country is compulsory, simply because it is internalized as if it were real just as our very selves are, to the extent that they are.

Thus in the collective aspect of life that we call politics, the conflict between the desire for authentic mutual recognition and the rotating denial of that desire is manifested as a conflict between the desire to emerge into a real-we and the requirement of deference to the false-we. Insofar as my authentic presence is withdrawn into myself and I experience myself as identified with the relatively hollow persona(e) of my socially-authorized self—the false self through which I have been recognized into existence—to that extent I believe that I am part of the imaginary "we" that is the American citizenry, which both compensates for and denies my actual withdrawn state. Consider the normal functioning of our democratic process. In reality to the extent that I am a withdrawn and socially separated, alienated being enmeshed in the pathos of my sealed-off everyday life, it is obviously an illusion to say I am "in" a democracy: to be withdrawn *means* not existing as fully present in relation to others, *means* that no true experience of "we" can occur in my world—and if we are honest, each of us knows that vast amounts of our lives are lived out in the quiet desperation that Thoreau named. In such an environment, "we the people" cannot really exist because there is no "we" to be part of in a milieu of mutual distance. Yet the requirement of deference to the false-we requires that we all act as though our participation in the we of democracy, of we the people, really does exist, that, as I have said, "we" were brought into being by our Founding Fathers long ago and that we are still "in" that community, carrying out their original intent in the collective action of our present political life.

Let us examine carefully what we might call the phenomenology of the false-we, the lived experience of our conditioning to believe in this false-we, by linking two experiences most of us share: the eighth-grade civics class and the act of voting in an election.

Civics class in which students are taught the political narrative of what I am calling the false-we could not be taught to very small children because the formation of the false self remains incomplete until later in childhood—until the adult voice, that constraining voice that psychoanalysis calls the superego and that the child imagines is "above" him or her, is firmly installed as part of the self and serves as the carrier of the symbolic imagery and normative beliefs which foreshorten the horizon of desire and funnel that desire into authorized channels.

Prior to that time we children experience ourselves to a significant extent as here with others, rather than in any official "out there" where, for example, "citizens participate in a democracy, and I am one of them." As a result, small children remain significantly in touch with the present moment; they/we "play together here" rather than think about "there" as if they live there. But by the time the child is eleven or twelve, compliance with being-for-the-other within the circle of collective denial allows group activities, like the civics class, in which children sit quietly and passively in deference to the authority of the teacher and can read about and be told about how "we" are constituted. Through the prism of this book, I hope you can experience the internalization of this official political narrative as the taking in of a kind of hallucination: The passive child whose desire for mutuality of presence with others has been decisively subordinated to the role-performances of the false self sits removed from any mutuality of presence with the children next to him or her—sits alone in a glass booth of reciprocal separation—and is told the story of the Founding Fathers and the creation of "We the People," and that we live in a democracy in contrast to "the others" who live in monarchies or under totalitarian states.

As I have said earlier, it is of course accurate that an earlier generation in the late eighteenth century really did exist and really did write up their version of how "we" should be politically connected and organized, but what I am calling a hallucination here is that a magical gloss is cast over the version of the actual story that gives an idealized or larger-than-life dimension to the story so as to glorify the child's entry into it—Washington, Adams, Jefferson, and so forth were not "here" as everyday beings in relation to others like us but were Founding Fathers who met in Independence Hall and signed a document that constituted us and can now be found under glass. Through this idealizing enhancement, the child learns, silently,

> I am doomed to suffer the withdrawnness of my true presence, I am cast "underneath" the authority of this teacher, the school, my family, the world, but I have another "me," corresponding to this outer self that they say I am and that they recognize as me, and "there" I am one of "We the People" touched by a halo of sacred community. From this I gain a sense of idealized substitute connection, although I am painfully unconsciously aware that my imaginary participation in this symbolic tableau also is in the service of the denial of my desire to come into true connection with those around me.

The child learns that while he or she is not here with others in a true mutuality of presence, or in a relation of I and Thou, he or she is at least "there" in the symbolic tableau as one of the children-citizens of the founding fathers.

Now to repeat I must emphasize that I am not saying there is no reality to the historical political narrative that the child learns in civics class, but rather that the narrative is false precisely to the degree that the present reality of the child's lived experience is corroded by an absence of connection to others. The "we" of the we the people is lived as a false-we precisely to the degree that the child has come to inhabit a false self by which he or she is divided, by an existential moat, from the person next to him or her in every room and at every bus stop and in watching television and his or her computer screen, in every situation and moment in which he or she really exists as a living, sentient being. The "we" of the political narrative is false to the precise degree that the self who imagines it is false, is "outer," is disjoined from the desiring center of the child's social being in the living milieu of the child's psychospiritual field.

Now if we fast-forward ten or twenty or thirty years to when the child, now an adult, participates in the electoral process on the first Tuesday in November, we can see how the false-we of the citizens, of "the people," is enacted in the larger political process. Most of the year, each person is enveloped in the patterning of rotating otherness that constitutes our reciprocally withdrawn life, a life always simultaneously punctuated by the desire for genuine mutual recognition that is partially realized in every moment in and through the mutual alienation that separates us. During the long period between elections, each person for the most part does not participate in any political activity because each person is suffering the routines of role-passivity in the rotating patternings of daily life: There is no "we" that can emerge into mutual presence through mutual recognition and that might assert its collective agency in public space. During what we might call this long period of down-time, each person shares in the same imaginary that corresponds to the narrative of the civics class (and countless other such transmissions), in the sense that "we" imagine together that the world we are inhabiting together was and is created by us, democratically. While real life corresponds roughly to the world depicted by the great underground cartoonist R. Crumb in his famous comic book *Despair* (on the cover the decaying wife says to her decaying husband "why bother?" in response to his last-ditch suggestion that they see what's on t.v. while inside the comic book people shuffle in isolation down urban streets lost in sexual fantasies), at the same time each person sealed in his or her routines of separation imagines we live in the greatest country in the world because it is created by us, by our own free collective political activity. Insofar as we are (mainly) sealed in the reciprocity of artificial roles that fills up the mould of our false selves, we share the same imaginary of the false-we that each false self is imagined to be one of.

But on Election Day we do engage in a collective political act, the act of voting. We do go out into public—perhaps to a local fire station—and are each separately treated as sovereign individuals as we choose who and what to vote for by touching a computer screen in secret. Yet even here on this special annual occasion, we normally cannot escape our reciprocal withdrawnness and we normally do not actually emerge into a real "we" because most of the time voting itself is a privatized, serialized activity: Most of the time each voter has been conditioned in passivity to choose among candidates who have promised through their own role-based and artificial personae to maintain the rotating patterning as it is, with slight modifications unthreatening to it. Thus in voting, most of the time each person remains withdrawn within him- or herself but "takes" his or her body out to the polling place and then moves the body, experienced as part of the outer self, through the act, enacting being-a-citizen in the same way that the newscaster enacts being-a-newscaster. Remaining withdrawn, each of us "goes about our business" during the day to return home later to "watch the results," to find out what "we" decided. This each of us learns by adding up the total number of votes, and the "we" is then constituted and "our decision" declared as a mere numerical sum, the sum of our serialized voting enactments. The "we" established by the election can only be found by totaling up the sum of our outer-performances, rather than being experienced as a collective, interior truth. Thus, in its alienated aspect, the we that is brought into being by the election forms itself *around* the isolated individual, but he or she does not enter into it.

And yet here again, the description must be decisively qualified by the fact that the desire for mutual recognition overflows the rotation of fear of the other and the mutuality of distance attendant to it. To the extent that particular historical circumstances permit the longing for true community to be manifested in our politics, in part through the act of voting, then the act of voting can become a manifestation of a real-we. To that extent, we as a real people actually do come into a partial existence. For example, when Barack Obama was elected president in 2008, his authentic personal presence, the idealism of his narrative about who "we" are (in his victory speeches after the primaries tracing "our" existence back to the abolitionist movement up through the labor movement to the civil rights movement to the present moment), and his symbolic incarnation as the first African-American person who might get elected, all gave an authentic meaning to his appeal to a "we" that might emerge from its collective hiding and form into a public mutuality of presence. Unlike the more common abstract appeals of other candidates to inflations of the false we (as in Donald Trump's promise in the

2016 presidential campaign to "Make America Great Again"), Obama coupled his call for Hope with the call "Yes We Can," which in tune with my description might be better heard with the emphasis on we, as in "Yes *We* Can." And after Obama's victory in 2008, unlike in the case of the normal election when each of us sits at home and watches the false-we come into existence by the gradual summary of numerical totals external to us, after Obama's victory there was a huge outpouring of joy and tears and a going out into public, signaling the success of our immense effort to "win," to make ourselves visible to each other, to risk vulnerability in order to try to recognize each other into a new, more human, more hopeful, more idealistic existence. And as I write these words in the winter of 2016, this same pulse has been awakened by the candidacy of Bernie Sanders, a 74-year-old man who might be creating the conditions for a cross-generational group-in-fusion of the 60s generation, carried in the being of himself, with the so-called millennials, who are 18–29 and as of today are just starting to risk joining this effort to emerge.

While Barack Obama was not able for various reasons to carry forward for long the incipient real-we that he helped to give birth to, or to be more accurate, while we in the real-we were ourselves unable to sustain ourselves in part because we were too dependent on Obama himself (on this point, please see my discussion of this historical hemorrhage in Chapters 7–11 in *Another Way of Seeing*), the point of the Obama example here is to show that democracy can be a genuine manifestation of we the people to the extent that an election can overflow what we might call its normal alienated container. If we were able to grasp together that the bringing into being of a mutually recognizing, mutually affirming, loving and caring life-world is our objective or even our sacred evolutionary task, we would not reduce the work of democracy to episodic acts of voting which cannot possibly be adequate to that task. Realizing that such a transcendent aim will involve a politics that works in a sustained way to build the confidence, in lived experience, that the desire for mutual recognition that exists in each of us exists in all of us and can be embodied in the practical texture of life, we will have to create a new more continuous politics linking us to our neighbors and local and wider communities in a spiritually uplifting, idealistic way. We might retain voting as a form of mutual declaration—this even seems likely—but our entire political process would obviously not be reduced to the single act of the socially separated secret ballot once a year. Let us recognize the great achievement of prior generations in winning with tremendous effort, over hundreds of years, our current form of democracy, and in protecting us against fraud and coercion through the creation and legitimation of the secret ballot . . . and let us now become conscious of the higher level of mutuality of recognition and presence to which we aspire, and move forward.

The Necessity of Building a Parallel Universe

That moving forward requires not that we invent a new more communitarian image of political life, a new mentally-pictured model that would appear in its outer aspect to be a more we-constitutive politics, but rather than we co-create in lived experience itself a parallel universe, alongside the official political process, whose aim is precisely to establish, in lived experience, a new ontological ground on which a genuine "we" can stand. As I showed in my essay "The Social Movement as a Parallel Universe" (see Chapter 11 in *Another Way of Seeing*), the upsurge of a liberatory social movement actually constitutes such a parallel universe insofar as we each, through the mutual recognition permitted by the movement and incarnated in it, become newly present to each other in a kind of radiant circulation of lightness and joy. Dissolving the weight of our inherited political identity as citizens, which we have known unconsciously since civics class has actually sealed us in mutually withdrawn separation masked by the appearance of having granted to us, "since the Enlightenment," freedom and equality, the movement ushers forth a ground of presence *here* that instantly contests the mutual absence institutionalized in the political process's official other world *out there*. During the 1960s, which as I have said achieved its highpoint as a collective lived experience roughly between 1965 and 1974 and is still not entirely subdued, the "rising" brought into collective life a strange doubling within public space, in which the official world transmitted via our alienated conditioning co-existed with the liveliness and lightness of the mutually present world being brought into being. We called this world the counterculture because it really did manifest itself as another cultural space, parallel to and co-existing with the received cultural space, that was playful, oxygenated, and characterized by discovery and inventiveness rather than the enactment of scripted routines that is so much the hallmark of conditioned life. A socially transformative politics always requires the creation of such a new ground for social being to stand on because, as

I have said, we cannot make the essential change of becoming mutually present by remaining mutually withdrawn and trying to insert a progressive program into a milieu of reciprocal absence.

Understood from within the existential psychospiritual framework of the everpresent conflict between the desire for mutual recognition and the inherited fear of the other that is repeatedly on the lookout to contain it, we can see that the creation of such a parallel universe remains a perpetual possibility of each present moment. For as I have suggested throughout this book, no matter how solid the so-called institutions of the society appear to be, they are actually always unstable, mere rotations of alienated patternings of outer behavior seeking, out of fear of humiliation and attachment to the defense of the substitute communities of the false self, to maintain themselves as if they were indeed fixed and truly substantial entities. In this respect, our social institutions are, as I have said, like spinning tops, with each actor doing his or her part to keep the top spinning, as the power of desire—its ineluctable longing to burst forth into a plenitude of authentic connection with the person next to us—threatens in each moment to "topple" it. Of course as Michel Foucault in particular has shown, what I am calling the "rotating otherness" that becomes the social order has developed immensely sophisticated means of stabilizing itself through the creation of disciplinary hierarchies through which the collective monitors itself. For example, the legal system is a vast and dispersed network of government officials (judges, legislators, sheriffs, bailiffs, court reporters), imposing law books that have now been digitized, hallowed buildings ("halls of justice"), law schools festooned by quotes of the founding fathers, law-focused television shows and the like, all of which are devoted in part to re-creating the legitimacy of and, through reification, the necessity of the existing social and cultural institutions. When the judge in his or her robes enters the chamber and everyone rises, it is not only the rotating patterning of otherness in that room that contains the desire of desire and keeps the top of the courtroom spinning, so to speak; it is also the deeply imbued knowledge of every person in the room that all of the other elements of the legal system are "out there" adding weight and realness to what is taking place here, in the room itself. But what is so important to see and understand is that the manifestations of "The Law" in all of those other instances "out there" are themselves merely spinning, rotating, wherever they are; they are in empirical fact never more than people in rooms reconstituting their part within the legal order with each person using his or her inflection of gesture to keep the legal top spinning and aright. In a very real sense, the entire, majestic "legal order"—"The Law" itself—is a vast and elaborate acting out of the Emperor's Clothes story to the extent that its social power is sustained only by people's belief in it, which belief is itself sustained by the commitment of each "legal actor" to act as though the order is real, is actually "there." But as occurred in the story of the Emperor's Clothes, and as has actually occurred throughout history when transformative social change has begun to become possible, the top can start to really wobble and threaten to fall over altogether when the present moment begins to become infused with the possibility of an outbreak of authentic mutual recognition and presence, and this can only occur, when it does occur, in the present moment itself.[1]

The first moment of the creation of what I am calling a parallel universe of social being arises when someone, potentially anyone, engages in an action which "de-reifies the pseudo-concrete," which challenges the apparent realness of the existing order and at the same time, in that very act, affirms the realness of another way of being which acts, in its social aspect, as an appeal to the other, to potentially any other who experiences it, to recognize this realness also. Consider the very famous example of Rosa Parks refusing to give up her seat on the bus in Montgomery, Alabama. In one respect, it is of course true and important that Rosa Parks was engaging in civil disobedience of the local ordinance requiring blacks to sit in the back of the bus. But in another very important sense, this action also denied the realness of the bus seating rules, not just their legality. Whereas in the prior moment, the white establishment of Montgomery was able to rely upon the reification of a collective perceptual field in which blacks simply "sat in the colored section" as a matter of fact, as if this perceptual field were a two-dimensional surface without depth, once Rosa Parks refused to give up her seat she revealed that the prior "fact" was merely possible, that indeed the entire bus as a travelling vehicle might not have any pre-ordained cultural order at all. Parks's action could only have this meaning because all of the other acts of non-violent civil disobedience that had preceded it had opened up a new possible space, as yet not fully revealed before Parks's action, that made her able to tilt the collective perceptual field by her refusal to move—made it possible for her to introduce into the social field the notion that "the colored section" might not be a fact and, by extension, that all such racial segregation might also not be "the way things are." Were it not for all the prior acts of civil disobedience, protest, transcendent spiritual oratory, gospel singing, and the like, Parks's refusal to move would not have had the same power to reveal the contingent or merely possible nature of the rules because she would have been summarily arrested in accordance with seating rules that the collective environment, according to its long-conditioned legacy, would have continued to perceive as fixed, as "real." In the instance of her actual refusal, she was of course summarily arrested just as she would have been without the prior seeding of the context, but properly prepared for, her action helped decisively to crack open the frame so that the existence of the colored section could appear arbitrary and the arrest appear unjust, or better, absurd.

Seen as an example of building a parallel universe, we must understand Rosa Parks in this situation as having been intuitively ready, by her grasp of the entire social context of the Montgomery bus boycott and the civil rights movement as a whole in which she had been and was continuing to be a participant, to spontaneously refuse to move.[2] And while it is true that this refusal was an act of courage, it is better understood in its social aspect as an intentional appeal to "everyone else" to now, in this present moment, join her in seeing the existence of "the colored section" as an arbitrary social construction rather than a fixed aspect of the bus. Of course, the white establishment of Montgomery would resist this alteration of perception by doing all that it could to close the space thus opened by its own appeal to "The Law." But when I say Parks was appealing to "everyone else," what I mean is she was appealing to the social field as a whole with all its constituent elements pro and con to shift its overall allegiance away from the passively endured facticity of the existence of the colored section of seats to a new perceptual universe that would dissolve this facticity, ushered into existence ontologically by a new and more real "we" emerging within it. It is this new and more real "we" that is the parallel universe, an autonomous self-constitution of transformative group presence emerging from a ricochet of mutual recognition that takes back what Heidegger called "the worldhood of the world" (*Being and Time*, p. 91) and regrounds collective perception and collective meaning on its own truly human, truly interhuman, terms.

As the movement develops, the capacity to create such moments of transformation—or perhaps better, transfiguration—becomes more and more widely shared as the "we" of the movement grows surer of its foothold in existence. Recalling my own participation in the movements of the 1960s, I can think at random of a very large number of such moments rich with symbolic and creative force: Abbie Hoffman leading a levitation of the Pentagon during a large anti-war protest; Jean-Paul Sartre and Simone de Beauvoir inspiring a whole generation to refuse to "enter into" the frame of holy matrimony (although marriage may also have a redemptive transcendent aspect); the Chicago 7 defendants refusing to obey the courtroom rules of Judge Julius Hoffman in order to delegitimize the charges that the anti-war protests against the Vietnam War held outside the Democratic Convention in 1968 were the actions of hooligans who had "crossed state lines with the intent to start a riot"; the decision by one and then a few and then many women to stop wearing bras and shaving their underarms; the growing of long hair by men; the explosion of hitchhiking; and so on. And while it may seem trivializing to mention such examples in the same breath as Rosa Parks's challenge to racial segregation, the point I am making is that the accelerating rotation of all of these actions really were bringing into being a new community by virtue of their character as appeals to one another to come out from the system of conditioned roles that had been containing us and to give birth to the moving force, to what we call "the movement" which is nothing else than this morally compelling moving force of creation, community, and truth. The "truth" of this moving force is precisely its rotating, ricocheting affirmation of the mutuality of presence to each other that, because of our inherited conditioning, we had been in denial of without knowing it. And it was this collective becoming-present that allowed us to make social and political change, because this transfiguration of being, perception, and "world" *was* the change, in the sense that the action of Rosa Parks, when she refused to give up her seat and as her action became confirmed by others through mutual recognition of its truth and realness, was the dissolution of the racial distinctions in bus seating that *subsequently* generated the verbal change of the law as a result of her successful incarnation of it in that creative present moment. Thus the parallel universe is the ontological vehicle that makes manifest the incarnation of the new world constituted and then inhabited by a real-we, as it makes an incursion into the psychospiritual field of the false-we and contests it for political legitimacy.

What I am calling "politics" is the work of bringing into being this real-we precisely by contesting the false-we that the collective false self, the alienated matrix of the conditioned world, defines as politics. Just as the false self reasserts its fear of the other by claiming in meta-silence that it is the real self—that it is "what is"—so the false-we asserts that it is the real-we and that its collective expression in political life is a genuine expression of what "the people" want. When a movement of genuine mutual recognition arises, altering the perceptual field as I have described and introducing into that field a new psychospiritual vitality and spreading radiance, it has not won, but rather has only begun to engage the fear of the other that still exerts itself with great force against the liberatory opening that the desire for mutual recognition has managed to create for itself, for all of man- and womankind. Through the movement, the real-we is able to form itself and make itself manifest by breaking out of its prior pooled-up condition through a ricochet of confidence—we might say it manages to momentarily outwit the fear that previously had been containing it with constant vigilance that had been externalized in the hierarchy and internalized in the underneath-self. And once the real-we enters public space with sufficient confidence, through the rotation of mutuality of presence, for us to experience that a parallel universe comprised of a plenitude of connection exists alongside the artificial hollow universe-of-absence of the false-we, we do have a place to stand that is a source of spontaneous relief and joy. But as quickly as this parallel universe emerges, the artificial universe tries to reassert itself and dissolve it, initially through overt opposition (everything longed for in the parallel universe is "against The Law"), and then eventually through co-optation (what you long for can be accommodated by The Law). And on the side of the false-we is nothing less than the weight of history, which in the present moment is simply the accumulated transmission of the normalization of fear of the other in all its forms, modified by the poignancy of all prior efforts of the desire for mutual recognition to make itself heard. We all know that we long for more—for a present reality that would realize our desire and transfigure our fallen state—but we know it mainly through the medium of fear's long, successful containment of that longing, as that has been transmitted to us as the real world.

So when Rosa Parks dissolves the racial classification of correct bus-seating, the civil rights movement whose ricochet has made her act possible must then seek to "change the law," which is to say the movement must continue, following the moment of revelation, to enter into a dialogue with the false-we to make the dissolution of racial segregation binding on the false-we. Obviously this is a paradox. For while the moral appeal of the real-we being carried forward by the civil rights movement emerges precisely from that movement's authenticity as the carrier, in this moment, of the desire for mutual recognition, and while that moral appeal because of its basis in truth is irresistible in the sense that it cannot, if sufficiently supported by the movement's parallel universe, continue to be denied by the false-we in such a way as to allow the false-we to continue to be *credible to itself*, it nonetheless remains true that the false-we and its fear of the other still holds sway over "the world" as a whole and still has all the resources of its long and heavy weight of history to call upon. The false-we says to the real-we,

> ok, we cannot any longer deny that segregated bus seating is wrong, is absurd, but to make this binding on us you must change the law and in that symbolic and verbal arena, we will reassemble our forces of fear and seek to recharacterize your momentary revelation in accordance with our hegemony, in accordance with the overall requirement of maintaining security against humiliation in the face of our fear of the other.

Thus while Rosa Parks's action in 1955 did lead, along with the ricochet of and accumulation of other such actions, to the passage of the Civil Rights Act of 1964 that banned discrimination in public accommodations like buses, the disalienating meaning of Parks's action was given an alienation-restoring meaning in the legislation and its subsequent interpretation. To see how this transposition of meaning occurred in this instance and occurs in law generally, we need only locate ourselves inside what we might call the Rosa Parks moment and contrast the meaning of that moment with the world-view and consequent meaning of the Civil Rights Act and of anti-discrimination law generally. Parks's act was a transformation of a present moment in which the moral truth of true equality was incarnated and made manifest. We could say that in refusing to give up her seat, she broke through the network of images that the instant before was spiritually imprisoning her and the entire alienated world within which she and the bus driver and the other passengers were all located. That was the world inhabited by withdrawn beings separated from each other by their mutual alienation and participating in the "settled" imaginary communities of "whiteness" and "blackness," of imaginary racial differentiation, that substituted for authentic community and also served to protect those withdrawn beings "against" each other, against the threat of mutual vulnerability and possible humiliation. We could say that at a deep, even unconscious level, everyone understood that the racial differentiation in seating, and racial differentiation itself, was absurd and imaginary, but they could not allow themselves to know this consciously due to the necessity of sealing themselves in their roles in accordance with their conditioning. When Parks refused to give up her seat, she declared invalid and imaginary this entire alienated matrix and, supported by the real-we of the civil rights movement behind her, she was able to both reveal the alienated matrix, to make the alienation itself conscious in everyone, and also to bring a moment of true mutual recognition into the world. Suddenly, the withdrawn actors in this drama were pulled out of their withdrawn state, pulled out of their heads in which they were identifying with their false selves and (in the white section) with their imaginary whiteness, and they were forced to become present to each other and actually see each other in the present moment. That concrete incarnation of mutual recognition of their social equality, or better, of their common humanity is what gave to Parks's act its moral power, a power that because of the power of the real-we behind it, the false-we could no longer succeed in denying.

But now please notice what I am calling the transposition of meaning that took place when, almost ten years later, the Civil Rights Act of 1964 was passed prohibiting racial discrimination in public accommodations like buses. Certainly, the authentic egalitarian meaning of Parks's act as incarnation of true mutual recognition of our common humanity had not been forgotten in the culture by 1964—in fact, it had in many ways been strengthened by subsequent similar acts of resistance, by demonstrations, by the morally compelling oratory of Martin Luther King Jr., by the development and radiant influence of the civil rights movement itself as a continuing and developing moral force. But when Parks's action was codified in the Law, the meaning of her action was also turned over to legislators, and to judges who would later interpret the law, and who were for the most part, although not exclusively, still identifying with their roles as representatives of the State and spokespeople for the wider society, for the false-we. Many of these legislators and judges were also undoubtedly influenced by Rosa Parks and by the civil rights movement as a whole and were also themselves pulled toward revealing their own desire for mutual recognition and for true community by the force of the movement as a parallel universe, by its pull upon them. But insofar as these legal actors were also attached to their roles as makers and interpreters of the law, they also remained attached to their valued position in the existing society, and insofar as they were removed from the moral energy of the movement, they remained loyal to their false selves and the false-we of their own historical conditioning. So when they together stated by verbal declaration of the law that discrimination in bus seating is prohibited, they did not "see" the mutual recognition of our common humanity that Parks brought into existence in that concrete moment, but rather they "saw" a bus of disconnected monads, of mutually withdrawn "passengers" each in their roles, and they declared that their seating arrangement could no longer be racially differentiated.

In other words, they restored to the bus its alienated character but added to all the other relevant rules the rule banning discrimination based on race. To the extent that these law-makers and interpreters remained far enough removed from the pull of the movement upon their real longings as mere human beings seeking loving eye contact with all other human beings, to that extent they remained withdrawn into themselves and so perceived the world that they were "legalizing" across a moat, as a world of the withdrawn rather than as co-inhabitants of the world of mutuality that Parks had in her moment of resistance, and in conjunction with all the other externalizations of authentic being comprising her movement itself, brought into existence.

In subsequent years, many legal doctrines were employed by the Supreme Court to acknowledge the illegitimacy of discrimination based upon race, but all of them have sought to reconcile the prohibition against discrimination with what I am calling the "false-we," with a mental picture of the community of the nation and its political morality as expressed through law that makes non-discrimination consistent with remaining withdrawn within the patterning of rotating otherness that constitutes the concrete lived experience of alienated life.[3] To the extent that, for example, affirmative action retained the morally transcendent meaning in its early years of King's vision and Parks's action—to the extent that it signified a vast effort on the part of the real-we and the rising community of true mutual recognition to acknowledge and heal the legacy of slavery—to that extent the legal doctrine carried forward the movement's aspiration to social transformation. But as that doctrine was gradually absorbed into an imago of the socially separated world of the withdrawn selves, the doctrine was increasingly interpreted to mean that insular minorities who had been subject to discrimination in the past could get a bump "up" in the market-driven competition to make it as socially separated individuals in an anonymous and anti-communal "American society." And as I have shown elsewhere (see "The Spiritual Meaning of Social Justice" in *Another Way of Seeing* and my earlier "The Meaning of Affirmative Action: Making It as Individuals in the Competitive Marketplace or Climbing Together to the Mountaintop" in *The Bank Teller*), this gradual shift to make affirmative action consistent with the false-we inevitably reinforced image-based ideologies like meritocracy and the legitimacy of vested rights and produced new binding legal doctrines like impermissible "reverse discrimination" against deserving "whites" that further cemented the marriage of anti-discrimination law to the re-reification of the false-we. The civil rights movement's exertion of authentic, loving mutuality against the pathologies of the system of social separation continues to be felt within the culture as an echo and a kind of subterranean reservoir of hope not wholly extinguished (not merely for a world beyond racism but for a humane, communal world generally), but that echo and that hope has been reconciled with and therefore subordinated to the restoration of mutual distance and separation. One might say that this process reached its apotheosis in the election of Barack Obama, as a black man was able to become president of a formerly all-white enclave, but could not stand for more than "being a black president" at the "top" of the false-we's political hierarchy, still carrying forward the echo of Martin Luther King and Rosa Parks but predominantly being enveloped within and speaking for the false-we that has retained its predominantly alienated, mutually withdrawn character.

Yet my characterization thus far of the struggle between the real-we and the false-we may be misunderstood from this entire description to refer to two separate forces within the culture, one brought into being by the movement and one aligned against that movement on the side of alienation. The movement as a parallel universe is an indispensable origin of a transformative collective politics; and through its realization of the desire for mutual recognition, it does give birth to a new social reality of human connection on an ontologically independent ground, in effect "rescuing" the dispersed and withdrawn relational beings that we were from our mutual spiritual imprisonment. "We" come into existence by "rising up" and then standing together in a new space where we can suddenly discover and see each other. But we do this within the psychospiritual field of the false-we that had enveloped us, and so the movement actually introduces into that field its own transcendent presence as a spreading "call" upon the conscience of the We-as-a-whole. This We-as-a-whole is therefore best understood as a unitary, moving (or rotating) relational field inhabiting a unitary social space—it is a single psychospiritual field—with the "false" vector in that space actually constituting no more than a continual, mutually reinforcing resistance to the pull of desire within the unitary field, a kind of mutual appeal by each person to the other not to give in to the desire that calls upon the relational field itself, *from within itself*, to let down its guard. Thus the rotation of collective resistance that is the false-we has as its top priority convincing itself that it is real and through that mutuality of hardened conviction warding off the temptation to succumb to the desire and longing within. Because human reality is at all times relational, my sense of the balance of the real and the false within the We-as-a-whole, decisively influenced by the totality of my past experience of this balance, will determine what I am capable of transmitting from my "pole" in the relational fabric to the others around me and whether I feel I can or cannot "call" upon the person next to me, and all the others with whom I am in contact, to come out from behind the personae, the anonymous false selves who appear to believe in the false-we that separates us.

To see how the balance of the real and the false occur as a political balancing act always tipping toward a breakout of the real that the false is always struggling to contain, or better, infinitely postpone, consider the present moment in American politics, February 29, 2016, the day before Super Tuesday during the primaries leading up to the 2016 presidential election. On this day as I write these words, the Democratic primary is a contest between Bernie Sanders, mainly representing the real-we, and Hillary Clinton, mainly representing the false-we.[4] This contest is taking place within a largely demobilized atmosphere characteristic of American culture at this historical moment. By that I mean that we are not currently as a community under the influence of a breakout of mutuality like the 1960s, but are living within what we fairly call normal routines more or less regulated by an apparent universal, or at least hegemonic, commitment to the ascendency of the false-we. If we were living within/experiencing/constituting the breakout of such a movement of real mutuality of presence, the election would have a different meaning, because we would be everywhere constituting ourselves as a real-we from *here*, from our own existential space being rotated into existence by each of us in relation to the other. But in today's historical moment, such a force field of authentic reciprocity does not exist and so "hope for the We-as-a-whole" is projected out onto the tableau of the presidential candidates within the hegemony of the false-we. We each hope we can "use the election" as it takes place "out there" to leverage ourselves out of our mutual separation toward the realization of our common desire. And we have reason to hope this because we feel we have no other access to each other within the We-as-a-whole since each of us is sealed within our mutual distance as "citizens," and because as "citizens" we can each rely on the agreement-within-separation that we will all "declare" by the act of voting tomorrow whether the real-we is ready to overcome the fear of the other sufficiently to confirm itself as real "in public." The leverage that we as a real-we might gain from the election is that we might be able to declare that we exist as a political community laying claim to the character of social reality, to the We-as-a-whole, in a way that will if successful increase our confidence that the other is "ready to go with us" out from behind our respective shells. If Bernie Sanders wins Minnesota, Massachusetts, Colorado, Oklahoma, and Vermont tomorrow, Tuesday March 1, or if he does well enough, whatever that means within the balance of the real and false in this moment, the real-we will be able to go forward to the next step in the next moment toward a more general emergence into a movement for mutuality of presence, for a loving community.

Now I have called Bernie Sanders the candidate of the real-we because he manifests himself as a real presence rather than an artificial one, because he is running on a campaign of "we are all in it together" embodied in a series of actual programs that ground the authenticity of that call, and because he has said directly in an evocative and beautiful way that he believes we each feel the suffering of each other, that all human beings do, and that if we stand together, there is nothing we cannot do. As a witness-participant in this actual moment, I experience the authenticity of Bernie's call—I "feel the Bern" to use today's vernacular that really does capture this call of conscience that has rotated Bernie Sanders into existence and that Bernie himself has been publicly transmitting in his being and expressive discourse through his campaign—and I experience the artificiality of Hillary Clinton, who has taken over some of Bernie's words without the presence, to add enough borrowed reality to her own campaign to make her call to maintain the false-we appear real in the face of Bernie's real threat. Hillary is making her appeal from within her persona of public speaker/leader-to-be as the candidate of "realism" who will not "dismantle" the false-we but build upon it by incorporating Bernie's real elements within it. And she will be president of the new false-we, the first woman to "occupy this high office" on top of the hierarchy just as Barack Obama was the first African-American person to do so. I have no intention here of discounting the possible movement forward that Obama's presidency and Hillary's possible presidency represent—they do represent a partial empowerment of their respective subordinated communities, just as they also by contrast represent a partial co-optation of the respective social movements that made them possible. But my point here is simply to accurately characterize the present moment on this day within the presidential primary season as we call it, so as to show how the real-we and the false-we co-exist in struggle within the We-as-a-whole. The significance of this day is that the relative realness of the We-as-a-whole is being contested on this day, because of the leveraging potential for the real-we of this series of Democratic presidential primaries taking place tomorrow.

As I sit here at my desk, I am still passing through my normal routine carrying out the activities of an average 69-year-old man existing under the canopy of the false-we, existing my world within its few-block neighborhood in a rotating patterning of average mutual distance. As I say, this world is not currently "mobilized" in creative mutuality, but rather I pass my fellow neighbors on the street, say "hi" to those whom I know, project a pleasant demeanor within the constraints of the available role-performances (I can't really appear grim or overjoyed without absurdly tilting the rotation within which I am recognized). Considering what I am saying in this book, I certainly pour as much of my desire for mutual recognition as I can into these passing encounters—I do actually look at those whom I pass in the average milieu of what I have earlier called "aversive presence"—but I am entirely constrained by the rotation itself, by the routinization of what someone of my age and class and race (all cultural artifices of the false-self legacy) can do and how I can be. And from within that relatively constrained, relatively conditioned patterning, I am daring to hope that Bernie Sanders does well tomorrow in the states that I listed. However, the very inertia of my own neighborhood here in liberal San Francisco is partly intensified by the fact that although Bernie won New Hampshire by a landslide, he has since lost Nevada by a little and South Carolina by a lot. Since Hillary Clinton's call is to accept "reality" and vote for the false-we, as she wins in these early primaries her victories mean that the immense advantage that the hegemony of the false-we starts with within the We-as-a-whole may well be strengthening, or increasing in weight. My own vulnerability to being humiliated by hoping "we" might decide to extend ourselves toward each other (as I have been by the large crowds Sanders had been drawing and by his more-than-four-million small donations and by the surprise big victory in New Hampshire) is heightened today as I feel the inertia that Hillary's recent victories and most recent poll numbers affect the dynamic in my own neighborhood, affect the step of each other with whom I come into contact (including Clinton supporters who have with unconscious resignation decided that Sanders is not a realistic candidate although they like what he stands for, meaning they would like to hope if they could but they feel they can't because of what they believe, resignedly, everyone else within the We-as-a-whole will do).

And if and when I "turn on the news," the weight of the false-we upon me will become that much greater because the newscaster, as I have earlier shown in discussing his or her persona, his or her "presentation of self," is on the side of the false-we and wishes to present its reality as inevitable, as real. When the media that is mainly *mediating* the false-we to itself predicts the inevitability of a Clinton sweep and that she now has the nomination within her grasp, I cannot but know that a certain number of college students in Minnesota and Massachusetts will be less likely to remember to vote, as they instantly sense with their youthful, still relatively unsubdued life-force, that perhaps politics isn't for them after all and shift to thinking about going out dancing. In fact, I am hesitating to turn on that news broadcast because I know that it will hurt me to do so; I'm willing to still hope for a Sanders victory or good-enough showing but I'm not willing to expose myself too much to the humiliation of being once again thrown under the bus of the newscaster's smiling, relentless persona, that false self manifesting itself as real and claiming to speak "neutrally as a journalist" for the state of the we, as a matter of fact.

Now I offer this very partial description, this phenomenology of the present moment, to show how "politics" actually unfolds as a struggle between the false-we seeking to maintain itself as if it were who "we" actually are, and the real-we seeking to make itself manifest, in the context of an election, in which the We-as-a-whole "declares" itself by the collective act of voting. If Bernie Sanders were doing better, meaning that those students in Minnesota and Massachusetts were going to be declaring themselves as open aspirants to a world of human connection tomorrow on Super Tuesday, I might be feeling and behaving quite differently, I might be making an extra trip or two to my local coffee house to see who is there to talk with me about our momentum. But instead I am exactly where I am, daring to hope as much as my anticipation of rejection by the other can tolerate, along with millions of others like me, in a historical moment decisively conditioned by the overall balance of the false and the real within the group, and with the very limited but not insignificant opportunity for "leverage" offered by the electoral process within a relatively demobilized milieu. Furthermore, although my description of this present moment may seem almost silly in its detail (discussing whether I will go down to the coffee house or not etc.), I have left out a vast number of other phenomenological factors relevant to the precise situation of the balance of the We-as-a-whole, including the refusal so far by African-Americans in the South to respond to the "call" of Bernie Sanders, and the decision by many women to support Hillary Clinton because of the redemptive hope they attach to a woman becoming the first "leader of the we," or if you prefer "our" president, even though they sense her tilt toward reinforcing the congealed false-we that otherwise spiritually imprisons them as universal social beings. A full description of a single moment in the struggle over who "we" are, particularly a moment in which this question is explicitly contested in the limited way that elections establish the We-as-a-whole's reflection of itself, would require many pages. The point here is simply to present to you a glimpse or snapshot of this struggle as it actually occurs in the concreteness of social existence through the experience of each person attempting—as I must here at my desk—to totalize the entire psychospiritual field and gauge his or her willingness to reveal his or her desire for mutual recognition as that desire confronts what Sartre called its "co-efficient of adversity," the fear of the other that rotates a patterning of "otherness" trying to resist the threat of vulnerability. The point is that the false and real co-exist in the political sphere exactly as they do in every two-person interaction, with the former seeking to deny the pull of desire through the regulation of "me" (here) and "them" (out there) and desire itself seeking from every pole to break past its regulatory constraint.

Beyond Reform or Revolution

Once we can see politics as a struggle between the real-we and the false-we within a unitary We-as-a-whole engaged in an interior collective conflict with itself, we can also see that the debate within the Left about whether to seek social change through reform or revolution must be superseded. To once again quote my friend Duncan Kennedy speaking to a group of critical legal studies activists in the early 1980s, "it's not about reform or revolution; it's about making the kettle boil." The traditional reform vs. revolution debate proceeds from a standpoint that tries to be outside society, looking "at" the world from an outside position and debating whether the right approach to change is to change "it" piece by piece or try to fundamentally reorganize "it" as a totality. Like most social thought, this traditional approach treats a living, breathing, radiating, constricting, experiential interhuman life-world as if it could be known and changed from the outside, like the alteration of a physical object. From an architectural standpoint, it is possible to debate and decide whether it is better to remodel a house or knock it down and build a new one, at least to the extent that a house is in fact an objective entity that can be looked at and analyzed externally with the help of architectural plans, but the social world can only be grasped from the inside as a collective lived experience at odds with itself.

"Making the kettle boil," as Duncan put it, means seeking to create experiences which allow a we of mutual recognition to emerge from a we of mutual distance, role-performances, social beings at arm's length effortfully separating themselves from each other by a moat that protects them against the humiliation portended, they fear, by the pulsion of their own desire, their own longing for the reciprocated vulnerability of mutual recognition. As we have seen from the revolutions of the left in the last century, making a "revolution" understood as a seizure of state power, nationalization of the economy, or any other such fundamental external reordering does not assure the creation of a society that fosters authentic human community because such a communal world, in which each person can recognize and fully experience the other as a Thou and be so experienced by the other, *must be spread into being* through building confidence in each other's desire. In part this requires breakthrough experiences that are captured metaphorically by the idea of revolution, moments in which social movement becomes possible in bursts, people suddenly become present to each other, and the force of that coming out toward mutuality gains the traction to ricochet across the face of the social landscape as occurred in the 1960s. But in part—and here prior social movements including the 60s have fallen short—the successful communalization of the world also requires healing from the fear-saturated legacy of alienation that has been passed on generation to generation and has been internalized by every one of us. Such a social healing requires a spiritual politics that builds upon the breakthrough power of the movement and that allows our mutual confidence in each other's desire for mutual recognition to sustain itself in the face of the fear of rejection and humiliation that inevitably accompanies it. As I showed in my essay "How the Left Was Lost: A Eulogy for the Sixties" (see Chapter 6 of *The Bank Teller*), a "mere" revolution must produce a powerful counter-reaction to the extent that it connotes an instantaneous reorganization of the We-as-a-whole because it is not possible to instantaneously transform the real social relations that are mobilized in the revolutionary moment. Breakthroughs of mutuality are always thrilling, but building sustained confidence in each other's "hereness" or presence for each of us is more difficult.

Although the idea of reform in the traditional sense has always been contradictory in the sense that it is not possible to co-create a real-we while maintaining the dominance and fixity and legitimacy of the larger frame of the false-we, the metaphor of reform does aim toward the more sustained work of overcoming our fear of each other and building confidence in each other over time. Thus within capitalist society socially progressive reforms like universal health care can establish patterns of collective care for each other and each other's families that reflect back to us our sustained connection in a way that a revolutionary moment of breakthrough cannot. To the extent that an "external" reform like providing universal health care is accompanied by spiritual cultural practices that foster social healing (including the healing of our bodies), that reform may help the real-we to gradually emerge and gain a foothold in the We-as-a-whole, as a kind of marker of our continuing presence for each other. But without the creation of a spiritual practice that creates and sustains the actual transmission of the *care* in universal health care, a reform like universal health care may tend to congeal back into a bureaucracy of the false-we, a collectivization without soul that is consistent with maintaining the wish to remain withdrawn and in which care becomes mere insurance of separated and externalized thing-bodies (on spiritualizing social activism, please see Chapter 10).

Thus a spiritual politics actually requires both revolution and reform as those words are reunderstood from the inside. In its revolutionary aspect, a transformative politics requires decisive breakthroughs of authentic mutual recognition that reveal the fear-saturated artificiality of the false world masquerading as real, bursts of revelation that gain the traction to ricochet our real-we into existence and to gain a foothold in the We-as-a-whole. In this revolutionary aspect, the desire for mutual recognition emerges and spreads through the We-as-a-whole with sufficient force and radiant ubiquity so as to challenge the entire framework of the false-we and bring, for example, the entire rotating patterning of otherness that is "capitalism" into question. In its reform aspect, a transformative spiritual politics requires a sustained spreading of confidence within the fabric of this real-we being born, through progressive social changes that retain their soul, that retain their enlivened sense of authentic human connection and solidarity. When universal health care means making manifest actual caring about each other's health, vitality, and well-being as opposed to merely insuring externalized and ontologically separated bodies against illness and injury, then it advances the effort to sustain a real-we beyond the revolutionary breakthrough that allows that we to be born.

We can therefore outline the building blocks of a transformative politics as follows: inspire into being incursions into the false-we of authentic human connection that make us aware of each other's presence and simultaneously dissolve the appearances to which we had been attached that separate us; build out of the movement of such a real-we being born a parallel universe that provides a ground for us to continue to stand on beyond the breakthrough moment; support reforms that sustain our mutuality of presence to each other over time with sufficient attention to the psychospiritual liveliness of the reforms to infuse them with their transformative meaning and purpose as building blocks of a new world; and continue to generate revolutionary experiences of mutuality of presence that can in turn support new sustaining forms that allow that presence to be reflected back to itself in a way that strengthens our own confidence that the desire for mutual recognition within each of us exists, and will continue to exist over time, within all of us.

Notes

1 There have been many examples of successful efforts by activist lawyers and their clients to break through the ritual choreography of the courtroom as a way of countering the way that these rituals elicit obedience and passivity not only in the courtroom itself, but across the entire social field that "The Law" seems to govern. The best known in my lifetime was the Chicago 7 trial (originally, the Chicago 8 until defendant Bobby Seale's trial was severed from the others). That trial occurred in response to the protests against the Vietnam War that took place outside the Democratic Convention in Chicago in 1968. Mayor Richard Daley famously permitted the Chicago police to very violently put down the protests, and then eight "ringleaders" were selected for prosecution, including well-known 60s activists Tom Hayden, Abbie Hoffman, Jerry Rubin, and Bobby Seale, whose trial was ultimately separated from the others. The defendants and their lawyers, William Kuntsler and Lenny Weinglass, refused to obey Judge Julius Hoffman and disrupted the ritual in various ways, among them Abbie Hoffman cartwheeling into the courtroom and giving alt-answers to standard questions (for example, when asked "Where do you reside?" Abbie replied *"I live in Woodstock Nation. . . . It is a nation of alienated young people. We carry it around with us as a state of mind in the same way as the Sioux Indians carried the Sioux nation around with them. It is a nation dedicated to cooperation versus competition, to the idea that people should have better means of exchange than property or money, that there should be some other basis for human interaction."* The judge then interrupted him and told him to just say where the place is that he resides.

Paul Harris and I have analyzed the significance of this trial in undermining nationwide support for the Vietnam War itself in "Building Power and Breaking Images: Critical Legal Theory and the Practice of Law" 11 *NYU Review of Law and Social Change* 367 (1982–83). Our main point was that the challenge to the ritual form itself weakened the power relations through which the entire rotational edifice of power relations supporting the war was legalized and legitimized. In the trial, the prosecutors were trying to enforce the perception that the defendants had simply "crossed state lines to incite a riot" (which was what they were charged with). And Judge Hoffman too was attempting to use his authority, as robed choreographer of the proceeding, to make sure the trial was perceived through that lens, whether the defendants were found guilty or not. But the defendants and the lawyers were trying to topple that spinning top altogether and put the Vietnam War itself on trial, to reestablish that the protests had not been a "riot" and had immense moral import for the entire country. Disestablishing and delegitimating the courtroom dynamic, reported nightly on national television, was central to transforming the perceptual field within which the war itself, and national obedience to the coordinators and justifiers of the war, were viewed. If the Chicago 7 defendants could emerge from their "hooligan" status and establish themselves as moral agents of a great morally inspired movement, the hierarchical, image-saturated arena of the courtroom might partially dissolve and along with it the larger hierarchical network that was conducting the war itself.

2 There is a debate about just how spontaneous Parks's decision actually was, since she had been an active member of the civil rights movement, had participated in non-violent resistance trainings at the activist Highlander Folk School, and was Secretary of Montgomery's chapter of the NAACP. Parks herself always insisted that her action was not planned (see her 1956 interview on Pacifica radio soon after her arrest) and she rebuffed those who attempted to portray her as carrying out a preconceived strategy. But assuming Parks was being truthful, as I do in saying her action was spontaneous, that does not mean that her spontaneity itself did not require the background context that empowered her to "move," or in this instance, not to move.

3 The relevant legal doctrines are explained and summarized in Alan Freeman's brilliant article "Legitimizing Racism Through Anti-Discrimination Law: A Critical Review of Supreme Court Doctrine," 62 Minn. L. Rev. 1049 (1977–1978).

4 I have retained this description as it was written in the present moment on Super Tuesday during the 2016 run for the Democratic nomination precisely in order to capture how the effort to create a real-we contests the pressure to maintain the false-we within social consciousness within a living present moment. In that moment as I experienced it, I did believe that Bernie Sanders represented/spoke for an emergent authentic community and that Hillary Clinton mainly represented and spoke for maintaining the world as it is, subject to ameliorating liberal reforms. As I make clear in Chapter 8, this "claim" on my part is but an appeal to you to recognize the trenchancy of my description, which of course you are free to do or not to do, or to do so subject to your modifications. I voted for Hillary Clinton in the general election.

Chapter 8

Knowledge, Truth, and Understanding

Suppose that everything I have written thus far were true and that all of us came to know that it were true. If that were the case, then all of us would instantly leave behind our withdrawn positions and begin with great relief to see and affirm one another, to recognize each other as the loving beings seeking love that we actually are. Our fear of each other would dissolve with the knowledge that the other would reciprocate our desire for authentic mutual recognition, and no one would have any reason for sustaining the false self, allegiance to the false-we, or the pretense that the patternings of rotating otherness or of deference to hierarchy are "real" in the sense of being simply manifestations of the way things are.

But if all that I have written is true, "we" cannot possibly know that in a clear and confident way precisely because the denial of the desire for mutual recognition that sustains and is sustained by our rotating social alienation requires the denial of that knowledge. To sustain our own alienation and the masks of self, other, and "world" attendant to it requires that we not see through the masks. And by contrast, to risk knowing the truth of our common longing as social beings requires actually experiencing the longing. This book—my reaching out to you right now in this moment with these words—is an appeal to the desire for mutual recognition within you to allow yourself to experience the longing within you enough to know, based on the self-evident truth (to yourself) of your own longing, that my descriptions of our mutual alienation correspond to your perception of the world as you and I and everyone else live it. I am making an impassioned appeal from my longing to your longing to help us recover from the mutual distance that separates us. Beginning from the self-evident truth of our common longing, from our (collective, universal) desire for mutual recognition, I reach out with impassioned descriptions to illuminate what we have conspired to keep in darkness, or more accurately, since the desire for mutual recognition always is palpable within us and always seeks to transcend what separates us, to "enshadow." Only to the extent that my descriptions are illuminating of the truth you know already can they constitute knowledge of that truth and can they contribute to constituting a real-we conscious of itself enough to be confident in itself.

In our world as we currently exist it, the hegemony of mutual distance and reciprocally withdrawn presence is supported, so to speak, by the linking of true knowledge with being-at-a-distance and by the concomitant denial of the status of true knowledge to being present. Following the model of the natural sciences, most of us take for granted at the level of reflection that the only way we can know that anything is true about the world is to suppress our vibrant spiritual presence and stand back in a detached and neutral space, from which we as "rational beings" can look "at" the world with what we call objectivity. However, this stance is itself paradoxical, since it is through this very detached stance that the world *becomes* an object to be seen objectively. The entire method of the natural sciences severs the bond between the knower as a vibrant spiritual being and the known as a vibrant spiritual environment and seeks to propose hypotheses *about* the world from which the knower has detached him- or herself that can then be tested by what are called empirical methods. But the empirical methods are not really empirical because they have *presupposed* that both the knower and the known are despiritualized, with the knower erasing him- or herself as a vibrant spiritual presence and by so erasing him- or herself inevitably placing in shadow any spiritual presence in the object of knowledge. The only kind of knowledge that can be produced by this self-detaching, distancing approach is the passionlessness of detached knowledge, through which being delivers to itself flat and despiritualized information "about" the object of knowledge apprehended as an object, as a despiritualized thing. Detached knowledge starts out by forcing itself to be in doubt because it renders itself incapable of actually grasping the living presence of what it is "looking at"; and it cannot ever arrive at the assurance of truth because the knowledge that it produces can never be more than information about the world apprehended as a surface. Hypotheses conceived in doubt always end in doubt, no matter how much information is gathered, summarized, and correlated along the way and no matter how successfully this surface knowledge is formed into provisional truths, temporarily confirmed hypotheses, "about" the world conceived as a universal and infinite surface.

This isn't to say that vast amounts of useful knowledge cannot be acquired by this detached method, by examining the world from the outside as an object. The history of machines and of medicine, for example, show that such detached object-knowledge can produce much that is of value, provided that the knowledge doesn't run off like a headless horseman by uncoupling itself from its humane psychospiritual ground (as has in fact occurred to a significant degree in contemporary culture). The problem lies rather in denying the status of true knowledge to what we might call undetached knowledge, to knowledge that seeks to grasp through one's own vibrant spiritual presence the presence in the world and to illuminate that presence through evocative description lively enough to make that presence palpable and accessible to our engaged reflection.

To create and disseminate true knowledge about the world requires that everything that has spiritual presence, or more accurately that is spiritually present, must be grasped by a spiritual presence that understands intuitively, or grasps, the presence in the other through the channel to it opened up by the encounter with the presence in the self. This "grasp" is the ground of truth. Knowledge of the presence thus grasped must then take the form of impassioned description adequate to illuminate for consciousness what it has already grasped, and the truth-value of this knowledge depends upon how completely the spiritual relation of presence-to-presence manifested in the grasp can see itself reflected back to itself in the descriptive mirror. The knowledge thus produced "goes alongside" and illuminates the truth in reflection through the anchoring grasp that is prior to it.

We can see then that the detached method of natural science and the embracing method of spiritual illumination are directly opposed to each other. The detached method separates the knower from the so-called object of knowledge, relying on di-stance to apprehend the world as an object and to thus produce objectivity "about" the world imagined to be "out there," *away*, so to speak, from the consciousness of the knower who looks at it. The knower using this method necessarily starts out in doubt, "not knowing anything" except what can be detected by the residue of sensation left when you have despiritualized sight, smell, taste, hearing, and touch, the only vestiges of presence left to this knower withdrawn into detachment, and the only remaining connections of the being of the knower to the being of the world that actually prevent the knower from drifting off into outer space altogether (and it is a paradox of this detached method that it would if it could, in the interests of maximizing objectivity, eliminate even these sensory vestiges of subjectivity, which would then deprive it of any relation to the world at all sufficient to know anything at all about it). Beginning in this self-imposed doubt about what can be known to be objectively true about the world, the detached knower correlates information about the surface of the world, forms hypotheses about the world's functioning, tests these by trial and error, and then presents to itself this information through the despiritualized, dispassionate, methods of scientific rationalism. Befitting a world from which one has detached oneself as much as possible, the knowledge itself thus produced is potentially interesting but "dry": descriptions of a world without presence to itself, or to the knower, or to the severed relation between them, a world of the observer-at-a-distance to an infinite surface, an infinite outside.

The embracing method of spiritual illumination by contrast begins by the knower throwing him- or herself forward with all of his or her spiritual effort into connection with the being itself of the world-to-be-known, understood a priori, self-evidently, as a world of present being, radiating its presence with the spiritual vitality of Being itself. Because the being of all so-called living things is social, the relation of knower to known is also a social relation, through the channel of which the knower seeks first to grasp the presence of the living field of which the knower is a vibrant part and exists in relation to. Rather than beginning in doubt and detachment, the grasp is a movement of confidence emerging from full engagement with the presence of the world to be known, a world that wants to be known through the knower precisely to the degree that the knower wants to know it (for the very point in engaging in the work of knowledge is to illuminate in the relation of knower to known what is understood in the grasp of the mutuality of presence but still "enshadowed" and therefore still opaque to reflection). Out of the confidence of the embrace through which the knower as a spiritual presence grasps the spiritual presence of the world in which he or she exists as participant and expression, the knower illuminates what has already been grasped, through evocative description of what has been grasped and making it known to itself through reflexive self-evidence, as in "yes that's it exactly." The truth-value of the description comes not from the testing of an anchorless hypothesis, but from the revelation of what was already grasped but not fully seen, from an experience of recognition.

In the world we now live in, in which we are still so much withdrawn into ourselves and guarded against the presence of the other (and against our own desire for mutual recognition with the other), we have deprived our fear of the other of knowledge of itself—or more precisely *protected* our fear of the other *against* knowledge of itself—by declaring the attempt to make visible this knowledge "just a matter of opinion." Withdrawn presence reinforces the necessity of its own detachment by insisting that only knowledge gained through detachment can be true, or more precisely, can be known to be true. For if engaged knowledge were to be accepted by us as true, we would have to let ourselves know that we are transparent to each other, that through our mutuality of presence we can potentially grasp and reveal all that separates us. Since securing our withdrawn state protected against the risk of humiliation by the other requires denial of the knowledge of this very fact, knowledge is in the odd position of having to be exiled from truth, except for the provisional truths of correlations of despiritualized sense-perceptions at the surface of the world. Thus the claim to know anything by a confident embrace of the world is undermined by characterizing such knowledge-claims as mere beliefs or opinions, and that which is valorized and given validity as knowledge is *also* undermined by limiting the knowledge thus acquired to a provisional relationship to truth—a proven hypothesis is only valid so long as it is falsifiable by the same methods that established its provisional validation, and all hypotheses are ultimately surpassed by more information. Engaged knowledge is understood to be merely subjective and just a matter of opinion while detached knowledge is in effect "merely objective," unable to ever establish itself in relation to the being of the object under consideration and unable to achieve the certainty required of truth. Everyone is "floating in space" in a world of surfaces, the existential analogue in the realm of knowledge to the actual situation of us as withdrawn beings alienated from ourselves and each other, imprisoning each other in spiritually impoverished isolation. Of course we also transcend this nexus of constraint at every moment, reaching toward the other and seeking the redemption and grace of mutual recognition, and to that extent we also *know* this as a *true* potential, but that knowledge is disempowered, undermined by the way our conditioning marginalizes and minimizes it in reflection as a kind of anchorless or rootless wish, a sighing "if only."

Now the importance of all this is that it demonstrates how we have, out of fear of the vulnerability of our own and the other's presence, cut ourselves off from knowing how to recover from our mutually enforced separation. Through our collective epistemology transmitted to us through the hierarchies of separation and accepted by each of us in our reciprocal withdrawnness, we have marooned ourselves on islands of doubt. The only way to get off an island of doubt is through an encounter with confidence, but it is the paradox of our marooned state that we are each surrounded by doubt and in our respective doubting states we inevitably primarily transmit doubt to the other. I described this earlier in my discussion of street encounters when I characterized these encounters as manifesting "aversive presence," a tendency to avoid each other's glance, to attempt to continually retreat from affirming that we are both *here*. And yet as I have said, at every moment, in every interaction, our desire for mutual recognition and our concomitant longing to affirm that desire as real and grounded in truth transcends the doubt in ourselves and leads us to find hope in the gaze of the other at the same time that we are conditioned to retreat from it. Thus when a liberatory social movement arises, we are able to come to know with self-evident certainty that the other who is suddenly coming toward us will actually be there, instead of receding away from us, if we emerge from our withdrawn state and affirm the presence of our connection. In that realized mutuality of presence, what had been moments before just a matter of opinion with no socially validated anchorage in truth reveals itself to in fact be true. That is why a movement can "ricochet": The rotation of revealed self-evident confidence overwhelms the rotation of doubt that had moments before denied that this confidence was epistemologically possible.

The Women's Movement's Knowledge of Its Own Truth

Consider the plight of women for hundreds of years prior to what we might call the epistemological breakthrough of the women's movement. For centuries men succeeded in controlling the airwaves in a way that denied the truth of women's experience of the men themselves. These men appeared to deserve their positions as "announcers of the real" in public space because their authority appeared to be self-legitimating. The Congress was made up entirely of men, the Presidents were men, the meetings were run by men, the big public decisions were made by men, all by virtue of the more or less universal acceptance of the meta-claim carried in the male discourse and posture and musculature and gestures that asserted, implicitly, self-legitimating authority and validity. The actual experience of women as social beings excluded from and demeaned by this format was that males were merely engaged in an authoritative performance, but they could not become conscious of the validity of that experience, of the truth of their implicit knowledge, until the women's movement itself allowed women to "arise" into mutual recognition and through that new ground of being confirm in one another the insight that they had necessarily held in silence, even in unconsciousness, up to that time. Men who dominated public space were pontificating, bossy, hyper-rationalistic, and violent, inhabiting false selves puffed up to protect themselves from their own vulnerability to humiliation that would result from actually being seen, and representing these artificial authoritarian personas as "real" instead of as mediums of denial. Only the upward force of the women's movement itself as an upsurge of collective social being could elevate women's awareness to allow them to emerge from their own false selves as passive complements of the male authoritarian false-self and to make their previously repressed understanding known. And since the knowledge was true, its expression inevitably began to create change in the false-self matrix, to undermine it, although, as we have seen from earlier chapters, the resistance of the false-self system, and its false-we, would inevitably begin to oppose, co-opt, and seek to compromise that emerging knowledge as the false-self system sought to secure itself against the dissolution that it simultaneously longs for and fears. It is the *truth* of emergent moral knowledge of this kind that supports the truth of Martin Luther King Jr.'s claim that "the moral arc of the universe is long, but it bends toward justice" (Wesleyan University Commencement, 1964). The truth, eventually, and through the multiple twists and turns of denial, co-optation, and every other effort of the false-self system to suppress that truth, sets us free.

One thing that has made the truth of this spiritually illuminated moral knowledge more difficult to see has been the dominant influence of liberal and progressive world-views that have participated in the denial of the truth of this very knowledge. Consider, for example, liberalism, Marxism, and deconstruction, which all still powerfully influence the channeling of liberatory impulses in the culture into social action to bring about change. Each of these world-views is actually a claim to knowledge about the truth of the social world. The liberal thinker looks "out at" the world and claims that he or she knows, a priori, that "we" as a social group are discrete individuals, all of whom are free and equal to each other, who form the social world and its institutions (out of an original state of nature) in order to protect life, liberty, and property, and maximize the general welfare in a way that would not be so protected and maximized if "we" did not form such a mutually binding social contract. The Marxist thinker looks "out at" the world and claims that he or she knows, a priori, that the liberal thinker is wrong, that "we" are and have always really been grouped as social organisms into classes who actually have not been free and equal as the liberal asserts in his or her knowledge-claim, but have rather been engaged in a struggle over the acquisition/production/distribution of the material resources necessary for material survival. The thinker influenced by deconstruction looks "out at" the world and claims that he or she knows, a priori, that "we" exist in particular groups embodying particular cultural identities each of which is distinct and unique, none of which can be enveloped in some kind of universal claim about "the nature of man" that can be known. The liberal thinker seeks to free "the individual" from the constraints of social coercion through creating an ever more free and equal society; the Marxist seeks to liberate the oppressed classes from the yoke of material deprivation and exploitation through creating a classless society based upon worker control of material production and material resources; the practitioner of deconstruction seeks to free each culturally produced identity group from the oppression of all totalizing knowledge and socially coercive forms of life. Each of these ways of seeing the social world makes knowledge-claims about the world that themselves are dependent on a priori assertions about the truth of their respective ways of seeing.

Yet from what I have said thus far we can see that all of these forms of social knowledge share a detachment that makes the illumination of the social world as a psychospiritual field impossible. Let me return to my example of the women's movement as a rising force of illuminating solidarity that enabled women to become conscious of an understanding that they already had of oppressive male authority. If you recognize my description as "valid," it is only because you yourself as a spiritual being identify with my way of illuminating, of bringing to light, the spiritual nature of both the prior suffocation of women and the empowered self-liberation of women from that milieu of forced passivity, deference to bossiness, and accommodating role-complementarity that had previously been enveloping them. In my description I was—based upon my own past participation in social movements that have in part liberated me from my own conditioning—attempting to grasp the social-spiritual, historical emergence of the women's movement as a transcendent manifestation of social being becoming conscious of itself, and through the intuitive bond of understanding linking me to that movement offer my descriptive knowledge to you by appealing to your parallel spiritual relation to that movement, to which you have access by virtue of your own partial liberation from your own conditioning. To the extent that my description was accurate, the desire for mutual recognition within you that at every moment seeks to surpass your coerced deference to the false-self system joined me in sufficiently identifying with my description of the liberating power of the women's movement as a movement of social being so that you could say to yourself, with me, "yes that's it exactly," or if not exactly, approximately. The sentences written by me as the one acting as the knower express my effort to channel my spiritual understanding of the women's movement's dawning power to you as an appeal to you to see it also, and in so doing we together gain confidence in the truth of our perceptions through shared knowledge of those perceptions. Together you and I as spiritual presences "use" our own spiritual presence to apprehend or grasp the spiritual truth manifested in the women's movement becoming conscious of itself and together we then confirm our knowledge of what had already been understood through apprehension, through our grasp of it. And if you feel that my description is "off" in some ways (which of course it must be, as we will consider in a moment), you might then reply, through our shared spiritual apprehension of the movement as a collective spiritual presence, with a revised description appealing to me to reconsider my own. The validity of my description itself, and of my transmission of it to you, depends entirely on the passionate illumination of a shared spiritual understanding of a "moment" of spiritually enlivened and shaped social truth, the truth of a moment of the women's movement.

Liberalism, Marxism, and Deconstruction

Neither liberalism, nor Marxism, nor deconstruction can illuminate the social world in this way because they each participate in the withdrawal of spiritual presence from their understanding of the world—or to be more precise, they each deny the relation of spiritual presence that unites them to the world as a social-spiritual reality and thus suppress their own understanding of that reality which they as spiritual beings co-inhabit. Liberalism, for example, as articulated in the writings of Locke, Hobbes, Adam Smith, and among modern writers by John Rawls, and also as expressed through the dominant common sense of present-day Western culture as a whole, begins by asserting that the social world simply *is* made up of free and equal individuals who simply *are* in discrete, socially separated space. This assertion of "is-ness" is a truth-claim, and liberalism presents this truth-claim as a knowledge of that truth . . . social existence *is* a collection of socially separated individuals. We can note at the outset that this a priori ontological position is not offered to the reader or listener as an appeal to his or her experience but rather is asserted as an a priori truth. And asserted in this way, liberalism presents itself as a "knowledge without a knower" . . . the liberal thinker places him- or herself outside of social existence, as a neutral cipher purporting to transmit a social knowledge to the reader or listener not drawn from the intuitive understanding of his or her own socially enmeshed existence. In reality, the liberal thinker is not neutral in creating his or her social knowledge, but is rather withdrawing his or her spiritual presence from the world by denying that this presence exists and then projecting a mental picture of the world that also erases the mutuality of presence in everyone: The free and equal individuals are represented as disconnected monads who then become the political citizens who will, out of mutual fear, enter into the social contract that will become the basis of liberal political theory. And in addition, because this two-dimensional, despiritualized, mentally-pictured tableau is simply asserted as "the way things are" or the way the social world simply *is*, it reinforces the denial of the desire for mutual recognition by purporting to simply "announce the real," which is to say that it is an authoritarian, fact-like, reification whose fixity (or is-ness) complements and secures the self-erasure and withdrawnness of the knower, the liberal thinker. Of course the liberal thinker would agree that he or she is "one of the individuals" in his or her own theory of social life, but that simply displaces his or her actual existence as a really existing social-spiritual being onto the reciprocally disconnected tableau that he or she has created. He or she gives him- or herself a double-existence as on the one hand an erased/withdrawn actual living, breathing social presence, and on the other a projected/internalized "free and equal" disconnected monad. Thus in its ontological aspect, liberalism involves one manifestation of what we might call the "rule of withdrawn presence": a despiritualization of the knower which corresponds to a despiritualization of the social world represented as an authoritative knowledge that denies to the reader or listener access to the truth and validity of his or her own social-spiritual experience.

In its historical aspect, liberalism sought to secure its "rule of withdrawn presence" within the several-century-long disintegration of the feudal order and the rise of market societies at the level of material production and survival, the rise of the bourgeois class in a newly conceived political hierarchy, and the displacement of religion by science in cosmology or world-view. In part this multiply-vectored rise of new social forms expressed a genuine liberation from prior forms of social alienation and manifested a genuine apprehension of human freedom and social equality, a moral upsurge corresponding to the upsurge of liberalism as a social movement incarnated eventually in, for example, the American and French Revolutions. But because of the still-existing predominance of fear of the other (of the person right next to you) in the evolution of interhuman life, liberal thinkers did not leap from the dissolution of the feudal social order to the creation of a truly loving social world characterized by an emergent experience of mutual recognition, but instead sought to align themselves with the absorption of the genuine liberatory impulse expressed in the long overthrow of the feudal hierarchies into a new, mutually withdrawn set of hierarchies that could become, so to speak, invulnerable to themselves. Thus Locke, Hobbes, Adam Smith, and eventually the writers of the American Declaration of Independence could incorporate their genuine impulse toward human liberation into a form of authoritarian reified social knowledge that rationalized as consistent with liberty and equality the murder of native peoples, slavery, the oppression of women, and the material suffering of the poor. The point here is not to single out these forms of inhumanity and non-recognition as evidence of liberal hypocrisy or evil, but rather to draw attention to obvious elements of the denial of desire for mutual recognition embedded in the liberal's truth-claims about the world and the social knowledge consequent to it. The historical impulse toward human liberation, genuine in itself and always pointing to an eventual authentic interhuman liberation through mutual recognition, is appropriated in liberal knowledge into a despiritualized ontological transmission that denies this very desire and re-rationalizes social hierarchy and human separation.

Does this mean that once its utopian elements were absorbed into a system of individual rights and social contract theory, liberalism's focus on "society" as a collection of free and equal individuals then meant that it simply became an ideology that legitimized the operation of the new free market and the hierarchical class relations of the emergent capitalist society, with the ideology being the appearance and the hierarchical class relations being the reality? No, because if we grasp these economic and class relations by extending our spiritual presence toward them and then apprehending the spiritual presence that actually suffuses and constitutes these capitalist hierarchies, we realize that they themselves are not "real"—they are not "moving things" hierarchically organized in an actual top-down fashion—but rather are rotating patternings of mutual distance, an alienated psychospiritual field or "flow" of separation, in which each of us holds the other at a distance mediated by our false self from which we withdraw our true presence and longing.[1] Illuminated by this spiritual understanding extending from ourselves and into these hierarchies as living social realities, these hierarchies are in truth no more than mutually constructed, imaginary,[2] and enacted orderings through which the rotating false-self system monitors itself in the service of mutual self-protection. And this is as true for the billionaire CEO at the so-called "top" of the hierarchy as it is for those who defer to him or her "underneath," in the sense that the billionaire feels as isolated and sealed off from love and mutuality of presence as every other participant in the hierarchy, materially more secure but spiritually just as impoverished (or moreso by virtue of his or her lack of a community of resistance). Thus apprehended as a collective, interhuman lived experience rather than a reified "entity," every hierarchy is simply a flow of social being seeking to secure itself, through the denial of the transcendent desire that undergirds and threatens it, against the desire to become fully present to and vulnerable to the other.

The relationship of liberal knowledge to the rotating flow of socially separated, hierarchically-mediated life is to reinforce this denial of desire by idealizing it, just as the false self seeks to displace and channel the desire for mutual recognition into perpetually trying to become what I earlier described as the Perfect Other. The transposition of the lived relational experience of social alienation—of mutual distance and reciprocally reinforced spiritual isolation—into a "society of free and equal individuals" robustly co-creating a world that realizes our actual longing for the experience of freedom and equality—this transposition secures in collective reflection each isolated person's attachment to the inflation of the outer or false self through its assertion that its imaginary, idealized characterization of our lived experience is "true." This collective, reflected idealization at the level of social knowledge does not "serve the interests of the ruling class,"[3] but is rather a way that alienated social life, in which we are each pooled up in our mutually enforced withdrawn separation, guards itself against its own desire to break on through to the other side of the moat that separates us, isolating those at the "top" of the hierarchy as much as those at "the bottom."

The "villain" in the piece is not the powerful individual or class, but the alienated false self and the legacy of the fear of the other that holds our universal desire back from its own redemption.

Thus just as the desire to become the Perfect Other condemns the false, outer self to chase an ego-ideal that it can never become (because the false self always understands within itself that it is false, that it is really "outside" of itself), so also the effort to become one with the liberal free and equal individual whose social success depends upon his or her merit and will-power within a competitive "society" supposedly incarnating our collective freedom and equality is also a fruitless quest. In reality, I want to encounter you, the person next to me, in a relation of authentic human connection that would realize our desire as inherently relational beings to truly meet each other, as Buber put it. The imago of myself as the liberal individual installed in me in the course of my conditioning is a manifestation of false social knowledge that weds itself to the desire to become the Perfect Other within my outer self, creating a "double" within me and within all of us that we cannot become and do not actually want to become.

We can now see that once its true liberatory impulse became absorbed in the creation of a new fear-saturated world, liberalism became a despiritualized form of social knowledge that manifests the very same characteristics of withdrawn presence and projection and internalization of a false or idealized outer unity that characterizes the rotation of the false-self system itself. Can Marxism, a form of social knowledge so thoroughly opposed in content to liberal thought, be a manifestation of the very same "rule of withdrawn presence"?

Like liberalism, Marxism emerged as a genuine moral revolt against dehumanization of some by others, in its case the manifest moral injustice of the oppression and exploitation of workers and the poor by those who controlled land, factories, and machines, the means of material production. But instead of apprehending this world as a lived interhuman relational field whose alienation from itself was creating widespread dehumanization and social injustice, Marx detached himself from his own spiritual presence and in so doing unmoored the "world" he was describing from its own interhuman social-spiritual rootedness. Instead of throwing himself forward as a spiritual being into the world of capitalist exploitation and describing the world within which he was imbricated in terms of the spiritual distortions of its ubiquitous fear of the other and the rotations of that fear, he detached himself from that world and from himself *in* the world, looking "at" the world as a despiritualized externalized object that he then transposed into a mental picture of externalized "material" relationships: people pictured in terms of their economic functions laboring to produce and distribute material goods to support the survival of their bodies, means of production (land, factories, machines) producing relations of production (social relations among workers, distribution of goods), with producers forced by competition to extract surplus value from workers measured in quantitative terms. What he did was to "stand back" from his lived experience in the interhuman world, look at it from his detached stance, and then "peel off" the material aspects of these real social-spiritual interhuman relations, converting the whole into a kind of "moving object" or materialized surface-in-motion. To this reified surface apprehended at a distance by Marx as the knower, the moral impulse for a genuine world of liberation from the manifest injustice of capitalist social relations was transformed into a "class struggle" for material survival, which is to say that the totality of the interhuman was theorized and presented as "real" in terms of a reified two-dimensional materiality. The existence of the class struggle as a knowledge-claim by Marx was based upon an a priori assertion of the *truth* of the despiritualized, materialized field as its ontological ground.[4]

If Marx had looked out at his nineteenth-century world with its manifest injustice, including its exploitation of the working class, its material suffering imposed on the poor, and including all the other forms of social injustice that he felt and perceived so powerfully, but if he had remained present himself as a spiritual social being and had grasped the world he saw as a field of psychospiritual distortion, what would he have written? If my descriptions have been accurate, he would have apprehended that what he characterized as the ruling class and the working class engaged in conflict driven by economic forces were actually rotating patternings of social-spiritual alienation reproducing themselves out of fear of the other, or out of the conflict between our fear of each other and our desire to transcend that fear in mutual recognition. He would have seen that the suffering produced and reproduced in capitalist social relations were in need of a spiritual-political healing rather than an externalized economic revolution, although the transformation required to heal the world would certainly revolutionize capitalist social and economic relations in very much the way Marx aspired to. And he would have grasped and then conveyed in knowledge drawn from and descriptive of that grasp how the hierarchies of capitalist production resisted with violence, co-optation, and every other means the vulnerability of self to other, the social vulnerability, that will be entailed in bringing into being the transformation that he so deeply sought. He would have understood that the material elements of the world apprehended in their full social-spiritual depth could not be "peeled off" from those spiritual elements but rather needed to be seen as the field of material survival on which the alienation of self from other was trapped into playing itself out. He would have understood and then shown that the reproduction of social alienation was the motor force in history of the reproduction of class society, rather than being a mere after-effect of the struggle over material resources, production, and distribution.

The despiritualization of the human and interhuman that was so much a part of Marxism and remains today a part of all materialisms including most contemporary forms of Marxism itself is in some ways more puzzling than liberalism's privatization of the spiritual. For unlike Locke and Hobbes who were intending to restabilize and legitimize the rotation of social alienation in its new liberal form following the surpassing of feudalism, Marx was a critical thinker revolted by the injustices of the capitalist world and the suffering that it was reproducing. He wanted to create a knowledge that would liberate humanity from this self-reproducing suffering, and yet in withdrawing his own spiritual presence from his descriptions of lived social experience, he created a false knowledge of his own that ultimately had destructive consequences precisely in its failure to see the necessary relationship of social-spiritual healing to a true liberatory transformation. By withdrawing himself from the life-world, and then superimposing materialist explanatory concepts on top of that life-world, he developed an objectified explanatory "master code" that defined a distorted idea of social truth for the next 150 years, absorbing much critical liberatory social energy into it. Ontologically, it led people to grasp themselves in an idealized "entity-relation" to economic production ("the working class") engaged in inevitably violent struggle with an opposing demonized owning class, with each antagonistic entity-group supposedly driven by despiritualized material interests that were supposedly pushing history forward. When Emma Goldman allegedly said, "If I can't dance, I don't want to be in your revolution," she was actually drawing attention to a distortion in the theory of Marxism itself and in its characterization of the real that wrongly subordinated the longings of the heart and soul.

Perhaps the feminist nature of Emma Goldman's insight was no accident and perhaps the reason for Marxism's own determination to control the world through rational, objectifying thought rather than express the world through illumination of its psychospiritual distortions was the result of Marx's continuing unconscious attachment to patriarchy and the fear of the other attendant to it. And perhaps the best way to understand what is actually true in Marxism is to understand it as a *literary* knowledge, indirectly capturing the social-spiritual distortions of capitalist society through the metaphor of their economic aspect—thus we can understand "exploitation" not as a scientized economic fact but as a manifestation of dehumanization of the other born out of fear, and "the extraction of surplus value" as a monetization of subjugation and inequality rather than a "real" mechanism of systemic functioning.

Certainly Marxism as literature is closer to the truth it means to describe than as a materialist science applying objectifying economic concepts to a materialized social field.

Deprived of the truth-illuminating ground of human presence, both liberalism and Marxism became harmful legitimators of worlds without spiritual presence, which is to say that they both asserted as knowledge of the true nature of human reality two-dimensional, spatialized tableaus "about" the world that supported the world's alienated character "as if it were real." And because knowledge emptied of spiritual presence is in truth the denial of that spiritual presence, both liberalism and Marxism have tended to become totalitarian—they have both legitimized hierarchical relations of separation by calling these relations realizations of their respective truths (liberalism's "free society" and "free world"; Marxism/Leninism's "workers' state"); and in their respective erasures of spiritual presence through withdrawal of the knower from the known, they both have not "allowed" the longings of the human heart to express themselves and challenge their respective versions of the false-self system. In the absence of the resistance force of revolutionary social movement against the false-self system (as was evidenced in my example of the women's movement becoming conscious of itself), the equation of truth with the unilluminated life of the false self has meant that listeners were conditioned in an oxygen-deprived epistemological atmosphere to not be able to affirm their own most impassioned desire—to truly see and be seen by each other. When women "rose up" through consciousness-raising groups and other incarnations to be able to affirm one another in a new way, they became able to illuminate in knowledge, as transcendent social beings, the truth of their own suffocation that had theretofore been "enshadowed," but the rotations of the false-self system had previously denied them that knowledge and had told them they were not "allowed" to know it, as films like *Revolutionary Road* and novels like *Mrs. Dalloway* have shown.

Against this totalitarian system of knowledge in the last several decades has arisen the movement toward deconstruction, which has sought to disassemble from the inside the ideologies of liberalism and Marxism, and all such "totalizing" knowledges characterized by Jacques Derrida as "logocentric." By this term he means something similar in some respects to the critique I have offered here, in the sense that he suggests the knowledge-claims of these forms of thought attribute a "metaphysics of presence" or "realness" to the world they describe that is achieved by suppressing aspects of that world that do not fit within it, and by privileging that knowledge as revealing truth itself. By centering all knowledge of the truth in linguistic categories that exclude the lived experience of whole populations of non-dominant groups, the official understanding of truth is linked to power in a way that can be deconstructed through an analytical critique that can show these truth-claims to be indeterminate and failing to produce the closure of meaning that they purport to do. In place of the totalizing knowledges of Western thought as a whole, deconstruction proposes that every event has a multiplicity of meanings, that there is no such thing as an authoritative interpretation of reality, and that interpretation of the social world in every instance is a political act of social and moral choice rather than a representation of truth "outside of" that interpretation. To avoid the logocentric (or in a more feminist characterization of the term, phallogocentric) error of asserting that there is a single master code for interpreting reality that is superior to others, deconstruction sees the world as a social "text" whose reality is subject to indeterminate, multiple interpretations, none of which can be said to be truer than the others, but only pointing in a better or worse direction for the community of interpretation. What I have in this chapter called "knowledge without a knower"—that is, knowledge which "hypostasizes" a truth "out there" that just *is so* by an a priori assertion and that concomitantly withdraws the presence of the knower from it—deconstruction calls logocentric knowledge manifesting a metaphysical assertion of an a priori presence of the truth that is signified by the privileged claim of knowledge. In liberalism, people "are" free and equal; in Marxism, people "are" materially-driven social organisms enmeshed in class struggle; and these are declared by epistemological fiat to be the privileged forms of social knowledge, the code for declaring the truth to which all other interpretations of reality are subordinated and must exist in relation to.

However, while deconstruction has had the virtue of undermining the truth-claims of totalizing rationalistic knowledges like liberalism and Marxism, it has also participated in the "rule of withdrawn presence" by removing the "deconstructor" from the production of his or her own critique. In place of the totalizing logocentric theories of liberalism and Marxism which assert an "is-ness" to the world they purport to describe "out there," deconstruction asserts an equally detached "isn't-ness" to this very same world. Because he or she cannot affirm with confidence his or her own transcendental grasp of the world that he or she exists in and in relation to as an intersubjective spiritual presence, the actual interhuman spiritual truth of the social-spiritual world dissolves into nothing and scatters itself into a multiplicity of "different voices" whose transcendent or alienated character cannot be critically described and known. The indeterminacy of deconstruction's social "text" thus is posited as a kind of hypothetical, detached entity "out there" and this floating, indeterminate text-entity is precisely paralleled by the lack of presence of the disengaged floating interpreter: The "text" can mean anything because the interpreter of the text cannot grasp it. As a result, in the words of Sartre making a similar critique to the one I have made here, "knowledge dissipates into nothing," and from a political standpoint, deconstruction cannot provide us with a spiritually anchored moral direction to move forward.

Or to put this slightly differently, the deconstructing non-knower detaches him- or herself from the object of knowledge and in so doing renders its contours indeterminate and unknowable, thus disaggregating social reality into an infinity of separate particular experiences. Out of the fear of the abuse of power through knowledge of purported truth, deconstruction renders everyone unable to grab onto the world at all. Supposedly deconstruction makes all interpretation political and therefore empowers everyone and every group to stand up for their own chosen experience and sense of the good, but at the same time, in its detachment it deprives us of the psychospiritual ground on which to stand to be able to know what is good. A mountain climber can only climb toward the mountaintop if he or she has anchored his or her pick toward the top and gauged his or her steps based upon that anchorage; but the deconstructionist must make his or her political choices without any such anchorage, and so does not know where to step in relation to his or her transcendent end, leaving us to wander around, armed with a kind of disengaged "choice," on the mountainside.

Thus in spite of its intention to be the ultimate negation of logocentrism and any "metaphysics of presence," deconstruction also participates in the very same flight from true spiritual presence-in-the-world and participates in the very same objectification, or two-dimensionalization, of a tableau or "world out there," a world it cannot grasp. Instead of imposing on the world a spatialized narrative that presents the world as a kind of coherent moving object, as in liberalism and Marxism, deconstruction imposes on the social-spiritual field a spatialized narrative (a "social text") that presents its object as incoherent, as unanchored and indeterminate in its unfolding. And because the presence of the knower remains withdrawn from the object of knowledge, the deconstructed world thus described remains metaphysically "present on its own," without the spiritual presence that makes the life-world human and gives it moral direction. Like liberalism and Marxism that substitute reified concepts for the spiritual richness of the life-world as collective lived experience, deconstruction *eliminates human reality* from its own two-dimensional deconstructed tableau, a world with no humans in it to make it known to itself as particular manifestations of the universal intersubjective social-spiritual being that make us *here* and *One*.

The negative consequence of the rise of deconstruction has been in its negation of any moral truth of social being and its consequent denial of a common moral direction for humanity in and through our infinite particular incarnations. We are left with a world dispersed into a disaggregated multiplicity of identities and projects not bound together by any common moral destiny. By insisting on the erasure of any social-spiritual truth from interhuman reality, deconstruction has supported the rise of a postmodern culture in which irony and laughter are the dominant way to approach the real insofar as irony and laughter constantly displace anything purporting to be true. Under the regime of deconstruction, the truth "isn't"; irony reveals that; and that's all that we can share across our disaggregated multiplicity of identities. But as good and as funny as Jon Stewart and Stephen Colbert are, we cannot get to the promised land only by undermining all the false direction signs that might be posted in front of us. It is more likely that others seeking some moral direction will seize the space abandoned by deconstruction/cultural studies/identity politics and the ironic stance to attempt to achieve at least a substitute sense of community and mutuality "outside themselves" to compensate for what they cannot realize within themselves in the moral truth of authentic mutual recognition. Thus xenophobia, English-only laws, family values, homophobia, and the like offer the spiritually isolated person forms of a false-we responsive to a universal longing for community that deconstruction refuses to affirm and speak to as a universal moral longing.

The specific cultural influence of deconstruction upon these cultural processes is that its hegemonic rise, supported by the ironic stance of postmodernism as a now dominant cultural way of being, defines the horizon of truth. To be sure deconstruction as I have described it is but a recent manifestation of the social alienation from our social-spiritual collective soul that I have been trying to describe throughout this book, but what is so important to see, and the reason that I have included this chapter in the book, is that what is understood as truth in collective consciousness, in legitimated cultural reflection, has a central influence on the extent to which the moral arc of the universe succeeds in bending toward justice. While deconstruction has perhaps helped to loosen the shackles of ideologies that people across the world have already begun to lose faith in, it has created new postmodern shackles all its own which themselves must be transcended if our social-spiritual truth is to become visible to us as the social movements of today seek to come to know themselves and their aspirations, to know these aspirations as manifesting a universal human truth of our common humanity rather than merely a political preference, one of a multiplicity of interpretations.

Assertion and Appeal

And yet we must now ask ourselves whether the claims that I have made throughout this book that we are interhuman beings in a psychospiritual social field, and that we are spiritual presences longing to complete ourselves, to realize our social being, through authentic mutual recognition–whether these claims are not just like the claims made by those I have just criticized, abstractions that I have imposed upon the world. And while as mere concepts, these ideas can legitimately be so criticized by deconstruction as being indeterminate in their concrete meaning (spirituality, love, and interhuman connection can mean anything as mere concepts, including their opposites), as I have used these terms these words are not intended as concepts imposing names on a world "out there" but rather descriptive evocations of my experience and your experience–of our common experience–which I do not impose on you or the world and in response to which you must be free to say "that doesn't feel right," "that doesn't really evoke the way I experience things." Because I am saying that human and interhuman truth is accessible only through illumination of our lived mutuality of presence, I have tried to write with enough style that you can "hear" me and feel my presence; I have tried to use examples drawn from our shared world that we may have experienced/sensed/felt in the same way; and I have tried to appeal to you by evocation rather than convince you through concepts and argument. Thus the knowledge that I am offering here is no more than an appeal, expressed with confidence that I am in fact evoking our shared experience as linked human presences, to you to recognize the truth of what I'm saying.

This is to say that human knowledge must link the knower to the truth to be known and be characterized by illuminating description resulting from and expressing a throwing-oneself-forward into the world that we, as a real-we, are in together, or better co-constitute together, as intersubjective beings. In this sense the idea of being spiritually present does not correspond to the "metaphysics of presence" that deconstruction criticizes because spiritual presence is not abstract or "meta-physical" but is wholly embedded in a social world that is itself spiritual—radiant, we might say, with its own self-presence. Neither truth nor true knowledge can be imposed on this world from above or from outside, but only *revealed through illumination*, through which the commonality of being that connects us makes itself visible through, but not with—*through, but not with*—language—as our truth revealing itself through our knowing it together. And in this sense the knowledge we seek and express is a vulnerable knowledge as vulnerable as the interhuman truth it is bringing to light, and can never be converted into "belief about the world" from a withdrawn or detached standpoint—in fact, if it is so converted, it becomes in that moment false knowledge even if the exact same "correct" words are used to assert it.

My use of the word "assert" here is important in distinguishing the knowledge revealed by illuminating description from that conveyed by abstract claims "about" the world conceived as a kind of social object outside of us. For assertion as a mode of characterizing directs the reader or listener to witness from a detached di-stance the is-ness of what is asserted about. The reader or listener becomes a passive "knowee" to whom a truth is told as if this truth existed "out there on its own" and is merely represented and "designated" by the authoritative knower, who denies that he or she is there except as a reporter or representor. This way of designating intends by its very assertiveness to suppress the presence of the reader or listener—actually to turn the reader or listener from a co-knower, or to be more evocative, co-illuminant, into a "knowee" cut off from his or her own co-apprehension of the truth to be known. Simultaneously, in assertion, the knower also suppresses his or her own presence by locating the knowledge outside of himself or herself and, through the despiritualization resulting from the erasure of presence, flattening its knowledge into a two-dimensional reification of the represented tableau. No matter how partially or metaphorically accurate the two-dimensional narrative may be—as in the Marxist claim about the class struggle, which really does to some extent characterize social life under material scarcity—the spiritual dimension of the life-world is rendered invisible when the class struggle is asserted as the truth of that life-world. And when through assertion "about" the world the spiritual presence of the asserter and also of the reader/listener are denied and erased, then the interhuman truth of this life-world is concealed and cut off from knowledge.

When, however, offered knowledge emerges through the voice of one already enfolded in the radiant psychospiritual field of real social existence, and when that voice in throwing itself forward into this field of mutuality reaches the reader or listener to whom it is extended as an appeal rather than as a telling or directing, then the conditions are possible for a co-illumination that lights up the world's spiritual distortions and invokes a moral direction that points the way out. When Moses appealed to the Jews to leave Egypt, he was not asserting to them that the Red Sea would open because God said so; rather, he was calling upon their emergent understanding that the dehumanization of slavery was a spiritual distortion that self-evidently marred the interhuman universe and that the life-world's own need to heal itself, brought into consciousness through the upsurge of their own overcoming, ought to make possible the opening of the Red Sea in accordance with G-d's will[5] as a moral direction. And the reason Jews retell the Passover story every year is not to redesignate their outer selves as "Jews," but rather to recover and re-hear the appeal to remember the best communal truth of our embodied heritage to strengthen us to continue to engage in tikkun olam with confidence in the moral direction that the story illuminates.

When knowledge takes the form of the illumination of lived truth emerging from the spiritual presence of us one to the other, we each become co-knowers and co-illuminants because we each are co-living, in mutuality of presence, the truth to which we are together testifying. This social-spiritual knowledge cannot become authoritarian because it is always co-created and its relation to our truth is only established in the moment of mutual recognition of its validity. And since we are each flawed by virtue of our conditioning and by the effects of the residual fear of the other that we are seeking to surpass, our appeals to each other, our efforts at evocation of the truth of the interhuman life-world, must always be open to self-correction. In this sense perhaps a good metaphor for the process of co-creating knowledge of the interhuman is the "call and response" practice of the black church. When the preacher as knower "calls," the listeners may urge him or her on or they may offer their own modifying cry in correction, but they are never being "told"—they are always co-evoking the social-spiritual truth of their shared lived experience and strengthening their own emergence as a spiritual community through the work and joy of their illumination of the life-world out of which they are being born, again.

Thus true human knowledge emerges from the Call that social being makes upon itself to become conscious of the interhuman truth that we are already living, however obscured by the masks of our alienation. And that knowledge "comes to us" through the emergent mutuality of presence inspired by the force of the movement itself, in just the way that the women's movement came to know, in its upsurge of transcendent reciprocity realized in consciousness-raising groups, marches, bra burning, and other ricocheting forms of resistance, the truth of the oppression of women (and men) that had been sealed up in unconsciousness—or more precisely "enshadowed"—prior to the movement's arising.

Yet we must see in this example that although the women's movement, like any movement, has been a particular, historical movement "upward" against the specific historical legacy of the rotating hierarchical patterning of the specifically patriarchal form of our alienation, that historical particularity is actually transcended in the breakthrough of mutual recognition that the movement itself brings into existence. In the *spiritual elevation* that dawns on a group in such a rising moment, the flatness of the world itself lifts, the dense inertia of our prior conditioning actually dissolves, and, in the case of the women's movement for example, women meet in a new higher space that incarnates the universal in the particular—*social being itself makes itself present through womanhood* as a newly empowered, spiritually elevated reciprocity of mutual recognition. And precisely because of its universal Call or "appeal" as I have been here using the term, this emergent spiritual elevation "reaches" across to men as well, who initially resist the challenge to their traditional role-system and the protection against humiliation that its "authority" has provided to them, but gradually, perhaps across generations, feel relieved of the burden to be the boss, to dominate and control meetings and other public spaces, to act out sexual virility, to wage war, and otherwise to keep up the spiritually imprisoning false self of patriarchal identity. In and through this experience of elevating radiance, we women and men experience the truth of our possible future as universal social beings, and also at the same time the truth of the alienated nature of aspects of our prior gendered identities that we are surpassing in an upward or rising clearing of mutuality toward that possible future. As we make that truth known to each other, as we communicate about our common experience through music and laughter, through illuminating discourse and even exclamations like "wow," that truth enters our collective reflection and our collective memory as knowledge of that truth, strengthening our confidence that this shared elevating experience is real and that we together recognize it as true.[6]

This appearance of the truth that the movement makes possible, because it is true, gains the power to ricochet across the social-spiritual field very rapidly and against every resistance, and it decisively alters the social-spiritual field as a whole. Because the social-spiritual truth is true, when it is made manifest through the spiritually elevating force of the movement, it—as I have said quoting King's words—bends the moral arc of the universe toward justice. In this sense, across history, truth as it emerges through upsurges of mutual recognition continually institutes moral gains in the social fabric and exerts moral pressure for all of humanity to take the next *particular* step in relation to its *universal* objective, which King called justice and which we might in the terms of this book call the realization of love itself. To the extent that we are able, in each such moment of elevation and overcoming, to share our knowledge of that truth through the illumination of our surpassing, we secure each moral gain in moral knowledge, and guide ourselves and future generations in how and where to place our feet in taking the next step toward the mountaintop.

The Universal and the Particular

Here we come to a hopeful and important final point. For when we realize that the movement enables us, via its "lifting" at the moment of its rising, to see each other as simply human rather than as man or woman, or black or white, or gay or straight, we realize that the ontological transcends the historical across every so-called identity or institution or structure that marks each historical moment. On the back side of our lived existence is our particular identity, but on the front side of every present moment, we aspire to the mutual recognition of each other in our universality, in our oneness as universal social beings, a recognition that is realized in the upsurge of the social movement. The priority that is customarily given to historical particularity in, for example, Marxism, and also deconstruction and identity politics, results from the fact that these ways of thinking and knowing are despiritualized and therefore attribute a mistaken objectivity to the social world, a world that they posit as "out there" and that they seek to describe at a distance from that "out there." Failing to grasp the world with spiritual presence and to illuminate the world through the relation of the presence of the knower to the radiant presence of the known, these thinkers/knowers tend to see the world as "all back and no front," reproducing through their own despiritualized detachment the fixity or reification of the alienated patternings we are longing to overcome.

But as the rising force of the movement underneath us enables us to dissolve this object-ness of the world back into its truth as an interhuman manifestation of rotating alienation seeking to surpass itself (and also seeking, out of fear, to resist that surpassing), as we through the elevation of social-spiritual insight become able to eliminate all "entity" thinking and see into the "spinning tops" to which we have attributed an undue substantiality as if they were fixed and real things, we can see also that our historical particularities do not limit our opportunities for transcendence. While it is true in the manner of dialectical reason that each step forward in the historical process must synthesize the particularity of our inherited conditioning in a new form, to the extent that these steps surpass the alienation embedded in that conditioning, they are sudden, ricocheting, incarnations of our transcendent universality manifesting the realization of our longing for mutual recognition. That means that while the rotating patternings of alienation are constraining to the point of near-objectivity, these patternings are always vulnerable in their being to dissolution by the upsurge of the movement toward mutual recognition, everywhere, all the time. Thus what we call "the 60s" was an outbreak of radiant mutuality that, in gaining the traction to ricochet, gave rise more or less all at once to the women's movement, the gay liberation movement, the environmental movement, the student movement—a *universal* movement of social being that was incarnated in each particular but that surpassed all of them as the true radiant energy of the transcendence. By respiritualizing our knowledge of the historical process, we need no longer confront either the social structure or institutions or our identities as heavy and impenetrable "things" to be somehow "changed," but rather porous, living, ephemeral manifestations of social being capable of dissolution. It is of course true that our social existence as we reproduce it in each moment is weighted down with our conditioned fear of the other that becomes coercive the more that we are encircled by the insistence that being alienated is the price of social membership. But we are always capable in our being of a mutual spiritual elevation, a spiritual movement toward one another, that permits us to meet "above" that conditioning and suddenly occupy a new universal ground of being that partly overcomes that fear and, slightly but absolutely, bends the social universe, against its own resistance, toward its moral redemption.

Notes

1 Of course, alienated flows produce real effects, and I am certainly not denying that class oppression is such a real effect. Rather, I am saying the alienated flow itself is not a thing or entity but an interhuman, enacted, incarnation of social alienation which must be healed and overcome by a social-spiritual politics.

2 Here again while the hierarchy is "imaginary' in the sense that no one is actually "above" another, the imaginary has real effects: domination and control of some by others.

3 And here again, liberal ideology does have the effect of "serving the (material) interests of the ruling class" but this fact must not be confused with the alienated, or alienation-serving, collective intention that creates this effect.

4 None of this is to deny that the conflict between owning and non-owning groups over material inequality is a real effect of the social alienation that produces it; nor is it to deny that a Marxist economic analysis of social processes can produce partially accurate descriptions of the behavior of alienated patternings reproducing their own alienation through struggle that is in part over material resources in a global context.

5 I use the word "God" when referring to the conventional notion of God as an entity or supernatural being. I use "G-d" when aspiring to sacred evocation of that mystical force in the universe that transcends all materiality, guides the evolutionary development of all Being, and, in the words of Rabbi Michael Lerner, makes possible the transformation from that which is to that which ought to be.

6 I believe this process of spiritual elevation is what George Katsiaficas was trying to capture in his concept of the "eros effect" that he perceived in the social movements of the 1960s, a process that he described as "a spontaneous cathexis between human beings at fundamental levels of social solidarity . . . which emanates from and reaches into the deepest dimensions of the souls of human beings." See his "Paper prepared for presentation at the 1989 American Sociological Association National Meetings in San Francisco," p. 8 (1987). And more:

> In this situation, an intuitive process of identification occurred in which individual and group self-interest were transcended as the universalized interest of the species emerged. It was not only the case that a new norm was created: Within a matter of 9 days, the entire value system and the institutions of France were transformed in the everyday lives of millions of people. Patriotic nationalism was swept aside by internationalism, and as self-managed factories, universities, and cities suddenly appeared, France was suddenly on the brink of revolution. How do we explain this sudden transformation of the whole society?
>
> (Ibid, pp. 8–9)

Here I am trying to explain the eros effect as a collective emergence of the universal spirit, on a new and higher ground, through the ricochet of mutual recognition.

Works Cited

Buber, Martin. *I and Thou.* Touchstone, New York, NY, 1971.

Derrida, Jacques. *Spectres of Marx: The State of the Debt, the Work of Mourning, and the New International.* Translated by Peggy Kamuf, Routledge, New York, NY, 1994.

Goldman, Emma. *Living My Life.* Alfred A. Knopf, New York, NY, 1931.

Katsiaficas, George. "The Eros Effect." *1989 American Sociological Association National Meetings in San Francisco.* 1989.

King, Martin Luther, Jr. Wesleyan University Commencement, quoting Theodore Parker, 8 June 1964, Hartford, CT, Wesleyan Baccalaureate.

Sartre, Jean-Paul. "Replies to Structuralism." *Telos*, Candor, NY, Fall 1971, pp. 110–114.

Chapter 9

The Movement's Lack of Confidence in Itself

On the Necessity of Spiritualizing Social Activism

If as I have been claiming the rising moment of the movement enables us to emerge from our experience of reciprocal isolation and to more fully recognize each other as *here* and as universal beings, as "one another," why then have such movements failed to bring into being a world that can sustain this redemptive mutuality? It should first be said that these movements when they arise do produce immense change—they do fundamentally alter the social landscape because, as I emphasized in the last chapter, these risings do introduce the truth of our universal longing into the manifestation of our social being. Thus, again as I have said, the upsurge of social being that was the 60s produced (or greatly advanced) more or less all at once the civil rights movement, the gay and lesbian movement, the anti-war movement, the women's movement, the environmental movement, the student movement, and the counterculture. Between, say, 1955 and 1975, the entire face of the culture was transformed by a singular alteration of the psychospiritual field itself, inflecting each particular movement into existence as an expression of the universality of mutual recognition that unified them as manifestations of a common rising of being itself. Seen in their most hopeful light, social movements are the vehicle of our evolution, with each new upward spiral of mutuality of presence providing the ground for greater and greater awareness of our moral direction in the long struggle against fear of the other, against fear itself. This was the basis of Martin Luther King Jr.'s conviction that it is "unarmed truth and unconditional love that will have the final word in reality": In this evocation of our common destiny, he was linking truth and love and projecting their co-realization forward in time as the realization of our universal humanity that will occur through the repeated overcomings, through these upward spirals, of the layers of alienation that separate us. "That is why right temporarily defeated," as King said in the next sentence, "is more powerful than evil triumphant" (Nobel Peace Prize Acceptance Speech, 1964).

And yet all of our prior movements thus far have been unable to sustain their redemptive mutuality of presence and have fallen back before the fear of the other that has, so to speak, waged war against them. It is a sign of the limitations of our current knowledge of what these movements actually *were* as miraculous risings that we have thus far produced no convincing explanation for why the movements have failed, or subsided, or better since they also have succeeded, why they have not sustained themselves as upward openings-up of the heart. Often the defeat of these movements is explained by the power of the opposition, as if the forces of reaction simply overpowered the attempts at fundamental social change–the new Soviet Union was attacked by multiple capitalist armies, the labor movement of the 1930s was under constant physical and legal attack by the bosses, Ronald Reagan harnessed the power of the silent majority to defeat the liberalizing opening of the 60s. Or explanations are offered that suggest a failure of reason on the part of the left, as in the idea that a rising movement did not have a plan that would work to create a new society. But if we talk about the millions of people touched by and changed by the rising social movements of the last 200 years, did we all abandon our glimpse of who we actually long to become because others sought to physically and ideologically oppose us?

The problem with blaming the forces of reaction for defeating our utopian impulses is that this way of picturing the conflict generated by the rising movement once again pictures the culture as a kind of entity perceived by an observer from the outside, as if one phalanx of individuals seeking change comes up against a resisting army of those opposing it, like an external image of Marx's conception of class struggle. But in reality, the "struggle" inspired by the upward movement of mutual recognition is internal to social consciousness as a whole–it takes place within what I have been calling the "rotation" of recognition that constitutes public space as a collective lived experience. The movement arises as an upsurge of authentic mutual recognition not "against" a wall of social alienation, but within a fear-saturated rotating patterning of a regenerating mutual distance, of "aversive presence." This is what we mean when we say a movement "arises"—the movement "moves" as and only as an upsurge of enlivening social-spiritual presence within the "fallenness" of the rotating mutual evasion that has cast us into reciprocal withdrawnness shielded off by a gossamer false self. When Heidegger refers to this collective state as "the they" and links inauthenticity with falling into "the they" (*Being and Time*, pp. 164–166), he is actually describing the mutual and rotating deferral of presence through which we seek to make ourselves "no one" so as not to become vulnerable to the threat of humiliation posed by the other's sight. The upsurge of mutual recognition that moves the movement "moves" into this vacuum-space of reciprocating fear, as an engagement and a challenge taking place within a collective consciousness as a living environment. While physical force is almost always one feature of the conflict that movements inevitably engender, that use of force is an externalization of an ontological and moral struggle taking place within collective consciousness itself, as the desiring breakthrough of mutuality released by the movement encounters the fearful resistance of the militant rotating withdrawnness that has been policing itself, as a kind of cultural superego, to prevent such an uprise within itself from occurring.

Thus the defeat of the movement, when it occurs, is a subduing of an outbreak of desire and longing and mutual vulnerability that causes us to withdraw back into our shells. Our own fear of the other, fear of each other, that is circulating within and co-constituting the culture as a whole employs physical force (the protesters are beaten and arrested), co-optation ("Light My Fire" becomes a Buick commercial), the granting of legal rights (the labor movement wins the right to organize unions but only to bargain over wages and working conditions; gays and lesbians win the right to marry if they will tame their rebellious sexuality and become normal role-abiding couples), and idealization of the false community (Ronald Reagan promises a return to "Morning in America") as a way of drawing off the vital energy released by the outbreak of mutual recognition animating the movement and channeling it back into the safety of our separation.

In the case of the 60s, I lived through both the radiant joy of the rising of the movement within the social fabric, and, very gradually, the long, drawn-out pain of the loss of the movement as the negative genius of rotating fear-consciousness succeeded in leading us to ebb away from each other. As the movement "rose," we as a new "we" came to constitute a parallel universe of mutual presence and liveliness co-existing with and within the dominant culture of fear-saturated separation (recall please the Vietnam War and also the legacy of lynching, burning of witches, castration of gays, the genocide of the holocaust, and the extermination of native peoples). But in spite of the fullness of mutual discovery permitted by the release of the movement-force within us, we were gradually persuaded to leave each other "out there," and cast each other once again into aloneness, onto poignant fall-back plateaus with friends and family leading lives of longing and pathos (and of course beauty also, because we do remain alive, always longing, always hoping, in every interaction). As a Haitian, New York cabdriver, perceiving that I was a likely denizen of the 60s, said to me one day in his cab in the early 80s: "How could you have let it fall?" In the phrase "let it fall" he captured precisely what did take place, what I mean by an "ebbing away" from each other that returned us, to a significant degree, to the mutually deferred, aversive presence of being "no one," false selves, the they.

And yet the above account of the way that fear of the other opposes the desire for mutual recognition leaves out the single most important element of the way this fear manifests itself—as an internal lack of confidence within the movement itself. For insofar as the subduing of the movement involves a persuasion to ebb away from each other and return to the safety of the alienated status quo, the fear of the other that conducts this rotation-of-subduing actually depends upon the residual doubt residing within the heart of the movement itself. And how could it be otherwise? As we rise with the movement that we ourselves are co-creating, we are running out from behind shells—or to retain the metaphor I used earlier in the book, we are leaping over the invisible moat that divides us—without yet having the certainty that the other will remain with us out there in our connection. The movement is rising with the desire for mutual recognition that we are urging into being, and through its erotic power, it is beginning to ricochet across social space with relief and radiant joy; but how could that very process occur without heightening our anxiety that the fear of the other that we have been conditioned to accept as "real," through the conditioned false "reality" of the identified-with outer or false self, will seize upon our revealed vulnerability to the other that the movement has made possible, and subject us to the very humiliation we have been for so long guarding ourselves against? Or as Rabbi Michael Lerner puts it in his book *Spirit Matters*, how could we expect our most powerful spiritual longings to be suddenly fully reciprocated when these longings have been denied and even ridiculed throughout the process by which we have been conditioned to form our normal selves?

To assist you in actually feeling the vulnerability that I am describing here, let me recall again the experience of Barack Obama's election in 2008, the election in which "Hope" and "Yes We Can" were Obama's main evocative words as he successfully sought to raise himself into the position to become the first African-American president. While the election of Obama was not itself a widespread social movement because it depended almost entirely on the erotic power of watching Obama speak and otherwise manifest his presence and our hope on television, the process by which he sought and then won election had true elements of a movement because he was able, for personal and symbolic reasons, to evoke a future communal possibility, the possibility of the rising of a true "we," that led millions of people to partially overcome the fear that otherwise would have sealed them, during a political campaign of this kind, in cynicism and resignation to normal artificiality, to electoral politics as watching role-performances of the political class. That is why when Obama won on election night, many of us burst into tears as it was announced on CNN that "Barack Obama is the 44th President of the United States"—his election meant that enough of us declared for hope to become a "we" symbolized by the vote total, and in that "we-ness" we all at once experienced the joy and relief of suddenly being together. We poured out into the streets, people honked their horns on street corners, and in the ricochet released by this collective emergence, across the world there was an outpouring of erotic, binding oneness and hereness (recall that Kenya immediately declared a national holiday). To use Joseph Heller's brilliant phrase to describe "hereness" suddenly emulsifying mutual distance/reciprocal deferral of presence/collective absence: "Something Happened."

And yet this moment of collective transcendence turned out to be not stillborn, but doomed for lack of a spiritual strategy to sustain it. The declaration of mutual recognition incarnated in the vote was made possible only by a vast dispersed collective "watching" on television of one man with evocative qualities under special conditions (especially his race, in the context of other factors like 9/11, the war in Iraq, and the Bush presidency) that made his authenticity, or better, his "pull," "come through" with compelling power. And because neither Obama nor we ourselves had any notion of how our confidence in our mutual co-presence could be sustained going forward in time, "we" almost immediately began feeling the distance reopening between us, and then among us. The joyous bond between me and, say, my neighbors in my building had no basis, no embodied or even discursive history, besides having together watched Obama. And so as Obama began to slip away into his role as "president," we inevitably began to slip away from each other also. Thus the internal bond of mutual recognition that had united me with my neighbors became a mere external "happiness" that Obama had won, a looking together at the inauguration, at the "first couple" dancing, at the increasingly vacant or role-bound inauguration speech three months after the moment of the election. Lacking a spiritual strategy to sustain the opportunity, the opening up of the heart, that Obama's election created, and only thinly bound together in the first place by the shallowness of the conditions that had created that bonding, we began to rapidly ebb away from each other. My neighbors began once again to pass me in the halls (and no doubt I, them) with an evasion of glance, each of us ebbing away as the other receded.

Thus Obama's election at once created an explosion of mutuality and truth releasing real energy into a previously dead or "fallen" public space, and an unsafe vulnerability to the other, to hope itself, that was the result of having dared to declare ourselves in a way that had made the explosion possible. And because Obama and we could not figure out how to sustain what we had created, we gradually suffered the humiliation of non-reciprocation: After opening up to each other, we were unable to be there for each other. Over the next two years, this vacuum of mutuality was the actual ontological reason for the rise of the Tea Party, as rage against the vulnerability to humiliation engendered by unrequited hope washed across social space. Yes there was already a small minority of angry people, including some "racists," waiting in the wings and ready to pounce on such a moment of vindication of their anger should it emerge, but the true cause of its emergence was the conversion of eros to Thanatos, or loving desire and longing to pain and rage, that flooded the intersubjective psychospiritual field. Or to be more precise, this pain and the rage that collectively expressed it was able to occupy the void-space left by the reciprocal withdrawal of us as wounded hopers, as a "we" that felt we had been "tricked" into rushing out from behind our well-defended conditioned selves, and in a kind of traumatic shock, sought to withdraw back into ourselves, creating a vacuum of presence into which those inveterately bitter, committed non-hopers on the right, waiting to react against the opening, could run. What followed was the dismal failure of the forces of hope in the 2010 mid-term elections, and the general conversion of the meaning of the Obama presidency from that of a rising incarnation of mutuality to a rearguard action hanging on to the residue of that rising moment while "relapsing" into the more conventional politics of role-performances and deference to hierarchy by us as outer selves, as "citizens" watching "the first African-American president" (and silently longing for the re-emergence of the "we" that we briefly were).

Now what I am asking you to recall, if you can, is the pain itself of that unrequited hope, and its humiliating nature. For that distinctive, corroding, even sickening pain is felt as the silent "other side" of what we become vulnerable to when a social movement breaks through the everyday constraints that normally protect us. For this breakthrough not only elicits a new vulnerability to the other in the present, it also evokes the unconscious memory of its original occurrence during the original formation of the "shield" of the false or outer self in early childhood. What Christianity calls "original sin" corresponds to an original loss that each of us suffers as we surrender to our alienated conditioning that is the condition of our social membership, of our social existence itself as recognized beings. And the threat of re-experiencing that original loss is the source of the quite extreme pain and flight into reciprocal withdrawal that the movement itself, the "rising" toward each other, seems to make us vulnerable to. As I have indicated earlier, those of us who lived through the San Francisco earthquake in 1989 experienced that pain when the explosion of mutuality generated by that natural disaster gave way after two weeks or so to the "return to normal" that was heralded by the then mayor from within his own normalizing role. And in 2001, the entire community of the nation experienced something of this pain of loss, with echoes of early childhood loss, that occurred following the emergence of authentic community after the 9/11 World Trade Center bombing. Then, to perhaps further your own recollection, the fellow-feeling of the John Lennon-inspired telethon concert watched by tens of millions of us, painfully gave way after a few weeks to the us-against-them war in Afghanistan and then eventually to the war in Iraq.

Thus the excitement and radiant joy that accompanies the rushing ricochet of mutual recognition that characterizes the rise of the movement is of necessity haunted by a felt risk of present loss of the other undergirded by the echo of our original loss, and this vulnerability is the source of the movement's tendency toward overstatement of itself, as if we could reverse in a single instant of "revolution" centuries of alienation passed on to each of us as the density of our own conditioning repeatedly reinforced over our lifetimes. And alongside the beauty and mutual discovery awakened by the movement (a mutual discovery that actually *is* the movement's internal motion), we see manifestations of this doubt about itself in a tendency toward the grandiosity of one form or another of political correctness and the tendency toward the demonization of those outside the movement who are not "with us" (and those inside the movement who show any sign of veering from the correct line). To the extent that the movement has rendered us suddenly "unguarded" in the presence of the other, to that extent our fear of re-humiliation is inevitably awakened also and is revealed in the distortions that manifest that fear while attempting to deny it.

It is this insight that can give us the key to why so many of our groups and organizations born out of the movement have tended to collapse upon themselves. For as these groups first form as joyful and hopeful gatherings, each dedicated to its own distinct socially transformative purpose, each composed of different people numbering in the tens or hundreds of thousands or even millions when the breadth of something like "the 60s" is recalled as the worldwide phenomenon that it was, each group is uncertain how to sustain its newfound sense of community, and each actually senses its internal doubt about whether and how this will be possible. If we hold in mind the pain and sense of humiliation accompanying the Obama dissolution, we can grasp how within these groups the joy of new community is fraught with a felt risk of danger, a risk that is accompanied by a gravitational pull within the group's unconscious to fall back into the accustomed state of the collective false self—the rotating patterning that we are all familiar with in which our collective life consists of "watching" the group from within one's withdrawn detachment while the group becomes a kind of object that "the others" are creating. Thus within each group there is a doubling: a vital force pulling us toward each other and toward true mutuality manifested first in the movement itself and then incarnated with particularity within each group, and a fearful, conditioned counter-pull tinged with the memory of pain and loss that so to speak "tempts" the authentic group to abandon itself and flee back to safety. This is the "material" out of which each group is created, and this material forms the conflicted psychospiritual field of the group as an emerging milieu.

In the absence of a spiritual dimension to the group's "activism" that would attend precisely to this internal doubt and to the conditioned legacy of fear of the other that of course haunts the group's heightened vulnerability, each group becomes vulnerable to the following dissolutive tendency: Initially, the group hurls itself toward its external task (e.g. stopping the war, ending apartheid, getting more rights for women) while the group's members also hang out together, fall in love, become inspired to change their lives in a moral and socially transformative direction. Then the underlying free-floating anxiety about the group's capacity to sustain itself on its new ontological ground starts to emerge in public space as the group's leader or leaders begin to exhibit flaws resulting from their conditioning and their own imperfection. Simultaneously, dissidents emerge within the group who are themselves fearful about the group's sense of communion being a "trick," and they attack the leader(s) or some "other" or "others" within the group who are deemed the cause of the group's risk of failure. Segments of the group begin to flock to private sub-spaces where they gossip about "the other side" or both sides, further undermining the group's confidence in its ontological integrity and solidness and its transformative capability. Instead of openhearted affirmation of one another as the dominant expressive and emotional quality of group life, the group begins to devolve toward a congealing around *interlocking points of opposition* which are actually public enactments of fear of the other by the resurgent "outer self." The content of these interlocking points of opposition is actually arbitrary because the conflict to be posited and enacted is not actually about its manifest content, but rather the latent "wish" of the group's latent fear of the other to be heard and acted out. Yes there is some historical specificity to the conflict's manifest content—in communist groups of the 1930s, the Trotskyists opposed the Stalinists; in the 60s the conflicts focused on gender and race, or on leaders vs. no leaders—but the latent intention behind the conflict is to seize upon partially-true perceptions of imperfection and use them to enact the latent paranoid fear within the group of humiliation, of domination of the vulnerable self by an abandoning other. Fear of the other leads to the increasing invocation of two "sides" within the group which emerge, slide, and turn like two sides of a Rubik's cube until the group's public dynamic can interlock on a point of conflict within which the latent fear of the other can play itself out.

In this developing milieu, within each person within the group's rotation there occurs a gradual but steady and accelerating *slippage* away from the experience of communion out-there-with-the-group and toward returning to withdrawn observation of "the group" increasingly conceived as an object with an externalized task and riven by "watched" mutually interlocking conflict in its public manifestation. Those performing the conflict enact their protest against their own and the group's own heightened vulnerability to humiliation by re-identifying with their self-protective false selves and insisting on the threat posed by the leader(s) or "the others" in the group to the group's supposed true purpose and constitution; everyone else—normally the large majority of the group's members—rotate inexorably toward reciprocal withdrawal without the ability to regain their footing within the group's dissolving communion. And this dynamic leads each person to privately think, in a rotating, mutually reinforcing fashion, that perhaps the experience of true mutual recognition, in spite of its own self-certainty of its own validity in the plenitude of its original experience and intimation that another world was and is possible, was not sustainable—that indeed, the "real" world was the world of each person's prior conditioning, with its inherited and previously recognized roles and performances. And accelerating the pull back toward the reestablishment of the false self's hegemony, within each person, is the appeal of the safety it offers. Although the cost is high as each person suffers again the trauma of loss of the real other that the movement had awakened into existence, a trauma that is accentuated by the perception that this same "ebbing away" is occurring in the other groups around him or her, the recompense is the quelling of vulnerability and the security of the return to the private space of withdrawn observation enclosed within the "substitute" recognition provided by the roles of the outer self.

Thus we see in this description of what actually occurred in so many groups during the ebbing away of the 60s the conversion of the group as a plenitude of erotic mutuality, of the binding-together of mutual recognition, into the group as a kind of outer manifestation of itself that has lost its transformative spiritual core. And once this conversion happens, the group has only one of two pathways: It can either disband and dissolve altogether, which many do and did, or it can continue and gradually convert itself into what we call a bureaucratic organization. The path of dissolution takes place by the rotating failure of the tentative, longing, but residually fearful majority to return to the group's public gatherings and activities where the group is actually constituted as a collective reality. One by one, and then ten by ten, people stop coming to meetings and return to the withdrawn space of private life—to watching television, smoking dope, and at the same time trying to reassume the conditioned roles within the false self's frame of reference that had been temporarily abandoned. In the case of the 60s, for example, the critical moment was Ronald Reagan's second election in 1984, which was the moment of closure for the gradual dissolutive process that I have been describing: At that moment, after years of gradual ebbing, vast numbers of the entire 60s generation took flight from their hopes, partially buried their unconscious pain as best they could, and applied to business school or law school or grabbed onto whatever slot they could within the existing rotating order (my own alternative 60s-inspired college, New College of California, lost over a million dollars in one year as students fled to more traditional institutions).

Greatly accelerating this collective flight was the rising New Right which both gave birth to Reagan and constituted his negative force field in the wider culture. Led by authoritarian politicians like Ed Meese and Caspar Weinberger, intellectuals like Milton Friedman, Alan Bloom, Robert Nozick, and William Buckley, and journalists like George Will and Pat Buchanan, as well as multiplying "return-to-the-ideal-past" organizations like the Family Values Coalition, the New Right was *primarily* devoted to bombarding the longing for a new world released by the movements of the 60s with the message that the 60s was a fraud and was harmful to the good world, actually the "perfect" world of the false-self matrix whose perfection served to deny the possible appeal of the power of the movement to those vulnerable to temptation. The decent, caring, longing, desiring person drawn to the movement's groups in the 60s—and here we are talking about not just someone reaching adulthood in a single decade, but a responder to the movement from the next or the prior generations—was not so much personally affected by the negative messaging of the New Right as by his or her perception that "the others," "the they" in its new incarnation, had closed the door on any access to transcendent possibility. Even being a liberal was demonized by Ronald Reagan himself as being touched or afflicted by "the L word," a demonization of the other that was intended, unconsciously, to establish both the reification and the idealization of the perfect outer/false self of the conservative role-matrix that was vulnerable to exposure. In the face of this saturation of the public sphere in the realm of words and images, that vulnerable young man or woman already rendered increasingly skeptical through his or her own participation in one or more of the movement's groups, was really prodded into full-scale retreat by such a profound delegitimation of his or her hope in the visible public sphere, and by the vote total of 1984's landslide general election of Reagan.

Thus many retreated to private life, never to completely forget the momentary realization of their desire for authentic community, but never to fully recover from the exposure to re-humiliation and the actual loss of the other that the movement experience, including their participation in one or more specific groups, engendered within them. But others, a smaller number but still many, many people, took the path of remaining within their groups but participated in the conversion of their group into what I am calling a bureaucratic organization. In the bureaucratic organization, the group gradually turns itself into a kind of machine assembled to carry out its external task. At first, as I have said, the group incarnates the spirit of transcendent community in pursuit of its universal, transformative objective—say ending the Vietnam War in order to bring peace and love into the world, dissolve "enemies," and fully recognize the other, each and every other across the planet. But as the group begins to dissolve internally through the rotation of doubt about the continuing confirming presence of the real other and to experience the "free-floating" anxiety that humiliation of the real self may occur, the group's members struggle to stabilize the process of dissolution by actually cooling out their transcendent aspirations, their aspirations to a loving new world confident in itself that would alter the whole of social space. To rescue itself from its own dissolution signaled by the slippage away from each other that follows the circulating tendency to withdraw from the group's community in the face of the often violent enactment of what I called the interlocking poles of opposition that more and more displaces the initial confirming energy in the group's psychospiritual field, the group's leadership unconsciously colludes with the group membership to gradually replace the group as a living and vibrant community of fellow-feeling with "the group" as a functioning organization, with each person having a role and function that can be represented in a two-dimensional flowchart and aiming primarily at the realization of the group's external goal. Within each person, this conversion process is lived out as a kind of slippage from being one manifestation of the unity of "us," to becoming once again split into an inner observer of the group "out there" and a performer of a role and function within the increasingly externalized group-entity. Just as the group gradually becomes outside-of-itself-toward-its-task, so also each member of the group contributes to this collective externalization by metastasizing into an outer performer carrying out a part of the group task and a withdrawn observer at a distance from the group's enacted collective activity (including his or her own activity). He or she may feel "I'm doing a good job" and may aspire to be praised, as an outer self, for his or her own performance in what has become "the organization" (to rise up the imaginary ladder), but internally he or she is once again a divided self, an actor behind the moat.

What we call the non-profit sector is largely comprised of organizations of this type, which work on highly specific, often policy-oriented, socially progressive issues, and whose members are often highly idealistic, but which are outside-of-themselves toward their task rather than manifesting an interior, transcendent unity in the realization of their common meaning and project. And without that interiority characterized precisely by a rotating mutuality of recognition and presence, each of these organizations falls into a kind of pocket or fissure of its own—the creators of each pocket do not experience themselves as transcendently connected to each other and do not experience their group as linked from within to other groups. We could say that the non-profit sector thus described is like the opposing mirror-image of what takes place in the rising phase of the movement, when the upsurge of civil-rights activism, women's emergence, environmentalism, LGBTQ mobilization, and student and anti-war protest are all born out of the same transcendent meaning and each fosters the other's co-creation. Once the groups produced originally by these very expressions of the movement devolve into bureaucratic organizations, they of necessity fall into separation. To be sure they can be listed together as advocates of discrete elements of a progressive platform, but their external correspondence as advocates of what have become externalized tasks cannot produce an internal, co-creative, mutually reinforcing unity and so they cannot co-generate forward-moving energy in the now passivized psychospiritual field. The organizations remain worthy and mentally identified with socially progressive goals, but they have to some extent lost touch with the common soul of which they were once a common expression.

When the movement and the groups born out of the movement devolve in these various ways toward dissolution or bureaucratization, the pain of humiliation associated with the loss of the real other, of the persons next to me who had been *here* and are now *over there*, leads each participant to repress the memory of the fullness of human connection during the movement's rising period and to actually forget the feeling of fullness itself. This forgetting is not total because the realization of human connection that was the movement—that was what moved—is truly unforgettable: As a realization, however brief, of each person's deepest social longing, and as a glimpse of what it would be like to fully complete oneself as a social being, the movement experience enters our collective soul in the same way that the manifestation of social truth permanently alters the psychospiritual field of "society" itself and moves forward social progress. But in just the way that the conditioning that produces the false self necessarily, to be successful, must transmit to us that the false self is "real," is who we actually are, so also the closing-up of the movement's opening requires for its efficacy that we forget in our consciousness the memory of that opening and the fullness of the mutuality of presence that the opening engendered. In other words, the opening actually cannot close so long as it is remembered as a felt memory of realized desire, and the resumption of the rotation of normal alienation cannot take place unless it experiences itself as immune to the desiring impulse that seeks to emulsify it. The "fall" is therefore accompanied by a forgetting of where we have fallen from, as well as a dissociation from the pain of humiliation that the movement, in its falling, required us to re-experience . . . and yet just as necessarily we do retain that memory as an "echo" that haunts us as a kind of pathos in our normal lives and that can help inspire us and future generations encountering us to try to break on through again.

As a visual example that may help to capture—in a before-and-after sense—the process of falling and forgetting that I have just described, one need only contrast photos taken during the movement's rising period with photos taken after the fall. In photos of groups large and small taken from within the eros effect of rising mutuality, we can often perceive with an intake of breath the joyful radiance expressed through a group's "manifestation"—a relaxation of the bodies, easy smiles, and a sense of unitary community largely free of presentation of any individual or collective "outer selves" being puffed up for the picture. In later, post-movement photos, it's hard not to see the re-separation of the persons in the image: What had been the organic creation of a small group expressive of the rising has become a "staff photo" in which roles appeared to be inhabited in a way that pools up the available energy in each person's stiff self-presentation. And parallels to this transfiguration in photographs can be found in many other artifacts—for example, the warmth of offices or other gathering-places giving way to professionalized architecture and modes of interior design that "hold up" the outside of the structures to "look" inflated with authority, emptied of erotic and welcoming presence. Certainly the graduations at my own workplace, the 60s-inspired New College of California, went through a similar transformation of manifestation of collective being: During the movement's rising period, students threw off their graduation robes in favor of flowing gowns and sometimes bare feet, but by Reagan's second election, they had returned to hotels and other status-signaling locations and had redonned the graduation robes to signal the external importance of what was being bestowed on their "outside." The very flight toward the outer identification with what "the others"—here the reviving "they" or rotation of deferred presence—increasingly appear to value requires the suppression of the memory of the earlier experience of communion, and also relieves each person, in the course of their historical falling, of the memory of the pain of and humiliation at the loss of the real other.

How then can we counter the tendency toward dissolution that plays upon the group's internal lack of confidence that appears phenomenologically as a rotating lack of confidence in the desire of the other, as a rotating doubt that this person next to me will continue to remember and have confidence in the authentic mutual recognition that the movement made possible? It would seem self-evident that the only way to counter residual doubt is through intentional collective practices that build our confidence in each other and, so to speak, put a floor under that confidence so that it can withstand the anxiety in everyone following from generations of fear of the other that preceded our lifetimes and were carried over into our own conditioning. Such social-spiritual practices would have as their aim re-creating, regularly, the experience of openhearted affection among all human beings participating in them, and at the same time aim toward elevating the consciousness of all participants so as to bring us all back in touch with our highest vision of the world that we are seeking to bring into being. On the positive side, such a practice would seek to intentionally keep open the space of mutuality of presence to which the movement has broken through by constructing a collective experiential "brace" that gives our co-presence a chance to breathe and get to know itself. On the negative side, such a practice would seek to quiet the fear of humiliation that otherwise exerts a gravitational pull on us all to run back into our false-self fortress and pull up the drawbridge. Can you imagine it, dear reader, can you see how indispensable such a thing is and how powerful it could be in sustaining our newfound sense that we are indeed here together, as impossible as it has been to sustain that sense thus far in our lives?

Furthermore, at a practical level such a social-spiritual practice, if successful, would address one of the most puzzling dilemmas that has beset all of us who have participated in social change movements—the capacity of an often small minority of people in a group to mobilize the group's internal fear so as to overcome the openheartedness and hopefulness of the majority, of most of us. For although we all risk the anxiety of humiliation by opening up to each other in transformative moments, it is most often the most unconsciously anxious and most unconsciously, determinedly self-protective who initiate the process of devolution by attacking the leaders and the legitimacy of the group's own constitution, and by trying, unconsciously, to slide the group toward the interlocking poles of opposition that gradually shift the group away from itself.

Spiritual Stitching

A social-spiritual practice of the kind I envision will have the intended effect of stitching together this majority, gradually and intentionally increasing the density of its occupation of the group's social space and at the same time, in direct proportion to this growing confidence among the many, shrinking the existential space available for fear to overwhelm that space. As we saw in the case of the Tea Party's response to Obama, and as really millions of us witnessed with confusion in the groups thrown up by the 60s opening, the fearful emerge and expand their reach in the void-space left by desire in flight from itself, and so the practice of spiritual "stitching" is important to minimize the tendency toward collective flight and, so to speak, leave the space filled with the presence of mutual recognition that the movement has made possible. With social space filled in this way, the most fearful will gradually heal themselves through the buoyancy created by the now visible majority which is also visible to itself, or retreat back to the pocket of collective fearfulness from which they emerged. Stitching through social-spiritual practice thus prevents the slippage toward dissolution, but it also prevents the descent into bureaucracy, into the group becoming a kind of mechanical object outside-of-itself that is solely oriented toward achieving an external goal (that is, a goal divorced from its own spiritual meaning). Since the group actually converts to bureaucracy through a process of mutual, rotating withdrawal and concomitant externalization and despiritualization of the group's own project, it is only restorative social-spiritual experience that can allow the rotating mutuality of the group, the mutuality that *is* the group, to remain in touch with itself, and to remember itself. In the face of the learned anxiety that pulls me away from you, I must remember, through practicing, that you are still here and that I can indeed still remain out here with you. Or as Roger McGuinn of the Byrds put it in his song "5D":

> Oh, how is it that I could come out to you
> And be still floatin'
> And never hit bottom and keep falling through
> Just relaxed and paying attention?
> All my two-dimensional boundaries were gone
> I had lost to them badly
> I saw that world crumble and thought I was dead
> But I found my senses still working
>
> And as I continued to drop through the hole
> I found all surrounding
> To show me that joy innocently is
> Just be quiet and feel it around you
>
> And I opened my heart to the whole universe
> And I found it was loving
> And I saw the great blunder my teachers had made
> Scientific delirium madness
>
> Oh, I will keep falling as long as I live
> Ah, without ending

And I will remember the place that is now
That has ended before the beginning

Oh, how is it that I could come out to you
And be still floatin'
And never hit bottom and keep falling through
Just relaxed and paying attention?

After so many movements have failed to sustain themselves and disappeared through the hemorrhaging of "ebbing away," and after so many tens of thousands or hundreds of thousands of particular groups have fallen apart through "the left eating the left" or become mere outer versions of themselves through bureaucratization, isn't it clear that we simply must find a way to extend the movement's idealism and plenitude of connection forward in time through intentional practices that accomplish the above goals: practices that stitch together the shaky majority unsure of its own presence and solidity, that enable that majority to overcome its internal lack of confidence so as to close up the space that otherwise will be flooded by fear led by "the crazies" who are the most fearful, that keep alive the spiritual and communal core so as to resist the incipient deadness of routinization of task and function, that reassure all of us that we are really here together, that we will come back to the next meeting, and that we will remain committed to our own collective salvation? Once we grasp the underlying reason for the group's tendency toward dissolution, it seems self-evident that practices that affirm and reaffirm our confidence in each other's desire and presence are essential to the movement's longevity and success, and have been the missing dimension of social activism up to this time, an activism that has focused on anger at an opposition, on class struggle, on contests over power and control, on economic redistribution, expansion of rights, and other externally conceptualized and articulated goals. Of course these goals are very important, but we must find a way to realize them that also realizes the aspiration to community that inspires them.

And there is an additional reason why the creation of such collective practices is essential for sealing in the group's confidence and collective strength—namely, the ability of such visible, public manifestations of our togetherness and reciprocal commitment to each other to enable us to *know in reflection* what we have thus far only grasped pre-reflectively in direct experience. Movements themselves are characterized by risings of mutual recognition that are ineffable in the sense they seem amazing or even miraculous, like a "dawning" that arises out of nowhere, and that also ricochets through invisible space in ways that surpass our everyday sense of cause and effect. The reason for this is that the desire for mutual recognition in *everyone* responds spontaneously to the other's willingness to cross the moat: Some may anxiously shore up their defenses in response to this spontaneous impulse in themselves, as in "I'm not falling for that impulse," and this is why there has been such a protracted culture war over the meaning of the 60s—but many others will also take the leap of faith across the moat and release themselves toward the invitation extended to them, both because of and in spite of the vulnerability that that leap of faith entails. However, so long as the movement remains exclusively in the realm of the spontaneous transfiguration of the invisible, so long as it remains a "dawning" that is suddenly simply "there," it cannot be grasped in reflection and cannot enter into the realm of knowledge. And that is why it has been so hard for past movements to understand why they could not sustain themselves, why it would have been so hard for me to have answered that Haitian cabdriver in the early 80s when he asked me, "How could you have let it fall?"

The creation of intentional, confidence-reinforcing, collective spiritual practices that seek to re-create and name our common experience can overcome this limitation because they allow us to intentionally bring into being experiences of mutuality, of realizing our desire for mutual recognition, that thus far seemed to happen by magic. And by coming to *know* what we are *doing* to secure our reciprocal social *being*, we will gradually gain the strength to withstand the flaws/shortcomings/imperfections that will certainly emerge in every group—those who talk too much, those who talk too little, those who say improper or accidentally offensive things, those who spread potentially painful gossip, and so on ad infinitum. There is no way for such imperfections not to emerge in every group, and if the fear of humiliation heightened by the movement's connecting force is not being properly responded to and "treated" by the group's self-awareness, the group's latent fear will seize upon it as evidence of danger and as cause for dissolution, for everyone running the other way.

But through collective practices whose aim is to sustain and extend the spiritual "dawning" that has given birth to the group, we can call upon our knowledge of the truth of our connection to accept our imperfections and prevent them from becoming a threat to the group's integrity. To the extent that the movement experience of mutuality of presence was and is true, introducing an intentional spiritual dimension into our groups and into our activism can help us also *know* that it was and is true, and thus allow us to cement at the level of collective reflection the otherwise fragile bond that the movement so beautifully and hopefully elicited. Although this knowledge may be conceptualized in words by the group to itself (through leaders or perhaps other processes), the nature of this knowledge is not strictly conceptual and its strength does not come from "rules" about how the group should think of itself and respond to imperfections or conflict. Rather because the knowledge is gained through the embodiment of collective spiritual practice, the knowledge learned is a wisdom-that-we-are-here that instills patience (knowing most others will be patient), that instills confidence (knowing that most others will remain confident), and that instills a sense of common direction (knowing that most others will continue to move forward with the group's psychospiritual and substantive project in spite of constant slips that would otherwise lead toward unraveling and dissolution).

Although as I have said every upsurge of mutual recognition incarnated in transformative social movements, and every attendant injection of truth into the social field that such movements allow, does advance human social consciousness toward its own eventual realization, that evolutionary process will be greatly advanced by the incorporation of knowledge of itself into that upsurge. While the movement's psychospiritual (or ontological) achievements are never wholly erased by their falling, and although these achievements remain, as I have said, as an echo of residual spiritual meaning even after the fall, they will remain in our hearts and minds with more confidence, and they will fall less far, when we find ways to ensure that knowledge of the *spiritual dimension* of these achievements is retained as something we know in our collective awareness and self-consciousness.

To again quote the words of Martin Luther King with which I began the chapter: "I believe that it is unarmed truth and unconditional love that will have the final word in reality; that is why right temporarily defeated is more powerful than evil triumphant." His belief, his conviction, emanated partly from his awareness of the universality of the longings in his own soul. But he had also seen in living actuality the way that each burst of mutuality "upward" does elevate in a kind of spiral social being's consciousness of itself, such that when it falls due to the continuing power of fear of the other, it does not fall all the way to its previous less evolved location. Those of us who lived through the 60s have witnessed this in our lifetime: Virtually every feature of American culture, and increasingly world culture, was to some extent transfigured by the outbreak of mutual recognition that took place, and the subsequent subduing of that movement has not erased that echo in us or the cultural heritage that has followed in the next generations. But imagine how much the evolutionary consciousness of humanity would be advanced, however beset by new problems, if we had found the way to deepen and strengthen our memory through creating a living knowledge of the change that had occurred that we were seeking to sustain, and also a living awareness of what had tended to undermine it that we were seeking to heal?

Works Cited

The Doors. "Light My Fire." *The Doors*. Elektra, Hollywood, CA, 1967.

Heidegger, Martin. *Being and Time*. Translated by John Macquarrie and Edward Robinson, Harper & Row, 7th ed., New York, NY, 1962.

Heller, Joseph. *Something Happened*. Scapegoat Productions, Inc., 1966.

King, Martin Luther, Jr. Acceptance Speech, on the occasion of the award of the Nobel Peace Prize, 10 December 1964, Oslo, Norway.

Lerner, Michael. *Spirit Matters*. Hampton Roads, 2000, Charlottesville, VA.

Chapter 10

Social-Spiritual Activism

Activism that Thaws the False Self and Fosters Mutuality of Presence

To the degree that my descriptions in this book have been accurate thus far, we can see that "social change" is not the reconfiguration of an entity but the redemption of a psychospiritual field alienated from itself. And if we are to transcend our alienation so as to actually "change society," we must heal and repair the life-world that we ourselves are living rather than fix it as if it were something outside of us. This means that social activism must in part be—to make use of an insight from Chapter 9—"a dawning that remembers itself," a transformation and elevation of social space that brings us into authentic contact with each other and makes us present to each other while also enabling us to *know* that this is occurring and gradually become what we are intending. Of course the projects of social activism are always particular and practical—fighting for universal health care, say, or for an egalitarian economy, or for the expansion of LGBTQ rights, or opposing fossil fuels and global warming—but their transformative aspect is in the universal intersubjective meaning to be realized through each particular project. To create a world that realizes our desire for a loving world, each project must be a healing and repairing of our alienation through the realization of each practical end.

We have seen that rising social movements and the upsurge of mutuality of presence that accompanies them—or really that *is* them—want to change everything at once: love each other across our differences, restore reverence for the natural world, release ourselves toward each other and toward the divine in a way that heals the world's suddenly evident insanity. But as we have also seen, the legacy of fear of the other and the residual rotating lack of confidence in the desire of the other gnaws at the movement's integrity and tends to unravel it or to sink it into bureaucracy. And through the hemorrhage of bureaucracy, social change work subtly converts itself into the performing of external tasks. I-and-Thou-and-We slide away from each other into becoming discrete mutually withdrawn actors no longer united to the total transformation of the field with each particular change incarnating a universal transformative meaning. The change subtly shifts its meaning from something lived to the alteration of an external entity, which is actually a mere mental picture of a world "outside of us" emptied of our actual presence.

To sustain the movement's rising mutuality in the face of the legacy of fear that corrodes it, and to sustain the spiritual dimension of each particular project so that its attempted realization carries forward the mutually recognizing or loving meaning of the project, we need to make use of our spiritual knowledge of the "we" that we are trying to sustain. This means starting with ourselves right now where we are, in whatever relationship to hope that we actually have, based on the raw material of our desire for mutual recognition and our relationship to past experiences of mutual confirmation of that desire within ourselves that we can call upon, and engaging in intentional practices that will deepen and strengthen our conviction that we are here with each other and for each other as we take the next steps.

While there is a vast wisdom drawing from religious and non-religious spiritual traditions regarding how to "bind each other together again" (the precise meaning of "religion"), up to this point this wisdom has not been well-integrated into sustaining the mutuality of rising social movements, because social movements have not been well understood precisely as a rising mutuality of presence. In this last chapter, I will specify three "levels" of practice that are important to the sustaining of our bond, of our experience of "we," and that correspond to three "regions" of social existence. We begin with the person—that is you and me as we sit where we are, as vessels bearing the contradiction within us of desire and fear—let us call that the innermost circle; then we move to the surrounding social field and the practice of building a parallel universe capable of confirming and therefore building our confidence in the mutuality of our desire—let us call that the second circle, the terrain of concrete mutuality of presence; and then we move to the evocation of the future to which we aspire, to spiritualizing social policy and other projected incarnations of the world we are trying to bring into being—let us call that the third circle, the evocation of a whole world that gives to all of our efforts a moral direction. Taken together, these circles form something like the context of Being, in the sense that they designate in a general way the whole of our existential social experience as we live it in time, from our presence at the moment, at any moment, as separate beings-in-relation, to our existential or lived social milieu as a confirmatory environment (to the extent that it is confirmatory), and to our projected future as a collective moral project, as our moral direction.

However, it must be emphasized at the outset that these three circles are sketches of regions of Being, rather than arguments for putting into effect particular, conceptualized forms or practices. To say, as I do to begin this chapter, that social change is not the reconfiguration of an entity but rather the redemption of a psychospiritual field alienated from itself means that any articulation of a possible social-spiritual practice must be read as an evocation of a possible thawing and a possible elevation of communal being rather than as a recommendation for the "implementation" of a particular social practice. Precisely because the social field is not an entity, no recommendation of a strategy for social change can be presented abstractly, outside of the living environment within which it might be tried out. That is why, to give a sweeping example, communism turned into its opposite: The Marxist-Leninist thinking "about" the social world that shaped the Soviet Union led in part to the creation of a Workers State that instituted a new collective form but did not bring about the realization of a communal manifestation of our collective being; or to give a tiny example drawn from my own experience of groups in the 1960s, having a rotating chairperson at the steering committee meeting did not produce the inclusive, participatory experience that was its formal objective. If our aim is to heal the world rather than to fix it, then we must engage in intuitively-based social-spiritual actions that may redeem our collective being rather than in rationally-based formal changes that we think will bring about social-spiritual effects.

Thus the sketch of the three circles that follows and the examples I give of possible social changes within each circle that may move the ball forward are offered as a kind of existential or "hodological" map that may offer pathways for healing and transcendence of the mutual withdrawnness that currently contains us and—if we think of the reality of nuclear weapons and of climate change—may also threaten the very existence of the world. The purpose of these pathways is to thaw out and partially dissolve the casing of the false-self matrix that separates us, and their value depends upon whether they actually do so, whether they actually allow us to emerge into each other's presence. The proof is in the pudding, not the recipe.

The Innermost Circle: Spiritual Practices that Strengthen the Presence of the Person: Meditation

Social movements have a way of flooding us with the joy of mutual discovery, but as we have seen, they do so on a shaky foundation conditioned in fear of humiliation and uncertain about the other's continuing presence. Meditation, yoga, chi gong, tai chi, walking in nature, prayer, and other spiritual practices can be of value in strengthening the solidity of one's own raw material, of the being of the person that each of us is, our incarnation.

At the present time, the rapidly expanding mindfulness movement, born of an actual evolution of human awareness across the West that the problems of the world are caused in some way by a spiritual void at the heart of capitalist culture, has been to a significant extent siphoned off into the private sphere. The mindfulness movement is for the most part proceeding as if each of us can find an "inner" private solution to the rotating alienation of the wider world. In this direction, mindfulness risks becoming a co-optation of the longing for a genuine reconnection with our being, one that will allow the fear-saturated world of capitalist culture to keep on turning with the mindfulness movement acting as a kind of spiritual safety valve through which the longing within each of us can momentarily assuage itself. As we have seen earlier in this book, there is no "inner" world as distinct from some ontologically separate "outer" world, but only an intersubjective psychospiritual field within which we become social together, either emerging into true mutual recognition and presence, or conditioning each other into maintaining the fear-saturated deferral of presence that is the world of the rotating false selves manifesting themselves as if they were real. We are either mutually withdrawn, in which case, in its rotation, the social world appears to be external to us, like an entity outside of us that we peer out at, or mutually present, in which case we rise into the fullness of mutual sight and become mutually confirming poles of togetherness. The idea that there is an "inner" world separate from an "outer" world is an artifact of our alienated reciprocal environment looking at itself from "the inside." Thus the pursuit of a salvation that can only come through one another as if it could come "from within" is an illusion and a co-optation of the very real longing to come back in touch with our true being, a being that is individually lived but is social through and through.

However, in our effort to spiritualize social activism so that our movement can remember itself and gain greater confidence in itself as a movement of the true being within each of us toward the other, meditation, yoga, and other person-centered spiritual practices can have real value. In meditation, presence quiets itself and seeks to attend to itself, in opposition to the fleeing from itself that is the imperative of our immersion in the anxious rotation of everyday culture. Recall that when we are immersed in the everyday alternation of excitement and depression of everyday life with others within the false-self matrix, we are caught up in a swirling congeries of images of self and other and world that purport to be real, and that we feel to be lacking (because we are in fact lacking in presence, are in flight from presence, the presence of each other). Therefore, we are erotically drawn to perpetual inflations of the "outer self," a mere image that is the source of excitement, and we are also deflated by our attempts to realize the "perfection" of that ontologically hollow image, which is the source of our depression. And recall also that this preoccupation with one's imaginary place in the imaginary social gradient is intended to actually protect us against each other in the guise of trying to achieve the recognition by and with the other that has been falsely promised by our conditioning. It is in this state that we approach meditation, as one step in the effort to recover the presence that we are, while in the same moment taming or quieting that image-self that we are not, but that purports to be who we are. In meditation, we engage in an intentional spiritual practice to try to close the gap between our being as actual grounded presence, and our false self that is continually demanding that we remain loyal to the world of our inherited conditioning.

It is often said that this practice, as we engage in it, is an attempt to quiet the "monkey mind" by focusing on a mantra or our breathing or by one of the other meditative methods that are in some cases thousands of years old. The idea of the monkey mind is that our minds swing largely on their own and out of our control from branch to branch, from topic to topic, from image to image, grabbing onto anything that can capture the mind's attention in a more or less chaotic way. But as powerful and accurate as the metaphor of the monkey mind is for how our anxious distraction seems to pull us this way and that, if we look more deeply we discover that the monkey mind is actually almost always the false self trying to relive and correct a past imagined humiliation, or rehearse for an upcoming moment in which humiliation must be avoided. Thus "O My God I haven't practiced the bass yet," meaning that I may be humiliated by rejection in the actual performance; or "I haven't heard back from Mary," meaning that the image-based pleasure that I was hoping for in her response to my email message may actually turn out to be a rejection of my overly flip reference to our last meeting. Having been cast out into the false-self matrix since early childhood, our fragile and vulnerable withdrawn being has been consigned to defend itself twenty-four hours a day (Freud showed in *The Interpretation of Dreams* how much these defensive maneuvers are on full display even while sleeping), and the wild "swinging" of the monkey mind is actually a manifestation of the effort of our being to correct, by rehearsal or reliving, an imagined flaw emanating from the inevitably lacking quality in the outer self's past or future performances. The monkey mind swinging like a monkey from image to image is actually the false self alone in its fort racing from turret to turret, from weak point to weak point, attempting to keep the projected threatening image of the other at bay. What we fear is the real other right next to us, but what we feel we must "correct" is the recent past or upcoming future encounter in which we fear we may have risked or will risk humiliation due to a failure of our false-self maneuvers.

Yet we must also recall, as I indicate in this book's first paragraphs, that the false self is not wholly false, that the love that our earliest others have extended to us also suffuses the false self as a longing and a memory; and this doubling within the social self is why we are not actually schizophrenic or split in two. Our conditioning contains both the loving holding that is a lovely metaphor for the total bond we have with others, and also the deflecting imagos of self and other that painfully keep us all at a distance. This means that the false self of our egos retains within itself the transcendental desire that is repeatedly short-circuited or blocked by fear of the other that normally dominates it, or rules over it. When we engage in meditation seeking to quiet our monkey minds by focusing on our breathing, what is actually taking place is that our authentic being that is our withdrawn presence itself, and that is precisely present to us and accessible to us as the ground of our being, forms a kind of alliance with the transcendental aspect of our social selves in order to elevate our presence more fully into our selves, like a mobius strip seeking to finally come in contact with its other side and escape its perpetual evasive motion. Or to show this more concretely, when "I" seek to focus on my breathing and "I" seek to quiet my monkey mind, what actually occurs is that my being intentionally exerts itself outward toward that aspect of my social self (that we call "I") that seeks to become present to the other, and uses that aspect of the self to attend to the breath as presence manifesting itself in the body, in a way that recovers the erotic ontological energy that would otherwise be drawn off into the aversive maneuvers of the monkey mind.

Thus even meditation, which appears to be a spiritual practice by the individual in isolation, is in truth a social practice and an effort at social recovery. When we engage in meditation together with a spiritual leader, the meditative environment is strongest because the leader can begin by invoking the quality of being to which we, as a we, aspire within the room and within the moment itself. And we gain spiritual strength to center ourselves—a fair and accurate image of recovering mutuality of presence—from the radiance of presence in the room, from all of us together engaging in our common effort. But even when we meditate alone, we are actually engaging in a process of social recovery insofar as the presence within us seeks to exteriorize itself the only way it can, through the legacy of mutual recognition that we retain as longing and memory within our "self-conscious" social selves. I therefore "tell myself" or better, tell my self, to focus on my breathing and then try to do so, and in so doing risk becoming present in the present moment through that very effort. As anyone who meditates will acknowledge, the effort to focus on one's breathing and quiet the monkey mind is a difficult and anxious effort, with the monkey mind frantically pulling at and trying to distract the emerging presence in the self from the vulnerable, grounded, openhearted being that we actually are.

Therefore, the work of meditation and other spiritual practices like it that strengthen the presence of the person by him- or herself are not actually individual practices, but practices of social recovery that we may engage in with other real others, or by ourselves with the support of the other within ourselves whom we as ontological presences call upon to assist us in channeling our ontological presence more fully into our realized manifestation. We use a part of ourselves to partially release ourselves from our withdrawn state and to some extent recover our social wholeness. That is why at the end of group meditation exercises especially, everyone in a meditation circle can normally make eye contact with each other, smile easily at each other, and otherwise palpably sense the co-presence of each to the other in a quite beautiful way, having emerged to some extent from the full-time "humiliation watch" that otherwise keeps us in a disembodied, solipsistic thrall.

The Second Circle: Social-Spiritual Practices that Strengthen the Internal Confidence of the Group in the Present Moment through Intentional Creation of a Parallel Universe

If meditation and other meditative spiritual activities are the most personal (or "individual") of social-spiritual practices, the next concentric circle surrounding the person in his or her separate space is what we might call the confirmatory environment. Even at the end of a meditation session, we can sense that whatever mutuality of presence we have been able to achieve in our social-spiritual work together will soon dissipate as we step outside of whatever room we have gathered in. While meditation may have a lasting effect that inflects us toward being present with others in the remainder of our day, we must also acknowledge that even as we speak our first words to each other following whatever emergence we have been able to achieve while meditating, we cannot but start to careen back into the realm of the outer self as soon as we start speaking. Or to be more precise, in starting to speak again, we cannot but feel ourselves becoming "outer" again in relation to an "inner" withdrawal from each other that is involuntary. The inherited voice and language that we first learned as children, with its limiting connotative range, floods in to fill up the space between us and draws us somewhat away from the mutuality of presence that we have fragilely given birth to while meditating.

Therefore, the next concentric circle that we must attend to in spiritualizing social activism is the creation of new social spaces in which we can each become other to each other in a way that confirms rather than disconfirms our desire for mutual recognition. To be quite specific about this, when we leave the meditation room, we must come to sense that we are not simply returning to the world of "the they" in which the rotation of alienation will inevitably sweep us up with its gravitational pull, but rather are to some extent entering a social world colored by a sustaining disalienating intention and sustaining disalienating rhythms of mutuality. Of course, the "wider world" will exert its pull, hooking us by virtue of our own conditioning-in-alienation toward becoming outer to ourselves and outer to each other, but co-existing with that pull, we must be intentionally bringing into being a parallel relational field co-existing with the "wider world" that carries forward the movement's transformative alteration of the social-spiritual space and sustains it through intentional effort.

The most widespread and visible example in everyday life of such a parallel universe existing alongside the dominant culture is the set of spiritual practices associated with religion. For many people and perhaps most people across the world, being with the other means both the secular rotation of anonymity that is "the market" and the co-existing, subdominant, "private" existential realm of the church/the synagogue/the mosque that forms a parallel milieu of silence, ritual, song, and togetherness that really does "compensate" to some degree for the anchorlessness of liberal secular life. And while it is fair to say that organized religion, or authoritative, routinized religious practice, has largely drawn off the spiritual longing for communion and channeled it into a hierarchical ordering of images, of deference and authority, of aboveness and underneathness, that supports rather than challenges the rotation of social alienation generally, religious life does offer much to guide us in creating a parallel universe supporting the spiritualization of social activism.

Imagine, for example, if accompanying our mediation practice, we were to intentionally gather once a year for a ten-day period in which we would publicly come together in rooms across the country, light candles together, embrace one another, retell to each other our highest vision of the loving world we aspire to create, sing and dance outside together under the stars, reflect on how in the prior year we had moved our lives forward toward creating a beloved community and contributed to bringing into existence such a world for all beings, but also reflect on how we had been limited in so doing by the weight of our conditioning and the residual fear of the other that had led us to miss the mark—and imagine also if we were to gather once a week during the year to engage in such sustaining communal activity intentionally aimed at easing our fear of each other and nurturing our recognition of each other as loving beings seeking to ground one another in each other's presence. This partial spiritualization of our lives would be simply the adaptation of the Jewish High Holidays celebrated in the period between Rosh Hashanah and Yom Kippur—what Jews call the Days of Awe—and Shabbat weekly religious practices for the purpose of creating a confirmatory environment in our social movements.[1]

Thus one rich social location to seek social-spiritual practices that can help to build a confirmatory environment for our social-spiritual evolution is in the religious traditions that have been developing them in some cases for thousands of years, but we can adapt these practices without any reference to any religion as such, and without the hierarchical elements that have often transformed these practices into incantations of subservience to the status quo. We must recognize that these practices often really do bind people together, and liberated from their own self-alienation, they can offer guidance in how to sustain our loving vulnerability to each other through ritual, movement, and song, and through mutual elevation and collectively elicited spiritual openness. Pursuing this path to creating a parallel universe would require overcoming the terror of spirituality currently felt by many on the left, a terror that results in part from a fusion of the valid liberal idea of the separation of church and state with the near-paranoid liberal fear that engagement in any spiritual practice will render one vulnerable to humiliation and control by a dominant other. But if we wish to succeed in sustaining our openheartedness and to sustain the vulnerability required to become fully present to each other, we will have to overcome the neurotic interpretation of separation of church and state that has reinforced the despiritualization of the public sphere altogether. To the extent that the social bond among all human beings (and among all beings) is inherent in our very ontological constitution, and to the extent that this bond is incarnated as a radiant, loving force through which we complete each other through the grace of mutual recognition and presence, to that extent social life itself is spiritual in its very essence; and our parallel social-spiritual universe, existing alongside the inherited fear-saturated world, must precisely release that spiritual force from its current, mutually enforced imprisonment.

Apart from the use of liberatory psychospiritual ritual, in creating the second circle of social-spiritual activism we can introduce what I am calling confirmatory practices into our organizations to alleviate the recurrence of fear of the other within them and to thus help secure them against dissolution or bureaucratization. As we saw in Chapter 9, progressive organizations are actually rotations of mutuality formed out of the cooling mass of the social movements that inspire them and so must sustain their socially embodied moral meaning to avoid slippage toward the revival of the fear-saturated outer self and externalization of the group itself that otherwise tend to undermine their social-spiritual core. The labor movement, for example, emerged from the mutual recognition among workers of their common exploitation and subjugation by owners of land, factories, housing, and more generally the "means of production" . . . but the mutual recognition that enabled workers to "rise" and transfigure Western societies between 1850 and 1950 pointed toward a universalist socialist vision that would transcend alienation itself and create an egalitarian, cooperative world. Yet within the labor unions that emerged from the movement and its universalist vision, the force of direct threats, co-optation through legal and other ideologies, and residual effects of fear of the other within the unions themselves has led unions to some extent to have forgotten the spiritual-socialist meaning that gave birth to them in the first place. The ensuing, gradual bureaucratization of unions—the shifting to an "organizational" focus on wage levels and working conditions within the existing system and a partial subordination of the spiritual meaning of the socially transcendent movement "upwards" that gave rise to them—has to some extent negated the union's radiant appeal as a continuing locus of mutual recognition and confirmation, and has contributed to the labor movement's internal and external decline. Yet sustaining that very radiance of mutuality, confirmation, and love is critical to supporting both the labor movement itself as a transformative vehicle of social change and the success of the unions as organizations fighting for such practical goals in the present as higher wages, safer and more humane working conditions, and universal health care for workers.

Unions can retain their capacity to generate this kind of binding radiance by embracing a wide variety of social-spiritual practices that intentionally regenerate communal feeling. Most unions have at least one large meeting room that can be used for monthly gatherings in which union members might give talks about their family and ethnic histories (I'm thinking especially here of hotel workers, for example, whose room cleaners, cooks, and bellmen- and -women often come from African-American, Latino, and Asian heritages rich in meaning to each of them and currently largely invisible to the membership); the history of the labor movement and the union might be celebrated and retold on an annual basis along with the singing of labor songs; a cultural center within or adjoining the union hall might feature films and plays about the historical role of working people in shaping the social world, in much the same way that the Federal Theater made socially progressive theatrical productions available to a wide range of Americans for just twenty-five cents in the 1930s; harkening again back to the 30s, unions might re-create the labor summer camps that created opportunities for workers and their families to bond with warmth, affection, and play while sharing vacations during the summer months. These are all examples of creating what I am calling a confirmatory social-spiritual environment, in the sense that their purpose is not to achieve an external goal by a group organized by role and function, but rather to sustain openheartedness and the experience of liberatory community itself as a prefiguring of what the larger social transformation struggle is about. All of these attempts at spiritualizing the group's activism are meant to sustain within the activism the rising up of the mutuality of presence and hereness in the present moment that originally characterized the disalienating force of the movement itself, and that originally made it "move."

If one dimension of creating this mutually confirmatory environment is ritual celebrations for the group as a whole (of which the Jewish High Holidays are a kind of model), and if a second dimension is spiritualizing and meaning-restoring activities within the organization, an important third aspect of what I am calling a confirmatory environment is our neighborhoods and families. As I showed in my discussion of street life in Chapter 3, neighborhoods in which we routinely "pass each other" are often diffuse rotations of aversive presence, with each of us passing the other (at least in the middle-class form) affecting a pleasant surface of the self but in reality pooled up in our isolation, creating ghettos of quiet desperation. But if we bring a social-spiritual intention to the neighborhood instead of accepting its passive and aversive rotation, we can bring it to communal life. Many years ago in my neighborhood of Noe Valley in San Francisco, a local health food store owned by an out-of-state corporation fired all its workers who were trying to form a union and closed its doors. Instead of leaving it to the workers to pursue on their own whatever legal remedy they might have had under labor law, the neighborhood "rose up," intuitively confident in our socially progressive heritage, and in addition to supporting the workers by attending their labor board hearings, we created our own farmers market to provide our own healthy food to our community. By rising up in this way and pulling each other out of our collective isolation into a vital and meaningful relation to each other, to the fired workers, and to our neighboring organic farmers, we converted a collection of people previously linked merely by the material practice of "eating" (growing, distributing, and consuming food) but invisible to each other behind our reciprocal anonymity, and converted ourselves into meaning-creating, mutually recognizing actors bringing into being a socially and environmentally just world—but not a "world" as an abstraction but the actual life-world of a concrete community. Through social-spiritual neighborhood activism, we as a real-we, a real relational latticework, in part transformed "Noe Valley" from a passively-circulating rotating gathering into an embodied living group. And it is still the case, some fourteen years later, that the communal spark of Noe Valley remains in these Saturday morning, public comings-together in which the parched, passer-by detachment of mutually aversive life converts itself into the sudden lively plenitude of mutual presence.

In the present historical time, farmers markets have become symbols across the country of communal liveliness of this kind, but like the mindfulness movement, these markets can only play a transformative role if they form but one piece of a social-spiritual strategy, as one location within concrete social space of the invention of the confirmatory environment across all the spaces we collectively inhabit. Still a fourth such space within the surrounding context that I am calling the second circle is the family, the arena of cohabitation that can either be—to cite two obvious extremes—a hermetically sealed container of routinized suffering masked by a veneer of perfect happiness (Ronald Reagan's "Morning in America") or an oxygenated life-world of devotion, security, love, and working-through in which we create, encounter, and raise the next generation. In its "haven in a heartless world" version, the family tends to convert itself into a reified entity threatened by its own internal vulnerability, with sexuality threatening each of us by virtue of its pulling our very being into visibility to the other, and with the perpetual loss of the other threatened by the heartless wider world leading to an internal tendency to rigidly bind each other through guilt to deference to the roles of the family's outer unity. But here again spiritualizing the family remains an opportunity as a way of emerging into each other's actual, as opposed to "outer," presence and converting fearful allegiance to an outer unity into the true security of freeing, mutually confirming love.

Engaging in social-spiritual activism within the family means seeking to thaw and open up the closed space through which the couple, and the family as a whole, may tend to imprison itself. To repeat what I've said in a very condensed form above, for all its beauty and aspiration to love and commitment, the family is a challenging group within which to realize the desire for true mutual recognition because of the contradiction within it between eros, which calls us toward vulnerability and opening up, and the "command to be alienated," which is the widespread condition of the wider self-protective world. In the face of this wider world of passing each other with blank gazes on the street, or accommodating ourselves to conditioned roles that pretend to be who we really are, or in short, simply keeping ourselves at a distance from the pull of the other for authentic mutuality of presence, we tend to flee into the family, pulled by our own erotic needs which are expressions of the desire for mutual recognition itself, and then engage in massive security operations to require of each other that we conform to the roles of husband, wife, and child. Thus the "outer" family devolves toward being "performed," and then idealized as a denial of artificiality, while the actual lived experience of each person within the so-called "family-unit" is withdrawn and, so to speak, gasping for air. The medium through which this conversion into an enmeshed or undifferentiated unit is carried out is guilt, through which each person sacrifices him- or herself so as to bind the other to conform to "the family" as a collective image of our togetherness. If you fail to act in accordance with what is expected, you risk excommunication, which is to say, expulsion from the image-world that was your hope of "belonging somewhere," of having a place in even a "haven" in a heartless world into which you may otherwise be hurled, becoming an exile from any erotic outlet or social security.

This may seem like an extreme description, but if we are honest with ourselves about the entropic tendencies within our most intimate relationships, if we refuse in the interests of our liberation and fulfillment as human beings to participate in the "everything's fine" surface of the world's existence, we can at least recognize these negative dimensions of family life as tendencies that of course must exist in light of the circulation of alienation that envelopes us generally. And if we do recognize these tendencies, we need not be surprised by the widespread existence of domestic violence on the one hand, and joyless or sexless marriages on the other, or children who thankfully rebel with youthful and not yet completely territorialized desire against the coercive path laid out for them on pain of excommunication and "disinheritance." And once we see the family as it is, or as it tends to be as beset with understandable conflicts that exist in all of us in light of our erotic longing and vulnerability in a wider environment that makes this vulnerability threatening to our ontological safety, we can begin with compassion to attempt to open the family nexus up and begin to heal and change it.

Releasing love into the family as a communal space or psychospiritual, intersubjective field requires "lifting" the grid of coercion through which we close ourselves off to each other by deferring to an imaginary unity of idealized, relatively fixed roles, conditioned in part by gender (normally man and woman) and in part by generation (parent and child), but also in other ways not reducible to these conventions and unique to each group. That means seeking to recognize the other as he or she actually is in his or her being, to allow the other to exist so that mutual recognition between us and among us emerges as possible. And this in turn means letting go of control of each other that we carry out through guilt and unconscious obedience, such that love is uncoupled from adherence to love's outer substitute, which we might call "love." In the 60s, we somewhat mistakenly thought we could accomplish this by non-monogamy, rejection of permanent commitments, open marriages, and other legitimate efforts that sometimes succeeded in creating freer and more loving human relationships, but often were actings-out against the repressive aspects of coerced loyalty to the couple without adequate compassionate and loving attention to the vulnerability that this acting out would inevitably trigger. Instead what we should aspire to are spiritually releasing steps that leave us free enough of each other's control to be capable of loving each other as present beings, but also compassionate enough with each other's fear of this very freedom that we can encompass each other's anxiety as we give up our "hold" on each other. This would seem to be the path toward co-creating a world in which erotic vulnerability and the freedom that is a condition of it can co-exist over time. It appears that this requires the permanent commitment of one's presence, whether or not the relationships stay together in a physical, temporal sense. Among the social-spiritual strategies that may help to open up the family in this way are: couples resisting becoming undifferentiated units by pursuing separate lives not wholly defined by each person's relationship to the couple, having dinners for people in the neighborhood one night a week to which everyone in the building or neighborhood is welcome and in other ways breaking down the family's hermetically sealed "unit-space" from which no one can escape and into which no one can easily enter; engaging in social and political actions together to facilitate the shift from the pressure to focus only on each other and toward instead seeking to look in the same moral direction; consciously seeking to release each other from the tendency to control the other by virtue of our own patterned strategies of making ourselves secure, and also voluntarily and compassionately trying to assist each other in coping with the anxiety that leads us, each in our respective ways, to repeat controlling patterns that interlock with our own.

Regarding the raising of children to help them to become present beings instead of compliant/rebellious products of a coercive family system, let me quote Eckhart Tolle's words in his book *A New Earth*:

> Many adults play roles when they speak to young children. They use silly words and sounds. They talk down to the child. They don't treat the child as an equal. The fact that you temporarily know more or that you are bigger does not mean the child is not your equal. . . . If you have young children, give them help, guidance, and protection to the best of your ability, but even more important give them space—space to be. They come into this world through you, but they are not "yours." . . . The more expectations you have of how their life should unfold, the more you are in your mind instead of being present for them.
>
> Many children harbor hidden anger and resentment toward their parents and often the cause is inauthenticity in the relationship. The child has a deep longing for the parent to be there as a human being, not as a role, no matter how conscientiously that role is being played. You may be doing all the right things and the best you can for your child, but even doing the best you can is not enough. *In fact doing is never enough if you neglect Being . . .*
>
> How do you bring Being into the life of a busy family, into the relationship with your child? The key is to give your child attention. There are two kinds of attention. One we might call form-based attention. The other is

> formless attention. Form-based attention is always connected in some way with doing or evaluating. "Have you done your homework? Eat your dinner. Tidy up your room. Brush your teeth. Do this. Stop doing that. Hurry up, get ready."
>
> What's the next thing we have to do? This question pretty much summarizes what family life is like in many homes. . . . Being becomes completely obscured by doing, by the "cares of the world," as Jesus puts it. Formless attention is inseparable from the dimension of Being. How does it work?
>
> As you look at, listen to, touch, or help your child with this or that, you are alert, still, completely present, not wanting anything other than that moment as it is. In this way, you make room for Being. In that moment, you are not a father or mother. You are the alertness, the stillness, the Presence that is listening, looking, touching, even speaking. You are the Being behind the doing . . .
>
> The longing for love that is in every child is the longing to be recognized, not on the level of form, but on the level of Being. If parents honor only the human dimension of the child but neglect Being, the child will sense the relationship is unfulfilled, that something absolutely vital is missing, and there will be a buildup of pain in the child and sometimes unconscious resentment toward the parents. "Why don't you recognize me?" This is what the pain or resentment seems to be saying.
>
> When another recognizes you, that recognition draws the dimension of Being more fully into the world through both of you. That is the love that redeems the world. I have been speaking of this with specific reference to the relationship with your child, but it equally applies, of course, to all relationships.
>
> (2016, pp. 97–106)

As I have said earlier in this book, every newborn child creates an opportunity for us who are to some extent alienated to partially heal our fear of the other through the child's grant of presence and through his or her unfiltered desire for mutual recognition. Therefore, all children, including "our own" children, can form an important part of the parallel universe that we ourselves need in order to overcome our learned internal lack of confidence in the desire of the other. To the extent that we are encountering our children within the family, and to the extent that we are also able to "throw open" the coercive closure that we often bring down upon our adult family relationships in order to prevent anyone from escaping, to that extent the family itself can be a locus of social-spiritual activism that incarnates the new relational plane that we are trying to bring into being and gain traction in.

But the family can no more foster this social transformation than can meditation if practiced in isolation from the surrounding psycho-spiritual field, from the normal rotating world, the spinning top, within which this transformation is constantly being resisted. To actually help create the wider confirmatory environment that can as a whole form a parallel universe within which to create a milieu of greater mutual recognition, families should co-participate in openhearted and elevating spiritual-or-religious gatherings, and to the extent appropriate participate in efforts to spiritualize organizations like the labor union and attend the local farmers market, as well as oxygenating the spiritual environment of the family itself. The point is to intentionally seek to create within social existence a parallel disalienating sphere that extends across our lives as a whole, so that the world we aspire to thickens bit-by-bit with growing confidence in itself as real.

Finally, special mention should be made of current efforts being made today to intentionally build this post-liberal confirmatory environment in the midst of otherwise routinized liberal social practices that have for decades—really centuries—been reproducing the very social separation that within the Second Circle needs to be overcome. Under the leadership of Cat Zavis and Michael Lerner, The Network of Spiritual Progressives has for many years been seeking to create a parallel universe within the professions that draws doctors, lawyers, psychotherapists, journalists, social workers and educators into small groups that are reconceiving their work as an effort to heal social distortions rather than merely providing professional help or information to separated, floating individuals. In the same way that this Network has supplemented its efforts with a magazine, *Tikkun*, that conveys the ideas that the Network is seeking to bring into practice, *Sojourners* magazine in Washington D.C. under the Leadership of Jim Wallis has created a living community seeking to embody and practice spiritual activism along with a magazine that articulates the philosophical and spiritual foundations of its new and connecting way of life. Episcopal priest Matthew Fox, along with a younger generation of colleagues including Skylar Wilson and Jennifer Listug, have recently begun creation of a new "post-religious" Order of the Sacred Earth, supported by a book describing its work, that seeks to combat the withdrawn detachment that produces "species narcissism" through the taking of a common vow of resacralization of the earth and engaging in common activities inspired by the vow that they hope will form the basis of a new transnational community. There are, of course, many such efforts already arising within our culture that are mainly still isolated from each other, but that are seeking to prefigure what we might call the transfiguration of public space away from its tendency toward aversion from the other, from the person next to you, and toward the confirmation in the other, in the person next to you, of the same social-spiritual longing that you feel within yourself. A new understanding of the importance of what I am calling the Second Circle, the confirmatory environment intermediate between the being of the person and the being of the world-as-a-whole, may help these many differentiated groups to discover their undifferentiated ontological unity.

The Third Circle: Spiritualizing Social Policy as a Way of Evoking and Articulating Our Moral Direction

If the innermost circle begins with where each of us is right now in our conditioned space and proposes spiritual practices, like meditation, that can begin to align us with our innermost being, and can ground us *here* so that we can step forward into the social-spiritual field more prepared to become present to the other within it; and if the second circle proposes that we seek to create a parallel universe in which we reciprocally call into being the presence of the other, a parallel universe co-existing with the somewhat cacophonous rotation of the wider world that will otherwise tend to sweep us up like a vacuum cleaner and absorb our presence into it, cementing us into its all-seeing fearful casing; then out of the ground of those first two circles must emerge our moral evocation of the future towards which we are heading, or more accurately towards which we are seeking to pull ourselves, the unity of who we already are as immanence (in unrealized form) with whom we seek to become as transcendence (in realized form). To recall once more the metaphor I used in Chapter 8, like a mountain climber who first throws his or her pick to the top of a mountain and then pulls him- or herself up and gains each foothold in relation to the end to be achieved, so also must we—having established our ground of mutuality of presence through co-creation of the first two circles—anchor ourselves in our moral destination in order to take each step forward in our real historical present toward that destination.

The very first step in this latter process is how we speak to each other across a dinner table, or in small groups, or in meetings of our political parties, or when addressing large gatherings such as rallies or protests. For my entire lifetime, the primary way that speakers have communicated with often thousands and sometimes tens of thousands of people who have gathered to protest current conditions and to call for social change has been with righteous anger accompanied by denunciation of the oppressor. Without meaning to discount the importance of anger in breaking through our compliant adaptation to the system that has conditioned us and often cordoned us off from our own authentic needs for a new and more human world, this dominant rhetoric evokes a picture of the world as divided into a good "us" who are present at the rally, and a bad "them" who are keeping us from attaining the social world that "we" want. The future world that is implied in this hortatory discourse is one in which "we" the good will triumph over "them" the bad; we will stomp them into the ground and sweep them into the dustbin of history, clearing the psychospiritual field of their evil so we can fill it with our righteousness.

The core problem with this anger-fueled us-them discourse is not simply that it involves a false splitting in which we dehumanize the other and idealize ourselves, but rather that it actually implicates the speaker in the denial of vulnerability that, as we have seen, masks the underlying fear of humiliation that is at the core of what is wrong with the world and what we must overcome. In reversing the demonization process and aiming it at the oppressor, we flatten out the world before us, concealing our own spiritual core in an idealized victimhood of the outer self while also concealing the spiritual distortion in those enacting the oppression by painting them in a despiritualized outer costume of evil. So long as we remain ensconced in this hardened outer-surface of the world, and so long as we obscure in our way of evoking the conditions of social injustice the social-spiritual depth-dimension out of which that injustice arises, we cannot point toward the moral direction required to heal it. It is the fear of humiliation that is at the core of all oppression and injustice, and we can only reveal that fear by opening the hearts of our own listeners to their own spiritual vulnerability and longing through which they become able to perceive the spiritual distortion underlying the social alienation of self from other that envelopes them.

Martin Luther King Jr. has been the great exception to the predominant us-them mode of public expression to large gatherings, and both his evocative moral power and his practical success in inspiring the movement forward should set an example for what we all should aspire to as rhetoricians and prophets, as evokers of the world we seek to bring into being. King, it should be noted, was himself deeply grounded in the first two circles: Although he may or may not have engaged in meditation, he sought to recover his moral center daily in prayer, and in *Letter From Birmingham Jail* he describes the self-purification involved in non-violent civil disobedience and in preparation for it. That work of spiritual preparation, like Gandhi's daily spinning of thread, helped him lead gatherings of resistance that revealed in the very presence of moral truth that they manifested the moral injustice of what they were protesting against (and this is the great moral power of non-violent civil disobedience: its capacity to reveal, through the innocence of unearned suffering, the immorality of the conditions being defended by those causing the suffering). And King also was supported in his moral resolution by his second circle, his parallel universe: The black churches where the African-American communities that he led and spoke for experienced the parallel universe of mutual recognition, of enlivened loving community, and of mutually strengthening conviction that provided for King and his colleagues the ontological foundation to be able to generate an upward movement of being.

Thus when King stepped forward to speak to large gatherings and evoke the moral world towards which the gathering was and should be aiming, his moral being was prepared to speak in a way that could align the moral being of the crowd with the moral end to be realized. Can you recall the incantatory power in these last words from his "I Have a Dream" speech?

> And when this happens, when we allow freedom ring, when we let it ring from every village and every hamlet, from every state and every city, we will be able to speed up that day when all of God's children, black men and white men, Jews and Gentiles, Protestants and Catholics, will be able to join

> hands and sing in the words of the old Negro spiritual: Free at last! Free at last! Thank God Almighty, we are free at last!

Rather than angrily denouncing the present state of racial injustice in the world in which the bad them who are not present are oppressing the good us who are present, King evokes a world unredeemed as yet aiming toward its own moral redemption. In and through his being and his words, every listener can feel the social alienation of the present resolved in the mutual recognition of the future, a mutuality of actual presence in which we "join hands and sing" ourselves into the real-we that is a moral possibility of the present but denied by our separation in the present moment. Following King's example and learning from it, we can, when we speak to others of where we are going in any setting, express ourselves with empathy and compassion for the pain of our common humanity that is unredeemed because unrecognized in the world as it is, and with hope and conviction that we can bring into being the redemption of our social essence that we all sense as a universal possibility in the world to which we aspire.

Precisely the same evocation of the world we long to bring into being can shape the way we speak in favor of practical social policies. Every practical issue of the present historical moment offers us an opportunity to evoke the moral direction stretching from the present world suffused with fear of the other and unrealization of our loving social core towards a world in which our desire for mutual recognition would be realized. Here are five examples drawn from present-day political discourse contrasting the way an issue is often argued for from within a despiritualized world-view presupposing the inevitability of social separation, and a spiritually enlivened world-view that speaks to and aspires to transcending the fear of the other that blocks our desire for loving mutuality. Although these examples are drawn from a standard list of reforms that one would find in any Democratic Party platform, they can become vehicles for a more radical transformation if they are spoken for in a prophetic voice as partial realizations of a transcendent end. Having centered ourselves in Being through spiritual practice, and having gained confidence in one another through our participation in a surrounding confirmatory environment, these social policies can align the practical requirements of the present with the incipient creation of another world.

1. *Social Security*: Social security is normally advocated for and defended on the grounds that older people should not have to suffer from material want. But this description participates in the creation of an image of the social world as a non-social collection of individuals, whose aging bodies are in need of a minimal level of material comfort without having to continue to engage in the sale of one's labor-power. While many people can identify with this "benefit" being granted to the older generation (every individual eventually grows old), the world so pictured is also vulnerable to the counter-argument that social security is just too expensive and imposes too great a burden on the young. And by focusing on this issue of social security's supposed financial burden, conservatives are within their rights in seeking to extend the age at which these supposed "benefits" vest. If the world is made up of socially discrete individuals each pursuing his or her own self-interest, why not expect the older generation to work as long as physically possible and limit the burden on the young?

   But if we understand ourselves as inherently social beings seeking in each new generation to better realize our interhuman bond, we can and should advocate for social security as an expression of intergenerational love, as an *opportunity* for the younger generation to fully recognize and express their care and concern for their elders. Thus conceived, social security is not a burden at all, but rather a morally redemptive way for the younger generation to more fully realize its own longing to connect with and support their own parents and grandparents, but not limited by the restrictive envelope of the biological family. Thus through social security, we can all as a society deepen our bond among grandparents, parents, and their children, a beautiful aspiration that we all long for rather than a "cost" to society that we as lonely individuals are weighed down by.
2. *Health Care*: In a world of socially separated and alienated individuals, health care is even more costly than social security, with great unevenness in how its benefits will be distributed. If we all pay for people to have coverage, how do we know that some will not overuse their benefit, or that doctors will not defraud the system, or that the health care system will not become a giant bureaucracy of impersonal and inadequate provision of often unnecessary medical services to people who don't really need them?

But here also if we allow ourselves to remember that our world is actually a social-spiritual community seeking to more fully realize the love that unites us, our call for universal health care becomes a moral call with profound appeal, again an *opportunity* for us to manifest our desire to recognize and care for each other if we or our parents or grandparents should become ill. Thus health *care* should be about caring about each other's health rather than insuring each other's bodies. And when conceived as a moral opportunity of this kind, the young may want to become physicians in greater numbers as a way of realizing their own deepest social needs. No longer will our public debates be mired in discussions of complex insurance schemes that will somehow provide cost-effective but limited medical procedures available to some of us but not all of us, an inherently absurd idea from a perspective that sees us as all inherently linked by a universal bond of love. Who would want to save the life of his or her own mother while letting another's mother die?

Thus here also, health care is beneficial not just to the recipient but to the provider, an expression of love for all others realized through the communal form of a government program. And once health *care* is seen through this connective, actually caring lens, its meaning must point beyond the mere question of access (via universal coverage) to the nature of the care being provided, to a mode of heartfelt concern carrying the element of love that is largely absent from the current biomedical model that treats the body as an insured or uninsured medical object.

3. *Foreign Policy*: So long as so-called "foreign" policy is linked to the security and interests of the nation-state, it will have the character of and partake of the maneuvers of the fearful false self to protect itself against the threat of humiliation by the other. Thus as we saw in Chapter 7, the false self through which we separate ourselves by a moat from the other, from the person next to us, aligns itself through a collective imaginary with the false-we of our political unity in the nation. That imaginary unity—established by language, culture, style, and conventions of many kinds (the pledge of allegiance), as well as the transmission of imaginary narratives ("we the people were created by the 'founding fathers'") and actual political practices like the collectively-witnessed collective act of voting on the same day at the same time—is insubstantial and not grounded in

true mutual presence. While as I have indicated national identity can sometimes fuse with the emergence of a real-we, it is normally the idealized opposite of that, a collective mental arena of perfect otherness guarding our mutually withdrawn presence from the real other, from each other.

Foreign policy generated out of this fearful imaginary is inevitably drawn to wars based upon the identification of ever-shifting demonized others who are projected carriers of the threat of revelation of our universal vulnerability. General MacArthur is afraid of his wife, so he must subjugate the Philippines. And to the extent that foreign policy is not about actual or obsessively planned-for possible war, preoccupied with the creation of threats and enemies who participate in precisely the same reverse, fear-saturated imagining, it is largely about collectively relating to other countries to advance "our" interests, understood as primarily what furthers or sustains the rotation of our socio-economic patterning, our particular spinning top that is always in danger of falling over, of succumbing to the temptation to try to love one another.

This isn't to say that by virtue of being identified as Americans we do not face real physical threats, nor is it to deny that "we," even to the extent that that "we" is largely imaginary, express the residue of caring for the real other, which resides within each of us, through the generous element in foreign aid, in participating in disaster relief, and the like. But it is to say that foreign policy as we generally practice it through a conservative or a liberal prism is primarily about the creation of images that protect the false self experiencing itself as under constant threat and the displacement of its fear onto "foreign enemies."

A social-spiritual approach to foreign policy must speak for the real-we within us, the transnational emergent community that seeks to heal the fear of the other that has led us for thousands of years to engage in and suffer the effects of intentional mass murder (eighty million dead in World Wars I and II alone). This requires spiritualizing foreign policy with the intention of "surrounding" arenas of fear-driven international conflict and engaging in actions that might "thaw" the compulsion to repeat the threats reproduced by the us-them divisions. In my essay "Spiritualizing Foreign Policy" (see Chapter 12 in *Another Way of Seeing*), I have given many examples of this kind of healing foreign policy: From using the United Nations Security Council to hear from and publicly televise the suffering of Israeli and Palestinian families who have lost children in their conflict, allowing the security council to emerge as an incipient real-we in response to the spiritual pain underlying the hardened us vs. them casing formed out of the trauma of the legacy of reciprocal violence, to the restorative practices of South Africa's Truth and Reconciliation Commission that expressed, partly through the transcendent presence of its chair Bishop Desmond Tutu, the possibility of forgiving, rather than avenging, the spiritual distortion that had been at the heart of apartheid by actually revealing this distortion on national television (some 22,000 separate instances of it) and having it acknowledged by the perpetrators. But the core of this spiritualized approach is to evoke by word and action a transnational future in which we transcend imaginary and paranoid differentiations and recognize each other as human. And by recognizing each other in this way I do not mean simply to "have an idea" of the other's humanity, but to actually emerge as a real-we capable of actually recognizing the presence of the real other as he or she is arising in and actually existing across the world.

As in the case of social security and universal health care, this way of evoking and articulating foreign policy is not merely more humane toward the other but also realizes our own desire for mutual recognition. In surrounding, thawing, and gradually healing our hallucinatory and fear-saturated world of us-them images, we also point ourselves in the moral direction of realizing the bond of love that unites us. To "call" for that as policy is to partly realize it in the present because the call itself aligns our future goal with our present longing and, so to speak, pulls it to the surface of our collective being.

4. *Affirmative Action and Race Relations*: We have seen in Chapter 7 the "ontological gap" that exists between the cross-racial and universal mutual recognition realized in and through the civil rights movement, and the partial co-optation of that cross-racial recognition that occurred in the absorption of the movement's communal elevation into the liberal-legal re-picturing of that movement as being about "non-discrimination" among strangers. The latter legal characterization that prevails today reflects, as we have seen, fear's recasting of

the movement's desire, since it deflects the movement's transcendental claim upon the community as a whole for the creation of a world of love across our racial differences into a mere recognition that in the system's normal unloving rotation, "we the people" will not discriminate against any individual because of skin color. "Everyone" in his or her anonymous capacity as one of the strangers among the they will be guaranteed equality of opportunity to, for example, compete in the marketplace or vote in a curtained booth.

Certainly, this change in the law has been an important achievement and represents a new foothold out of the dehumanization and violence of slavery and other forms of racialized oppression, but to the degree that legal non-discrimination *replaces* the transcendent message of love across our differences realized in part in the movement, to that degree the movement itself tends to vanish because it can no longer see itself reflected back to itself. The loss of the moral horizon pointed to by the movement, as an embodied movement of being toward that horizon, tends to disaggregate the movement back into a scattering of withdrawn social individuals. And once this dissolution takes place, it's once again everyone for him- or herself: As we saw in the case of the history of affirmative action, a social policy that originally had wide appeal because it embodied the movement's own moral call for the realization of the desire in everyone for a truly human world (King's call for black men and white men to *join hands*) became a deeply controversial policy about whether blacks would receive a special benefit because of past discrimination in claims against whites who were otherwise deserving of success in a competition among them as scattered individuals. If we are but scattered individuals in a fearful social world whose best hope of salvation is making it within the zero-sum competitive system, it's hard to see why the white person who has fulfilled all the requirements of making it should be hurled down the ladder when he or she has not engaged in "discrimination."

A social-spiritual approach to affirmative action and every other attempt to overcome the legacy of and continuing presence of racial oppression must link the "call" of the social policy with love itself, with the morally redemptive realization of a new world in which we will become fully present to each other as social beings, as "I" and "Thou." We do not need merely an objective change in the policy but rather a new way of calling for the change that evokes a desire-realizing future that will be partially realized through the policy and gives profound meaning to it (in contrast to Bill Clinton's "Mend It, Don't End It" slogan that reflected his liberal-legal way of defending affirmative action). This way of calling for change inherently challenges not only discrimination whether present or past, but also mass incarceration and racially segregated cities in which African-Americans are begging on the streets and living grouped in the poorest sections of town. And most important, this social-spiritual call directly takes on, and offers a moral alternative to, the needs spoken to by racism itself, by the imaginary community provided by the puffing up of the outer self of those attached, due to their inner sense of humiliation and non-recognition, to their hallucinated sense of superiority for "being white." To the extent that our social policy offers the possibility of becoming part of an actual morally redemptive community, to that extent it will "stitch in" those who would otherwise be thrown back into their dugouts of humiliation if left only with their "equality of opportunity" within an isolating, socially separated world.

5. *Protection of the Environment*: The predominant way that environmental activists today argue for protection of the environment is to emphasize the risk that our existing socio-economic practices will soon cause physical destruction of the climate and of the natural world that will make life on earth unsustainable, or at a minimum cause great human suffering. The discourse used to demonstrate the probability of this outcome is mainly a scientific one, with organizations like 350.org emphasizing the quantity of carbon dioxide in the atmosphere, or documentaries like *An Inconvenient Truth* shocking its viewers by showing the increases in the earth's temperature created by the proliferation of greenhouse gases.

   As necessary and valuable as this discourse of science has been in awakening people to the physical dangers of such real ills as global warming and air and water pollution, it has thus far had limited success in persuading large numbers of people to support the fundamental changes needed to forestall and if possible reverse these destructive effects. And the reason is that we are addicted to our own alienation, in the sense that we cannot imagine making radical changes in our life practices without giving up the security of our place in the rotating patterning of our false selves within the false-we.

I may be aware that scientists say that some coastal cities may have to be abandoned and that some people, perhaps many people, may die as a result of coming environmental destruction, but this comes to me as mere factual "information" reaching my so-called rational mind, which has been in large part disconnected from my heart and is preoccupied with maintaining the self-protections and substitute gratifications of my outer self. The apparent ontological necessity of maintaining my place in the rotating patterning of the "outer" world is more compelling than any factual information that does less than threaten imminent death. As the continuation of wars and the proliferation of nuclear weapons demonstrate, people in a certain sense would rather have others die and perhaps would rather die themselves than respond to a call that they abandon the protection against the threat of vulnerability provided by the hardened casing of the false self.

A social-spiritual approach to the environment must evoke the restorative power of nature and our longing to reunite ourselves with the sacredness of life itself, embodied in the innocence and beauty of the natural world: the breathing of the plants and the chirping of the birds right outside my window, the miraculous purple of that flower that has simply appeared out of nothing, bursting out from the green fuse that channeled its mysterious energy into spectacular manifestation. My friend and ally Rabbi Michael Lerner often describes this kind of spiritual response as reacting with awe and wonder to the grandeur of creation, but I would add to this that such a response is also a social response because opening oneself up in this way requires a reconnection of the head and heart that inherently makes one vulnerable to the risk of humiliation by the other. To be able to respond openheartedly and with love toward nature requires a vulnerability that inherently opens one also to the person next to you, or to put this inversely, requires an overcoming of the fear-saturated casing of the false self that was constructed to respond to the threat to our social being posed by the other, by the person next to you. A social-spiritual approach to environmentalism is therefore one that evokes at once becoming present to each other and becoming present to the life of the world itself, which in nature reaches out toward us with innocence and vulnerability in every moment. Seen through this social-spiritual lens, the destruction of life resulting from the abuse of nature that has been objectified and exploited merely for economic production is revolting to the soul, rather than simply being the physical threat to the planet that makes it a cost not worth the benefit in a scientific analysis.

And so understood, the great advantage of spiritualizing environmentalism is that in itself, in its very way of articulating itself, such a spiritually expressive activism at once enlivens the activist as it enlivens nature, exerting through that very enlivening a moral claim on the listener that points toward the very recovery of his or her own being that he or she actually longs for.

Radical Pathways

The foregoing social-spiritual strategies for the most part presuppose actions that we can take within what we might call a relatively inert background—that is, a background social context in which the rotations of social alienation appear relatively fixed in the sense that everyone in his or her isolation feels compelled to "obey" them. This assumes the absence of an emergent transformative social movement that begins, as it "arises," to thaw out the seeming inevitability of "the system" and in which a true society-wide struggle begins to take place between the real-we and the false-we. When the system appears fixed and inevitable to each person in his or her isolation—when we each, peering out from our withdrawn space, see each other seeming to play predictable roles and enact predictable routines in such a way that we ourselves feel compelled to do the same in order to preserve our social membership—then it is important to try to generate experiences of mutual recognition within the inert field, within "the institutions" (although we have now seen that these institutions are merely "spinning tops" as I have called them rather than the entities we are accustomed to thinking of them as).

Although this does in a certain sense amount to "working within the system," that does not make the kinds of actions that I have proposed moderate, or merely reformist. On the contrary, the forms of social-spiritual activism that I have proposed are potentially transformative in the sense that they are intended to and may introduce authentic mutual recognition into what we might call the open space within the system, the space that is always available because the system always lacks closure. As we have seen, the patterned rotations of social alienation are always hollow in the sense that they consist mainly of a passing-around of the false-self as it were real, and the desire for mutual recognition is in every moment trying to challenge that very hollow surface, to break out into the open. The maintenance of the rotating system requires constant work and vigilance on the part of the fearful false self in each of us, and our spontaneous movement out toward one another at every moment transcends that so-called system and tries to topple it. So the social-spiritual strategies that I have proposed "within the system" should be seen as efforts to existentially stretch and expand the open space within every institution by building social confidence that the transcendental desire that exists in each of us exists in all of us, a desire that would otherwise be mainly pooled up within each of us in our reciprocal isolation. Trying to form a radical utopian collective during a relatively inert historical moment may be less effective at creating change than a spiritually elevating, socially conscious High Holiday service or a farmers market in an otherwise merely pleasant neighborhood.

But we must certainly make room in our social-spiritual thinking for more radical pathways, meaning attempts at creating more radically transformative social experiences that make a greater break from the inherited background of the conditioned world and help us to prefigure what the world we aspire to might actually be like. Here I am thinking, for example, of the social-spiritual practice of ingesting entheogens—substances, often psychoactive plants or drugs, that "generate the divine from within" in its Greek translation, or more simply are "generative of Being"—that can suddenly open our hearts to the wonder of the universe and the radiant and innocent beauty in each other;[2] of the formation of communes that played such a significant real and symbolic role during the 60s in liberating us, in reality among those who joined them and in imagination in those who only heard or read about them, from the apparent sealed-up fate of life in the institutions; of festivals like the Rainbow Gathering or Burning Man, which today attracts up to 70,000 people to the Nevada desert for one week a year to build a temporary city based upon a gift economy that aspires to collectively manifesting artistic creativity, a loving and embracing spirit, and a measure of holiness (however much that may have been partially co-opted or commercialized in recent years); and of those who simply grow their hair long or die it orange or blue or otherwise radically alter their "appearance," and those who create new schools (as I helped to do) or churches or workplaces or farms that model communal principles in ways that try hard to manifest in form what they hope they will actually bring into being.

And I am also thinking of historical examples of socio-political experiments that succeeded and failed in various ways to "totally" challenge the seeming necessity of social separation: the efforts of Gerrard Winstanley and the Diggers in 1649 to seize back the common lands that had been enclosed by wool merchants for the grazing of sheep and to create a radical Protestant community based on sharing and communal principles; the Black Panther's Free Breakfast for Children programs that removed the barrier of money from the feeding of thousands of poor African-American children across the country and showed that we could, if we wished, feed the entire world breakfast based on love and solidarity; Gaskin's Farm, which was inspired by the 60s counterculture and which led to the creation of a still-existing multi-generational community in Tennessee based upon non-violence and the sacredness of human relationships and the earth, and committed to the sharing of vegan food, the provision of free and adequate health care for all members, and midwifery in the birth of children; the Anarchists in the Spanish-Civil War who briefly controlled Barcelona and opened up the Ritz Hotel to provide free food for all in the hotel's fancy dining room; and really countless other examples of efforts to revolutionize the forms of social life in the hope of making real the Beloved Community that we intuit is within us.

As beautiful and inspiring as these many spiritual practices and historical efforts are or have been, however, what I have tried to show in this book is that the very social-spiritual nature of the transformation of the social world that we all openly or secretly long for requires the gradual building up of a confidence in the desire of the other, of each other, for the mutual recognition that each of us seeks. The most transcendent psychedelic trip must land back on a ground, and it is (mainly) the ground and not the trip that determines the trip's transformative impact. And great leaps forward that radically seek to alter the forms of life in a more communal direction do not in themselves alter the social being that must realize the potential in the form. For a social-spiritual transformation to occur, each social-spiritual step forward must take account of the vulnerability of each of us, the legacy of fear of the other within us that has saturated our conditioning. How often—as in the case of some communes and other idealistic collective attempts—have we seen the form get ahead of the Being in such a way that the form ultimately collapses and for a time undermines people's confidence that a radical transformation of the world that would realize our deepest desire is even possible!

Thus while more radical pathways have the advantage, in attempting to really break free of the existing conventions of the inherited world, of both revealing the non-necessity of the existing world and of prefiguring in intention and form the transformed world that we sense is possible, they have the disadvantage—during relatively inert historical moments—of not "bridging back" to the received world within which we think we know how to recognize one another safely, however poignant the limitations on that recognition may be. That is why in the previous sections of this chapter I have emphasized social-spiritual strategies that introduce transformations of social being within the spaces available within the existing "system," in the hopes that further opening and expanding those spaces will spread confidence in the experience of mutual recognition so as to create an emergent force field sufficient to at first gradually and then more rapidly begin to dissolve the hardened casing, and the apparent necessity, of the false-we altogether as our mutuality of presence begins to manifest itself. Because the false-we is actually always hollow, always an absence of Being presenting itself as if it were real; as Presence begins to arise within it a kind of conversion begins to take place—the psychospiritual field begins to "move" and the rotating artificial world itself begins to literally vanish, its non-being, its *evasion* of being, replaced by the fullness of the social being of the movement itself.

At moments like this, the leap to more radical pathways becomes especially important. For as the movement begins to spread its newfound mutuality throughout the absence in the inherited psychospiritual field, like the example of Japanese Go pieces surrounding and then flipping their opposition, at that moment more radical efforts at social change transmit actual confidence to those emerging into the real-we that we really can invent new social forms expressive of our newfound presence to each other while also pointing out a road to break free of our loyalty to the world of our conditioning. Thus as the force field of the movement rises, I may not immediately leave my inherited world of images and roles and routines to join a commune or other manifestation of the revolution, but I might begin to imagine doing so or doing something else that would allow the real me to continue to emerge into existence rather than remain within the hologram of a life that my withdrawn self will otherwise have as its destiny. As the movement accelerates, the emergence into visibility of more radical ways of being and living can accelerate the acceleration.

Yet while these more radical pathways may help to build the movement by seeking to incarnate the felt being of the movement within new and experimental social forms, they must incorporate into themselves the same grounding elements that I have emphasized earlier in this chapter and throughout the book. The joy and beauty of true mutual recognition as it arises, as we suddenly see one another more fully for the first time, must nonetheless remain haunted for the time being—and for a time going forward—by the fear of vulnerability and humiliation that is the legacy of the thousands of years of conditioning that has preceded our birth. Precisely what is distinctive about a social-*spiritual* strategy for transforming the world is that it measures its progress by our actual developing confidence in the spiritual bond that unites us, a confidence that requires constant attention to and compassion for our limitations as we seek to emerge from our withdrawn spaces and come to know that we are really here together as we let go of the masks that have separated us. If we recall the strength of the effort that has always been mounted by the collective false-self to undermine and defeat our efforts, and if we recall our own vulnerability to these very efforts occasioned by the fear and doubt that subsist within us by virtue of our conditioning, it seems clear that self-conscious social-spiritual practices supporting our effort to remain present must continue for time enough for us to become one with them.

Final Words

Let me repeat here in my final words that all of the foregoing examples of social-spiritual activism are intended to evoke in your mind possibilities for the recovery of being. No matter what *form* our activism takes, the goal must always be the creation of a) intentional actions that b) release us from our mutually withdrawn locations by dissolving the moat that separates us and bring us into each other's recognizing, loving presence, and c) does so in a way that we *know* with reflective wisdom that this coming-into-connection is taking place in such a way that we may d) become sufficiently confident in the solidity-across-time of our newly emergent bond that we can overcome the legacy of humiliation that otherwise might undermine our continuing movement forward. This kind of activism that consciously links each practical objective with the realization of our longing to more fully recognize and love one another, and that couples this elevation of our social being with knowledge of itself, will both greatly strengthen our capacity to generate and sustain future social movements, and also support the conscious evolution of humanity itself toward the full realization of our social nature.

It is natural enough from the standpoint of our fear, within our mutually withdrawn locations, to feel that such an unqualifiedly idealistic vision of the possibilities for social life are unrealistic. But if you take a moment to sit calmly with yourself, and to feel your own needs inside yourself and the longings in your own heart for the world you actually want, and if you then let yourself realize that every other human being on the planet is an incarnation of the very same essential being that is present in you and longs for precisely what you long for, then you may see that such a hopeful vision is simply the realization of who we already are in unrealized form. From birth we have expected to live in such a loving world, and we have already been trying to bring it into being, in every moment, in every interaction with another. In this book I have sketched out some of the obstacles that have limited our success thus far, but as you look up from the book and turn toward the next person who comes into your field of sight, you will extend yourself toward him or her with the same desire for mutual recognition, for mutuality of presence, that is occurring everywhere among all of us social, human beings. If this is our universal longing and aspiration that pulses through us in every human interaction, then only we ourselves are preventing ourselves from realizing it; and yet the paradox that has stymied us thus far has been that we can only do so by releasing each other from the enclosure that reciprocally contains us. Once we truly come to know together that we together hold the key to each other's liberation, and once we find the social and political path to spread this collective awareness sufficiently across social space, then the loving world to which we aspire will begin to be born. You may say that I'm a dreamer, but I'm not the only one.

Notes

1 I owe my understanding of the connecting power of self-conscious spiritual practices like these to my long relationship with Rabbi Michael Lerner, whose Jewish

High Holiday services I first attended in my late thirties. Up to that time, I had only experienced the breakthrough of mutual recognition through my participation in social and political movements, and I conceived of the spiritual as a strange and alien realm involving supernatural "beliefs." But gradually, Michael prevailed upon me to attend my first Jewish High Holiday services, in which he as Rabbi showed me that conscious, intentional creations of communally deep experiences were possible and could be confirming of the breakthrough I had previously only experienced in the spontaneity of the movement. Because I was at that same time witnessing (and experiencing the pain of) the tendency toward devolution occurring within 60's-inspired activist groups that I was often a part of, I simultaneously came to understand the importance of adapting the connecting and confidence-building spiritual practices of the best of religious traditions to the strengthening of our movements themselves, of which the Jewish High Holidays, the Days of Awe, are a powerful example. I encourage you to read Michael's brilliant book *Jewish Renewal: A Path to Healing and Transformation*, not because of its profound insights into Judaism, but because of its relevance to what we otherwise would consider secular social and political activism.

2 The ingestion of entheogens is often practiced, as in ancient indigenous cultures, in communal sacred ceremony. My assistant Jennifer Listug, who recently hosted an Ayahuasca ceremony, described the practice:

> In these medicine circles, participants often use their experience and insights as an offering to the gods, the earth, the world, the future, etc. For me, this is as much the power of the practice as the psychedelic experience is. During the ceremony, time, space and identity all become warped and melded and irrelevant. There is nothing quite like sitting in a darkened room in a circle of twenty people singing, praying, sweating, crying, chanting, listening to ancient indigenous songs, in an altered reality, totally melted into oneness with the group—and then, remembering suddenly that you are in a human body; you are an "individual" with a name and a story and an identity that no longer feel as concrete, real, or necessary as they did just hours before.

Works Cited

Freud, Sigmund. *The Interpretation of Dreams*. Translated by James Strachey, Basic Books, Inc., New York, NY, 1955.

Gabel, Peter. *Another Way of Seeing*. Quid Pro, LLC, New Orleans, LA, 2013.

King, Martin Luther, Jr. "I Have a Dream." Speech. Lincoln Memorial, Washington, DC, 28 August 1963.

King, Martin Luther, Jr. "Letter From Birmingham Jail." *Why We Can't Wait*. Beacon Press, Boston, MA, 1963.

Lasch, Christopher. *Haven in a Heartless World*. Basic Books, Inc., New York, NY, 1977.

Lerner, Michael. *Jewish Renewal: A Path to Healing and Transformation*. G.P. Putnam's Sons, New York, NY, 1994.

Tolle, Eckhart. *A New Earth*. Penguin Random House, New York, NY, 2005, 2016.

Glossary

Although I have tried to make this book as free as possible of obscure or technical language, I have used some words that may be unfamiliar to some readers ("phenomenology" or "ontology"), or I have occasionally invented words or phrases ("the Perfect Other," "underneathness") that I hope capture the feeling of a certain way of being or of existing with others in the world. This glossary is offered to clarify some of these unfamiliar or invented words, phrases, or images.

Absence (as in "presence haunted by an absence"): In moments of authentic social connection supported by the fullness of mutual recognition, we experience what I often call "mutuality of presence," an invisible sense of "hereness" with each other that has a unique solidity or groundedness. When we are enveloped in a social milieu of role-performances, however, what we experience is precisely an absence of presence, a kind of "surfacy" and ungrounded emptiness in which we are all pretending to be real without actually being so. This quality of absence "haunts" the false self, not only in extreme manifestations of artificiality (as in the newscaster of Chapter 2), but within the self of our everyday conditioning with its conditioned roles and routinized self-manifestations, within the performances of "the personality" that we each inhabit.

Alienated Reciprocities: Appearing mainly in Chapter 6 on the economy, this term refers to the way that a socially alienated environment is actually constituted by a circulation of reciprocal performances of the self that are enacted on the "outside" of the self. In the current economy, these alienated reciprocities shape the material practices of producing and distributing goods and services—that is, they actually "support" the practices themselves "from the inside" and therefore form what we might call the inside of the economy. From the standpoint of Social Being, they *are* the economy.

Assertion: Assertion is a mode of utterance, or way of communicating, that pressures the listener toward agreement through designating, with some force, a "right" way to describe phenomena. In Chapter 8, I contrast assertion with an "appeal," which intends to free the listener from such pressure, and which captures the way I wish for this book to communicate.

Aura: An aura as I use the term is a radiant manifestation of presence. Although our presence to each other is "invisible," it is nevertheless palpable as a kind of energetic field of Being, or emanation.

Authority: Authority as I use the term throughout the book refers to the coloring of "aboveness" which the false self attributes to some "higher" Other and which it always places itself underneath. In the formation of the false self cast onto us coercively by others in the course of our conditioning, we find ourselves "enacting ourselves" ungroundedly at the surface of our being, and so project "out" a "higher" authority that gives the false self a kind of pseudo-anchorage or basis, which the false self then internalizes so that it can feel real, rather than intolerably ungrounded or floating.

Being: The word being as I use it most often refers to the underlying foundation of all of our experience. Being is therefore prior to thought and language, the very ground out of which meaning is born. And our being therefore is what expresses itself through all our cultural manifestations. To the extent that we feel "here" beneath all our feelings and thoughts and words, and to the extent that we sense this very core of ourselves is expressing itself through our feelings and thought and words, that is what I mean by our being. (Note: Many philosophers use the term Being differently from me or address questions such as "the being of things" as opposed to the "being of consciousness" in a way not central to this book; others, including some postmodernists and poststructuralists, deny the existence of "being" altogether as a made-up concept added on to, and trying to attribute a "metaphysics of presence to," what are really simply cultural effects. I disagree with this latter group for reasons explored in Chapter 8.)

Cathects: "Cathexis" was Freud's term for what takes place when what he called an instinct—for example, the "sex instinct"—invests itself in (or "cathects") an object of instinctual desire. I use the term once or twice simply to convey the act of intensely investing energy in a person, idea, or image. The term "hyper-cathexis" means investing such energy in an excessive or fixated manner.

Deference: Deference refers to that quality of the false self that places itself "underneath" the authority of the father, the mother, the boss, the supervisor, the founding fathers, the Law, the People, or any figure invested with the coloring of "aboveness."

Despiritualization: I use this term to describe the flattening-out of perception and feeling that tries to strip a social milieu of its spiritual quality, of its vitality. Despiritualization effaces a liveliness that would otherwise be there.

Di-stance: I sometimes break the word "distance" into its two parts to emphasize the separation that perception and thought may create between the perceiver or thinker or "knower" and the perceived, the "thought about," or the known. This "doubling" or separation occurs whenever the perceiver/thinker/knower withdraws from his or her lived immersion in the life-world and, from this withdrawn or pulled-back space, looks "at" the world as if he or she were outside it.

Epistemology: This word means either the study of knowledge or the theory of knowledge, and addresses the question of how we know what we know about ourselves and the world. This question becomes important in Chapter 8 when I show how important it is that we come to know that our desire for the authentic connection of mutual recognition is "real," and that it exists in all others.

Eros Effect: This term is used by the sociologist George Katsiaficas to describe the intense communally binding experience that can happen in the rising moment of a potentially revolutionary social movement. Katsiaficas emphasizes that over and above any objective reason that a revolutionary group may come together, there is an everpresent invisible energy that may also emerge from the group's social relations with immense unifying and transformative potential.

Erotic: I often use the term "erotic" to describe the spiritually binding quality of a coming-into-connection, as in the binding quality of human relations during the rising period of a social movement. Because in these moments the bonds among people can properly be described as loving or manifesting loving energy, it is appropriate to call them erotic, whether or not they have a sexual character or aura. But I do not use the term in an explicitly sexual way.

False Self: The false self is the conditioned self in a world in which fear of the other, fear of humiliation by each other, colors the psychospiritual field as a whole to the extent that we cannot become fully present to each other in our being. I often describe the false self as an "outer" self because we actually do experience the self thus created as an enacted performance unmoored from the center of our (unrecognized) being, although we are normally not fully conscious of our false self's enacted quality because the falseness of the false self has been denied in the course of our conditioning. The false self is never entirely false or we would all be schizophrenic, and the residue of love and sensual communion that subtends our conditioning always moves us forward toward the next encounter with hope, and with the potential for true transcendence through the movement of social change.

False-We: To the extent that we are each "other to each other" and are unable to ground each other in a true community of mutual recognition and authentic social presence, to that extent we displace our desire for true community into an imaginary realm in which we "believe" together that "we" exist, as is to some extent the case with being-an-American, for example. In this false-we, I am with others "out there" in an ungrounded imaginary, while here on the ground of my actual present being, I am silently withdrawn within. The false-we always tends toward idealization due to its imaginary character (it "knows" it is false), and therefore toward demonization of "the others" constructed to support this idealization and to mask its true, internal fearful origin.

Fear of the Other: To the extent that others have "recognized us into existence" as other than we are and in so doing have coercively transmitted to us that we must not enter into a relation of true mutual recognition with them, to that extent becoming fully and truly present to the other becomes associated with the risk of "ontological humiliation," humiliation in our very being. Thus adaptation to the personality of the conditioned self is achieved at the price of denial of the vulnerability of the longing for true presence, for true mutuality of presence. Fear of the other inevitably corrodes a social milieu imbued with this kind of alienated adaptation, as the pull of the desire for mutual recognition in each of us threatens to render us vulnerable to a traumatic social excommunication.

Hegemony: Hegemony as I use the term means dominant sway. An ideology like liberalism or Marxism may become hegemonic to the extent that it comes to have a predominant influence in a particular time or place—not that it "dominates" other ways of seeing or feeling or thinking, but that it "holds sway" over alternatives in such a way that it is difficult for other ideas to be heard and gain credibility.

Hereness: This term is meant to capture the "region" of our actual present experience, as contrasted with the "thereness," or "out-thereness," of our enacted or imaginary experience. *Here* I may be withdrawn at the same time that "out there" I am pretending to be "really" myself (while not knowing that I am doing so to the extent that the existence of this division is denied in the social environment).

Hierarchy: Hierarchy as I use the term refers to an imaginary top-down ordering that an alienated group gives itself, spontaneously, to provide itself with "ground" or the appearance of realness. Through the hierarchy, we each monitor our own and one another's conformity to the rotation of the false-self matrix, so as to contain the tendency of the desire within each of us to "break on through to the other side," thus "requiring" (via the hierarchy's "ordering") that the false-self matrix be taken as real. The ricochet of mutual recognition, when it occurs, spontaneously dissolves the hierarchy as an alienated mode of being (which may produce a violent response by defenders of the false-self matrix threatened by the fear of humiliation).

Hodological: The word, borrowed from Gestalt psychologist Kurt Lewin, describes the kind of existential or "felt" space that we feel before us when we discover a pathway forward out of a constrained or blocked situation.

Humiliation: Humiliation refers to the ontological trauma of unreciprocated vulnerability. We can experience an echo of such ontological humiliation when we endure the quite sharp, even sickening, pain of unrequited hope. The humiliation caused by real or imagined slips in the false-self's performances reveal to us the vulnerability of our center-of-being that has been coercively denied recognition in the formation of the false self.

Ideology: Ideology refers to the "world" of images and ideas that represents the rotation of the alienated world as if a) it "is" the way it appears, and b) it ought to be the way it "is." Since the desire for mutual recognition perpetually overflows the alienated boundaries of the false-self matrix that as a whole seeks to deny this desire by claiming that the rotating false selves are "real," ideology reflects a work of the imaginary to continually absorb into itself the ever-varying manifestations of desire and to "co-opt" those manifestations by representing them as consistent with the false-self's world.

Imaginary Community: Imaginary Community is really a synonym in the book for the false-we, with the term false-we being used more frequently to describe the political form of the imaginary community, and imaginary community being used more frequently to describe the ontological displacement of our collective being from the hereness of true mutual recognition to a collective image "out there" that we each imagine we are "in" and are "one of."

Is-ness: An aspect of both reification and assertion, is-ness is the attribution of a fixed character or realness to how the self and the world are presented in alienated being, and are represented in language and images.

When the false self manifests itself "as if it were real," its very being transmits to others an implicit conviction that it "is" as it seems. Similarly, when the false self represents itself in language and images, it implicitly "states" its world as if it "is" as represented.

Moat: "The moat" refers to the existential distance, a kind of infinite distance, that our false selves place between us to the degree that we each enact an outer self that is not who we really are in our being. The moat is therefore a metaphor for the lived distance between our unconscious-because-unrecognized co-presence as social beings and our terrain of conscious-because-recognized, enacted social connection. The moat is always being "crossed" (by the desire for mutual recognition that seeks to surpass its distance) and re-established (by the false self seeking to monitor and secure its boundary as a condition of social membership). To the extent that social movements succeed in "rising," they dissolve the moat.

Ontology/ontological: The word ontology means either the study of being or the theory of being, but I use the term primarily in its adjectival form to describe the most fundamental, lived dimension of an experience, or of experience in general. For example, psychologically, I may feel unhappy if I feel I am merely passing through the routines of my life, but ontologically, I may become aware that at its foundation, this unhappiness expresses the absence of being that characterizes my experience, as if I am outside-of-myself in the routine and feel like "no one" from the inside of the routine. The ontological dimension of my existence in the routine describes the meaning for Being of my experience of the routine.

Otherness: "Otherness" refers to the outerness of the outer or false self, in the sense that it describes the not-being-oneself-ness of inhabiting a kind of alien persona. When we are recognized as "other" and therefore become "other" to ourselves, we experience a painful distance between our (relatively) unrecognized center and our enacted self that is somehow "other" to us and "other to the other" as well, a disturbing lack of presence that we nevertheless "are."

Parallel Universe: This term refers to the creation of a new interhuman life-world founded upon and manifesting true mutual recognition inside the existing rotating alienated frame. When social movements "arise" with great force, we can feel ourselves actually existing in a double-reality—on the one hand, we remain attached and still drawn to the pull of the alienated world that has conditioned us; on the other, we can feel the emergence of the lively new co-existing psychospiritual field that both calls upon and supports us in transcending the claim on us made by the received world of our conditioning. Chapters 7 and 10 in this book emphasize the importance of intentionally building a parallel universe as central to the success of social-spiritual activism.

Patternings of Rotating Otherness: This phrase is meant to describe the circulation of social alienation as we each pass on to the other next to us (or to millions of others through an electronic screen) the requirement of loyalty to the false self pretending to be real. The unusual formulation of this phrase results from my effort to resist participation in the reification of what we might call "nouns about the system": When we refer to "the economic system," or "social institutions," or even "society," we tend to treat what are actually moving, emerging-and-dissolving social phenomena as if they were fixed things, and therefore we participate in treating these phenomena as if they were "real." But in the actual reality of lived intersubjective experience, these entities only exist as passings-around, or rotations, of the otherness each of us feels compelled to enact, which is then internalized by each other person drawn into the alienated milieu of recognition. As I try to always emphasize, these patternings are always being transcended by the desire for authentic mutual recognition which renders every such patterning unstable and at certain moments capable of dissolution and change.

Perfect Other: This is a term I use to describe the tendency of a person who is not seen for who he or she actually is in his or her being, but who is mainly seen as "other" or as an "image," to seek to "inflate" this image of self-as-"other" in order to try to fill up what in it appears to be lacking. Since such an image disconnected from and therefore floating on the outside of one's actual being can never "find" the authentic recognition and connection that is missing, the image can never be "filled up" no matter how much it aggrandizes itself, and the person suffering within the image lacking in being knows this.

Therefore, the person—alas, all of us, in part—seeks to become a "perfect other" that would no longer feel the lack, the absence, the ontological hole at the core.

Phenomenology/phenomenological: Phenomenology is the study of Being as it appears or is revealed to consciousness, and has given rise to an important philosophical tradition, especially in twentieth-century Western Europe, but also in the United States. The work of Husserl, Heidegger, Sartre, Merleau-Ponty, and many others is associated with this tradition, and all of these writers make use of a method in their thought that tries to use no preconceived abstractions in describing "phenomena" in the world, including consciousness, but simply to describe experience itself. My description of the "perfect other" above is an example of a phenomenological description in that it relies solely on describing the actual experience of not being seen as I am in my being but only as I am an image for the other cast onto an experiential "outside" of my being. This book as a whole is a phenomenology of social being, a description of our interhuman reality as it appears and is revealed to our consciousness. One could say that phenomenology is a kind of "reliving" that goes alongside our lived experience while taking an x-ray of it.

Point of Social Being: The "point" of social being refers to the very center of our being from which, as inherently *social* beings, we receive and transmit mutual recognition. This point or center always subsists within us in every encounter, but it may be relatively inaccessible to the extent that our social being is primarily absorbed into the enactments of the false or "outer" self.

Pre-reflective/reflective: Pre-reflective consciousness describes our immediate experience of the world and others, prior to any reflection on that experience. Our encounter with the other, with each other, is always pre-reflective, an immediate co-presence that aspires to the completion of mutual recognition. The desire for mutual recognition means, for me, the desire for the realization of that immediacy of co-presence, of "withness," that would liberate us from the withdrawn space of our alienated world's mutual detachment emanating from fear of the other, of each other.

Presence: This central term describes the experience of the hereness of your own existence which emerges in relation to the other. Even if you are right now sitting alone "with your self," the presence to yourself that you may sense has its being and origin in an original relation to another being. Or to put this slightly differently, because we are social beings, the hereness of presence can only be consciously experienced to the extent that you have been recognized as present, and here with us, by an other. To the extent that you have been "thrown" into a false or outer self by the way you were recognized into existence, to that extent you may experience yourself as mainly not here, but "out there" in your self, and more haunted by an absence of presence (like the newscaster of Chapter 2) than actually here with the other, with the person next to you. Our unceasing aspiration to full mutuality of presence is the aspiration to the ever more complete realization of our social being, and it gives to history its moral direction.

Psychospiritual Field: This term refers to the interhuman life-world itself as a vital and alive milieu. I find this descriptive term more phenomenologically accurate than words like "society" or "the social world" because these latter terms are lifeless abstractions that imagine the interhuman life-world from a distance. My use of the term "psychospiritual field" is an attempt to dissolve "society" back into the spirited environment that it really is in its lived dimension; and in the book I try to locate myself amidst the field as a describer of a milieu that I myself am also living. I use psychospiritual and social-spiritual more or less interchangeably, but later in the book I place somewhat greater emphasis on the social character of the psychospiritual field because of my focus in Chapters 9 and 10 on social-spiritual activism.

Real-We: The term real-we is intended to express the authentic ontological ground of interhuman connection that occurs in the rising moment of social movements, in the creation of the parallel universe, and sometimes even in response to natural disasters or other extraordinary occurrences. The real-we is actually real in the sense that it expresses the palpable mutuality of presence that gives to true mutual recognition its substantial character, its fullness or weight. In the book the term appears mainly in Chapter 7 on "Politics as the Struggle Over Who 'We' Are" and is meant to contrast with the false-we that describes the empty or "absent" interiority of imaginary collective identities often exemplified by nationalism, skin color, and blood relations.

Reification: Like despiritualization, reification (from the Latin "res" meaning thing) describes a flattening-out of the life-world or aspects of the life-world that robs them of their spiritual liveliness and "createdness" and gives them the character of a fixed thing. When we are withdrawn from others within a "circle" of collective denial of desire, we tend to give the existing, alienated world a fixed character that protects us from experiencing our own longing to transcend the existing world and the risk of humiliation that would be attendant to it.

Rotation: See "patternings of rotating otherness." Rotation is an important idea because it is meant to capture the created character of all social phenomena as we together, almost but not quite instantaneously, "pass Being around" with whatever degree of presence or absence, through our reciprocal, circulating manifestations.

Social Movement: A social movement refers to an actual liberation and vitalization of social being that "arises" in response to a ricochet of authentic mutual recognition across a group's psychospiritual field. The "force" of a movement results from the emergence of mutual presence triggered by the rotating recognition of that presence, a kind of existential chain reaction. As I use the term, true social movements are inherently "good" because in their very "movement" they dissolve the fear-induced separation that is at the heart of the world's problems. The hyper-excitement of reactionary upheavals like Nazism are not true movements but rather paranoid inflations of the collective outer self, coupled with a parallel intensification of demonization of an Other conceived as a threat to that inflated outer self.

Spatialized Narrative (Spatialized Tableau): These terms describe the way we actually experience historical events and stories about events when they have been transmitted to us in an unreal, alienated manner, as if from our detached standpoint, we were "watching" them on a two-dimensional, "spatial" mental screen. The idea that the founding fathers created the country and then we were born and became citizens of it and must follow the founding fathers' intent as a condition of our membership "in" it is an example of a spatialized narrative of this kind, in contrast with the recovery of an actual historical lived experience through empathy and recovered, existentially true knowledge (to the extent that this is possible).

Spinning Top: This metaphor is meant to capture the true psychospiritual character of what we normally call institutions. In reality institutions are rotating patternings of otherness being held in place by a circulation of other-directed "behaving" with each of us seeking to behave like the others. Yet because the desire for authentic mutuality of presence is always, at every moment, surpassing and threatening to surpass the rotation of our mutual containment, the spinning top is always in danger of toppling. The more that we can grasp the "spinning top" nature of the seemingly fixed institutions of the psychospiritual field, the more porous the field appears and the greater our sense of the possibility of change.

Tikkun Olam: This Hebrew phrase means to heal and repair the world. The idea of tikkun olam is beautifully expressed in the kabbalistic idea (attributed to Rabbi Luria) that we are all shards of light scattered across and trapped within the material world as the result of an original shattering of a part of the being of G-d, and that our responsibility is to reunite the shards to make G-d's energy manifest in the world.

Underneathness: Because it is always ungrounded and therefore cannot be confident in itself in its being, the false self always experiences itself as "underneath" an authority that it projects and then internalizes in order to give itself the pseudo-anchorage of a pseudo-ground outside of itself. "Underneathness" and "aboveness" are the paired existential qualities both within each person's enacted self and also throughout hierarchy in all its social manifestations.

Undetached/Detached Knowledge: Especially in Chapter 8, I sometimes refer to detached knowledge in describing the kind of knowing that is possible when we stand back from phenomena and look at phenomena from a distance. This "observation at a distance" is the basis of the scientific method, whether applied to natural or social phenomena, and can produce useful "objective" knowledge about aspects of reality that are capable of being known objectively. For spiritual knowledge, the opposite method is required, since the spiritual dimension of the life-world can only be apprehended through the illumination of what has been first apprehended or grasped "subjectively." Since the being of the knower corresponds to and is a manifestation of the same being as that of the phenomena to be known, the phenomena can be grasped "undetachedly" or wholeheartedly, and then described through the enlightenment of illumination.

Unmediated: This term refers to immediacy of co-presence, or mutuality of presence. This immediacy is unmediated in the sense that while it is always expressed *through* an historical and social particular mediation (language, gender, racial identity, class position, or other cultural "channel of being"), the co-presence itself is not itself mediated by the particular expressive form that transmits it but rather transcends that expressive form. Most identity politics, cultural studies, Marxist analyses, and also philosophies of social recognition take a different view on this essential point about the nature of social being itself in that, however consciously, they subordinate social being to its historical and social mediation.

Verstehen: The German word for "understanding" has been used commonly in Continental philosophy to refer to the inherent understanding that consciousness has of its own projects. To carry out a project of any kind, we must inherently grasp the meaning of our intentions prior to any thought "about" the project as a rational task. To even walk across the street, we must, with understanding, synthesize all of our movements toward the realization of our action through a pre-reflective "grasp" of the action's direction and meaning. The word verstehen roughly corresponds to my use of the word "grasp," in Chapter 8 especially.

We-as-a-Whole: This term refers to the whole of the social field at any given moment as this field carries and expresses the relative balance of the real-we and the false-we within "politics" as a contested ontological terrain.

Withness: Because being itself is social, the psychospiritual/social-spiritual field on which it unfolds always possesses the quality of withness as a felt measure of social presence. Even when we are most withdrawn into ourselves and are therefore most absent and scattered into the false self, our relations with every other, with each other, carry whatever residual presence and "withness" that they have, in the sense that we always remain in present relation to each other even when we feel most compelled to deny that presence. In moments of true mutual recognition, our sense of withness is most palpable and most fully embodied.

Acknowledgments

First and foremost I want to acknowledge and thank my friends and colleagues Michael McAvoy and Gary Peller for their continual support and encouragement in the writing of this book and in seeing it through to publication. Michael and Gary read every chapter and revision, often more than once, and talked through with me whether important ideas were getting across and what modifications were needed to deepen and strengthen them. They were just incredible friends and allies over the entire time that I was writing the book, and I really am forever grateful to them for their help and also for the pleasure they gave me in talking through the ideas themselves with me.

I thank my lifetime friend and partner in many ventures Rabbi Michael Lerner for helping to shape my thinking over many decades, and especially for introducing me to spiritual-political understandings and spiritual-political practices that influenced the whole book, but especially the ideas in Chapter 10 on social-spiritual activism.

And I thank yet another lifetime friend, critical legal studies comrade Duncan Kennedy, for his insightful responses to the manuscript and for pressing me to recognize the microphenomenological opportunities for liberation and transcendence that exist in every moment.

Jennifer Listug, who appeared by near-magic out of the ether to assist me at a critical moment in preparing the manuscript for publication, has helped me and the book immensely in responding to the text, suggesting revisions, and offering clear and decisive reactions to aspects of the text that I was unsure of. Jen made what might have been an arduous task—the completion of the manuscript and the technical aspects of readying it for publication—an enjoyable and sometimes elevating experience. Jen and I were able to connect across generations in a way that I hope the book will do.

Thanks are due also to Robin West, Shari Motro, Ross Brockway, Richard Delgado, John Henry Schlegel, and Mike Seidman for sharp insights both affirming and critical.

Special thanks to my friend and great photographic artist Robert Bergman for creating the cover art for all of my books, including this one, and for the use of the beautiful portrait of the woman in red in Chapter 1.

And many thanks to Natalja Mortenson of Routledge Press for her confidence in the manuscript and her patience in waiting for me to finish it, and to Maria Landschoot, Helen Bell, and Tina Cottone for their assistance and support in guiding the book through to final publication. Thanks also to Sylvia Coates for her excellent work on the index.

Index

Note: Page numbers in italics indicate figures.